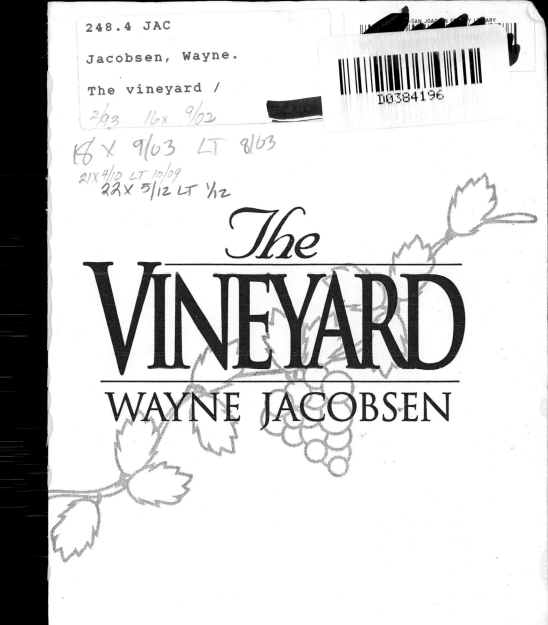

The VINEYARD

WAYNE JACOBSEN

HARVEST HOUSE PUBLISHERS
EUGENE, OREGON 97402

THE VINEYARD

Copyright © 1992 by Wayne Jacobsen
Eugene, Oregon 97402

Library of Congress Cataloging-in-Publication Data

Jacobsen, Wayne.
    The vineyard: finding fruitfulness and fulfillment in God's kingdom /
    by Wayne Jacobsen.
    ISBN 0-89081-925-4
    1. Christian life—1960- .   I. Title.
    BV4501.2.J315   1992   91-37785
    248.4—dc20   CIP

Printed in the United States of America.

To my father and mother,

Gene and Jo Jacobsen,

*on the occasion of their retirement
from their earthly vineyard;
and to parents like them everywhere
who have invested their time and energy
to teach their children how to grow
in the Father's vineyard.*

CONTENTS

Foreword

Come to the Vineyard

Part One: The Way of the Vineyard

Part Two: The Seasons

Foreword

It was a bewildered group and a puzzling moment.

They had just left dinner together; a disconcerting set of hours during which their host had alternately jarred their minds and comforted their hearts.

Now He stood with them, looking across the sharp defile which suddenly fell away to the east, rising with equal suddenness to the slopes of the hill called Olives.

Scanning the scene, brilliantly lit by the full moon filling the Judean sky, His eyes sought the *exception* on this mountainside...and there it was, small and lowly among the sweeping groves of olive trees. A vine. A grapevine.

And in that setting, perhaps but an hour after having declared His new *covenant* by sharing the fruit of the vine with His dining partners, the Son of Man now drew them to study the vine as the essence of the new *relationship* He was announcing.

Three days before, on this same terrain, He had cursed a fig tree. The morbid message of its shriveled frame was mute testimony to this Prophet's word of power: *The old order is dead.* The tree that symbolized a disappearing era of God's dealings and reflected the fruitless response to God's call may likely have been silhouetted against the moonlit backdrop somewhere nearby.

Winding their way down the Kidron's banks, then up toward the garden they frequented as a rest stop, Jesus pauses beside the vine which is just beginning to put forth its springtime shoots, and there He declares the nature of the new order: "I am the vine. You are the branches" (John 15:1).

While no one can confirm my description of the setting in which our Lord gave us the words which John's Gospel unfolds so poetically, powerfully, and preciously, none of us can escape the importance and implications of their content. Since my training days for ministry these words have kept my soul very low at His feet: *"Without me you can do nothing"* (John 15:5). And since my first pastorate these words have encouraged my heart: *"Your fruit shall remain"* (John 15:16c).

On the night before He died, Jesus not only unveiled the rite by which the New Covenant would be celebrated in continuum, He also engraved a symbol on the minds of His disciples. The vine was to be the key to their understanding how both relationship *with* God and fruitfulness *for* Him would be realized. Just as surely as the Lamb shortly satisfied all the legal demands of the Old Covenant, the Lord of the New Covenant testified to the pathway of life just about to open through the expiating redemption of His cross and the explosive release of His resurrection.

From the day I sat as a teenager in a California church building and heard the Savior whisper to me, "You have not chosen Me, but I have chosen you" (John 15:16a), I have been increasingly aware of my dependency upon living out the vine-branch relationship with my Savior/Commissioner. And that's why I welcome this book.

In a sometimes stirring, often heart-touching, probing, and personal way, Wayne Jacobsen gives us a fresh look at timeless truth. His experiences as a boy growing up on a grape ranch provides resources full of insight, which I think you'll find as enriching as you'll find them well written.

No one can write such words without having experienced more than a ranch. Here are the words of a man who has tasted the reality of a growing, impassioned, deepening life with Jesus Himself. And that's why I want to read—and listen with my heart. Because Wayne is talking about *how* Jesus spoke of our deepening relationship with Him. And I think that you, as I have, will hear Jesus' voice drawing you closer to Him through Wayne's words. May it be so for us both.

Jack W. Hayford, D.Litt.
Senior Pastor
The Church on the Way
Van Nuys, California

COME TO THE VINEYARD

This is my favorite time of year in the vineyard—the waning days of winter.

It is still only mid-February, but in the short winters of California's San Joaquin Valley, spring is just around the corner. The ever-lengthening days are already clawing at winter's grip, and it will soon succumb.

It's just after 5:30 in the afternoon, and the long yellow rays of the setting sun have surrendered to violet-tinted shades of pink. Though it was in the 70's earlier today, the evening chill comes quickly. I zip up my coat against the light breeze, pulling the collar up around my neck and thrusting my hands into its pockets.

Lights from distant farmhouses already twinkle against the subdued landscape, and out of the diaphanous shroud of evening ground fog that obscures the horizon, rows of grapevines curve over the hills and completely surround me.

The vines are all neatly trimmed, their branches gently twisted around the wire strung from the posts that stand as sentinels beside each vine. The labor of winter brings a surrealistic order to the vineyard. Should anything in God's creation be so tightly clipped and neatly arranged?

The vineyard is at rest, waiting patiently the glory of springtime and another season of fruitfulness. I guess that's why I like this time of year so. At the moment in battle just before twilight, the wispy fog and the sense of order combine to grant me that marvelous gift of secluded peace. Except for the softened whine of a few cars far away, the only sound I hear is the crunching of dirt clods underfoot.

Only a few months ago the air was filled with the dust, voices, and churning of tractor engines that mark the frenzied drive of harvest to get the raisins in before the first rain. A few weeks from now those same things will fill the air as the process of fruitfulness starts all over again.

But now it is quiet. And though a glance from a distant farmhouse might lead someone to believe that I am alone, it is not so. I have come here at this time often to walk and talk with the Father.

This has been my cherished prayer closet since I was a young boy. It is a sanctuary of greater reverence than I've known in any cathedral built by human hands. No place on earth more quickly draws me to him, because it is here that we first met, and here we have met so often. This is where I learned to walk with God—to hear his voice and surrender my life to his pleasure.

This is my father's vineyard—a 35-acre ranch in the heart of California's Central Valley. My father is a second-generation grape farmer and has for almost all of his 65 years lived within a mile of this very spot. The farthest he ever traveled, interestingly enough, found him in another vineyard in northeastern France where he was wounded in battle just before New Year's Day, 1945.

After the war he purchased the farm next to the one on which he was raised. This vineyard became his tool—not only to provide for his family but more importantly, to teach his four sons about God and his ways. I've learned more about God in this vineyard than in all my years of Bible training and study.

I learned from the lessons Dad taught us, lessons he always backed with the obedience of his own life. I learned about the cycles of the seasons, of God's faithfulness, of overcoming adversity, and of surrendering to his will. Most of Dad's lessons came straight from God's Word, but many others came from his personal observations and encouragement.

I also learned from my own budding relationship with God. In my long walks, usually at dawn or dusk, I read his Word and learned to speak to God, telling him my deepest secrets. Eventually I began to hear him respond—simple stirrings, gentle insight, deep convictions—the voice of God superimposed over my own thoughts. I could know what was on his heart in the same way I was letting him know what was on mine.

In these rows I also preached my first sermon, at ten years of age, just over by that muscat vine. Do you see where the branches split to form a natural vee? I propped my Bible between them, and it fell open to Ezekiel 34. I read the words and preached to my dog, Penny, and the other muscat vines nearby.

It was a child's game, to be sure, but something incredible happened that summer morning. The Word became alive in my heart, more so than at any time previous when I had sat down to read it. The words that flowed from my lips, the passion from my heart, were not the doings of a ten-year-old. As I came to realize that, I grew frightened.

What had I touched? It was a presence undeniably distinct from my own. I felt wonderful and foolish all at the same time. I realized how loudly I had spoken, and thought how silly I must have looked acting as a preacher in this row of vines. I looked about to make sure no one had seen me, tucked my Bible inside my shirt, and wandered back to our farmhouse.

But I couldn't deny that something special had happened, that I had connected with the presence of God in a way I had not before. I had no designs at the time to be a pastor, being far more enthralled with the airplanes that sailed over my head, hoping one day to pilot them. It was just a game that had unexpectedly taken on a life all its own. I didn't realize it then, but looking back I know that was the day my life was indelibly stamped with an affection for God's Word.

The vineyard has always been my special place, and it is no wonder to me that when Jesus wanted to reveal the secrets of the kingdom to his followers he made rich use of farming illustrations generally, and vineyards most specifically. No other image offers such a rich source of instruction, encouragement, and challenge as the vineyard.

The passages of Scripture that deal with vines and grapes are among my favorite in all of God's Word. I have not only studied them but lived them, and they have changed my life. The vineyard of my childhood is not so very different from those which Jesus walked through with his disciples. I can almost see him leaning up against the sturdy trunk of an old vine as he told the parable of the wicked tenants of the vineyard.

One evening in particular, as Jesus faced the longest night of his life, he wanted to convey to his followers where to find the rich spring of personal fulfillment and the keys to living fruitful lives. Where did he take them? To a vineyard—his Father's vineyard.

Fulfillment and *fruitfulness*. No themes recur more frequently in the vineyard than these, and who among us is not stirred to our deepest desires by their mere mention? Who doesn't want joy and inner peace deep enough to take us through any circumstance, and a sense of success that comes from knowing our lives have made a difference?

For too many people, however, these qualities remain an elusive dream. Though pursued with fervor they are rarely reached.

Many things in this world promise fullness, and though they may provide a moment of happiness or satisfaction, none of them offers the enduring joy and peace we seek so ardently. And who can ever be sure that they are fruitful, especially in things spiritual? Many of us are not even sure what it means, and most of us can honestly admit we don't think we've found it. We might think we're the only ones to feel that way, but we are not. Even those Christians who try to convince others that they have found the secrets of fulfillment and fruitfulness often prove by their own personal stress, immorality, or spiritual emptiness that they have not.

This is especially tragic because Jesus didn't want his followers confused or groping for either one. That's why he drew a picture of a vineyard and invited them to take their places in it.

I have long since left the ranch and moved to the city's edge. My days are filled less with vineyards and more with computers, automobiles, and other machinery of our technological society. But somehow these never quite measure up to the lessons that come from the heart of God's own creation. We are organisms, not machines, and even our spiritual growth patterns have more in common with the four grape vines I have growing today in my backyard than the computer on which I type.

Before we are completely urbanized, it would serve us well to take a look back to our agrarian roots. Scripture makes such vivid use of the images of plant growth and fruitfulness to teach us about our own spiritual life. Here, with less clutter lying between us and God's creation, we can learn the rich lessons he taught about his spiritual vineyard.

Previous trips to my father's vineyard for study and reflection have been alone. Now I invite you to go with me, not to his vineyard, but to a far greater vineyard that belongs to God himself.

Let's walk the rows of vines together, peer into the leaves and watch the grapes mature. There we will find the fullness of joy and the fruitfulness that he has promised to every believer.

Including you!

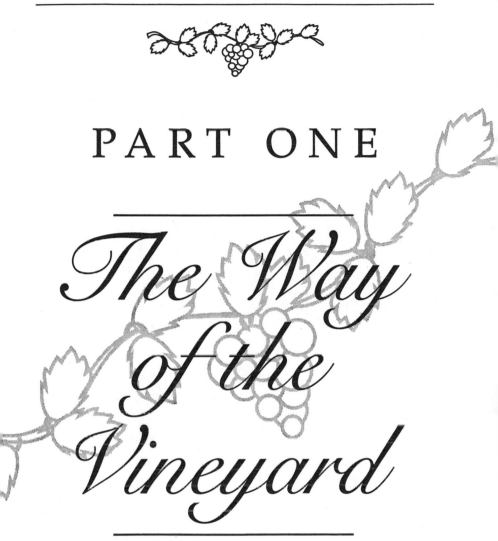

PART ONE

The Way of the Vineyard

1

AN AMAZING INVITATION

I have told you this so that my joy may be in you and that your joy may be complete.
JOHN 15:11

It had been the strangest of evenings. They had never seen Jesus so deeply troubled. As he served them a Passover meal he made ominous comments about the bread being his broken body and the wine his spilled blood. He said that from their own number one would betray him and another deny him before the morning sunrise.

He warned them that he was going somewhere they could not go, and he promised them a new companion, another Counselor, who would guide them in his place. He told them not to be afraid, and who ever says that without good reason?

Judas had fled the room earlier for reasons none of the others understood. Now they had left the safe confines of that upper room and were headed in the darkness toward the Garden of Gethsemane. Suddenly Jesus took the conversation in an unforeseen direction.

"I am the true vine."

Eyebrows must have popped up around this little band of men as they looked incredulously at one another. Vines? What did vines have to do with the events of this strange evening?

Perhaps Jesus had just spotted a small vineyard in the garden. I can see him walking over to a grapevine growing on the outskirts of the garden, affectionately taking one of the canes in his hand. He might even have squatted down near its trunk, inviting his disciples to gather around him as he launched into one of the more tender metaphors of his ministry—one reserved only for his closest friends.

He compared himself to a vine, his disciples to branches, and his Father to a gardener. He spoke of their need for pruning so that they could bear even more fruit, and of friends laying down their lives for one another.

Before we take in his words, let's look at his intent in speaking them: "I have told you this so that my joy may be in you and that your joy may be complete." Even in the midst of all the fearful unknowns he had introduced throughout the evening, he promised his followers complete joy.

What an unlikely group to be beneficiaries of such a marvelous promise! Take a look at the men sitting around that honored grape vine. Which of these 11 men deserved it? Four years earlier, which of these would you have chosen to dine with any king, much less the King of Glory on the last night of his life?

None of these men had been invited to state dinners at Herod's palace, and none were likely to be in the future. They weren't outcasts necessarily, but most were nondescript people that you would pass on the street and not give a second thought.

He found some of them at the docks, frustrated fishermen who had spent the night and come up empty. One he found in a tax office, another sitting beneath a fig tree. None were remarkable figures in their community, none had been leaders.

But they had just shared the Passover with the King of Glory on the last night of his earthly life, and now they were being told how they could embrace total fulfillment. Who would have thought such a promise would be given to men like these? Certainly not their friends or neighbors, or the Pharisees.

To this unlikely group of men Jesus promised joy to the fullest measure they could conceive. Their culture had not given it to them, and that is not surprising. Cultures only reward a sliver of people with success, and it usually comes to those people with the right abilities, backgrounds, breaks, or achievements.

There's much we don't know of these disciples, but one thing we do know: These are not the kind of people who are supposed to find fullness of joy. They were ordinary people who at times demonstrated the same weaknesses we face— anger, jealousy, greed, and incredible thick-headedness. Though the world only offered them lives of quiet desperation, Jesus extended to them an amazing invitation to absolute joy.

This is the reason he paused in that small vineyard on the way to the olive groves in Gethsemane; to teach these men how to embrace joy at a level far deeper than their circumstances would ever allow. He wasn't talking about mere happiness, a temporal feeling of satisfaction that results from favorable circumstances. Such happiness is always fleeting, for it only lasts as long as the current circumstance.

Joy on the other hand has a different source. It springs from an inner sense of fulfillment that reaches to the depths of our being. All is well. God's purpose in our life is being fulfilled. This joy often results in happiness, but it also leads us to peace, contentedness, and rest. Because it is produced by God's work inside us, true joy is impervious to any change of circumstances.

I have seen joy radiate from people who are in the midst of sacrifice and great loss. It is not a contrived facial expression, but a spring that bubbles up from inside, often in the face of the very circumstances they are enduring.

Our discovery of joy that is real is at the heart of the lesson of the vineyard. You may seem as unlikely a candidate as the 11 men that surrounded Jesus in that garden, and unless you are convinced that the same offer is yours you will never pursue it with the fervency necessary to apprehend it.

I've met many people who cannot believe that such a rich inheritance is theirs. They all have the same hollow glare in their pain-filled eyes. They all ask the same questions: "What hope do I have of ever being happy? Can God help me find the same fulfillment in Christ that you have?" Some were brought to that point through years of abuse and torment, others through willful sin or after years of disappointed pursuit of spirituality. They had not been able to find the God who could fulfill them with his joy.

One of these people came to me very recently. Judy had been rejected by everyone who had ever been close to her, from her birth parents to her adopted parents. She was a real-life Cinderella, but without the carriage and glass slipper. She believed in God, but believed that God had made her only to help expose the sins of others. Her own personal pain mattered not a whit to him.

She hadn't come to that conclusion easily—only after her many pleas for healing had seemingly gone unanswered. Everything she tried had failed, and she was left to the bitter throes of a loneliness that could only be temporarily held at bay with wanton bulimia.

Is there any hope for her? Just as importantly, is there any hope for *you*? Many of you may be reading this book because you have just such a hope. Hold on to it. Your hope today is the most decisive ingredient to the development of your relationship with God tomorrow.

But others of you may be reading this skeptically. You've tried to find a vital friendship with Jesus any number of times, but your experience, like Judy's, may never have lived up to its promise. Let me assure you at the outset that the promises made in the vineyard truly work for all of us who respond to God's work in our lives. There is no favoritism with him; he loves all his children equally. If his Word is valid only for people who grew up in safe, middle-class homes, it is not the gospel of Jesus Christ. If it's not real for whoever seeks him, then it is a fraud for everyone else.

Jesus offered it not only to the 11 in the garden that evening, but also to rich young rulers, hardened Pharisees, lonely beggars, and brazen prostitutes. Not all took his offer, but those who did never expressed disappointment with it.

I can't always explain to people why their past attempts have not been successful; for those who want to build their hope by just such an explanation, I'll not be able to help you here. No general answer could cover every possibility.

You will need to bury the past and all its unanswered questions and start fresh in your walk with God. Let the hope of his promise resurge in you, and pursue it even through difficult moments. Finding fullness is not an easy task, and the cost of that relationship is great. You will see the enemies arrayed against your success in that relationship, but the process cannot even *begin* if you have no hope that God wants to have such a relationship with you, or if you doubt that he is capable of forging it with you.

"Without faith it is impossible to please God, because anyone who comes to him must believe that he exists and that he rewards those who earnestly seek him." Without that hope we won't seek him hard enough or long enough to get through all our baggage and discover the joyful Father and his compassionate Son.

But I promise you now: There is no brokenness he cannot mend; no pain he cannot still; no life he does not want to invite to the fullness of his joy. *He desires a warm friendship with all his creation*, and he wants to speak with a voice that can offer direction and comfort every day.

That's why he told the story of the vineyard, and why he told it to a group of people about to face the greatest trial of their young lives.

2

THE GENEROUS LANDLORD

*The kingdom of heaven is like a landowner
who went out early in the morning to hire men
to work in his vineyard.*

MATTHEW 20:1

Jesus begins on familiar ground, "I am the true vine, and my Father is the gardener."

Though his change of subject might have been abrupt, this was not the first time he'd spoken of the vineyard. Many times before his parables had taken them into the vineyard. This, his final lesson, would build on all the others. For us to fully appreciate the depth of John 15, we'll have to depart now and then to visit the other parables and lessons Jesus had already used to embellish his picture of the vineyard.

Nowhere is that more critical than in our understanding of the Father's role in his vineyard. How we perceive the Father is the key to everything we'll learn in the vineyard, so it is here that Jesus begins. Though this is the first time Jesus referred to him as the gardener, the focus on the Father would not have surprised the disciples. Nothing stirred their hearts more than the intimacy they witnessed between Jesus and his father.

The most important lesson Jesus sought to impress on his disciples was the relationship the Father wanted to have with each of them, and how their absolute trust in him was critical to that relationship. To drive home that lesson he had told them another parable, probably only a week earlier, identifying the Father as the landlord and owner of the vineyard. This is the groundwork for the tale he now tells. Let us start there, for the gardener we will speak of is also the landlord.

If it had happened to me, I'd have been incensed!

I wouldn't care if I had agreed earlier to work all day for 40 dollars. When quitting time came, if I stood there and watched my father give the same 40 dollars to one of my brothers who had only come for the last hour of work, I'd have been furious.

But my father never did it. Whether he paid us by the hour or by the vine we pruned or the trays we picked, we got paid only for what we worked. If I worked two hours, I got paid two hours. If I pruned 180 vines, that's what I got paid for—no more, no less!

I've gone out at 6:30 in the morning to chase a dust-spewing tractor around the vineyard, picking up raisins and putting them in boxes. It's not too bad starting out, but somewhere after noon the pain intensifies. One hundred and three degrees of searing heat beats down on the back of your neck. The dust is so thick you feel it grind between your teeth. So much dirt fills your boots that they feel like cement blocks as you lift them one after the other out of the deep powdery dust.

If at that time more workers were hired, I was never disappointed—only grateful for the extra help. I remember those late afternoons when we tried to get the raisins out of an approaching rainstorm. On those days we weren't working toward a specific quitting time—we would be done only when the crop was safe, even if that came after dark. Any extra help was welcome indeed, but I certainly didn't expect them to receive the same pay that I did.

It is exactly that expectation that makes Jesus' parable of the workers in the vineyard (Matthew 20:1-16) such a powerful teaching tool. In his story the landowner goes to the marketplace five different times during the day to hire workers for his vineyard. We are not told why he does this. Was the work pressing before a destroying storm? Was he demonstrating compassion for those who had not found work earlier in the day? Whatever the reason, each time he finds those willing to help, even to the last hour of the day.

At the end of it all he instructs his foreman to do something most curious: pay the workers, beginning with the last ones hired and proceeding in reverse order to the first ones. What must the first workers have thought when they saw those who had been hired last receive the amount that they had been promised? I'd have been a bit concerned at first, but like them, I would have been hopeful that I would get more than I was promised. They said nothing until they received their wages.

What a shock when they received only the amount they had been promised! They received the same as those who had only worked an hour and that in the cooler time of late afternoon. Were they ever angry! "You have made them equal to us who have borne the burden of the work and the heat of the day." I understand exactly how they felt; that's why this parable has not traditionally been among my personal favorites.

This seeming unfairness is exactly why Jesus told the parable. It hits us so hard because we're left with the incomprehensible feeling that those who started early in the day were not treated fairly. What reasonable person would think otherwise?

But that is the very point of the parable. We don't bring our reasonable expectations to God and demand them satisfied. The landowner's actions in this parable were not unfair toward those who were first out in the field, but simply represented generosity to those who had come later.

Did he not pay the laborers what he had promised them? There is no unfairness here. "Didn't you agree to work for a denarius? Take your pay and go. I want to give the man who was hired last the same as I gave you. Don't I have the right to do what I want with my own money? Or are you envious because I am generous?"

Doesn't God have the right to do whatever he wants in his own vineyard? Doesn't he know best? Can't he be generous without inciting my envy? He is the owner of the vineyard. If we're not ready to trust him to that degree, we will find no joy in his vineyard.

Those for whom the landowner would have had the greatest appreciation were those who worked throughout the entire day. He gave more to the others out of compassion for their need, not because they held a greater place in his heart. But their gratefulness, coupled with the complaints of the first workers, reverses the tables. Jesus makes the saddened conclusion, "So the last will be first, and the first will be last."

The meaning of this parable applies far beyond the way the Father rewards us. It has to do with the way we view *him* in our lives. Is he ours to control, or are we his to serve? Those who started the day first in the Father's heart ended it last, because in their own greed they judged the landowner as unfair even though he had given them exactly what they had agreed to.

If we're going to find fulfillment in the life of Jesus we have got to have a good understanding of who's who in his vineyard. Only as we embrace God's place as the gardener and Jesus' as the vine will we know how to respond to him as branches.

I never had a problem with knowing who was who in my dad's vineyard. Throughout the restlessness of my adolescent years, I had many occasions to second-guess his ideas and decisions. But one area in which I never questioned him was the vineyard. In my eyes he was the master farmer and I his worker. Whatever he said went. He knew best.

Regretfully, the same hasn't always been true of my relationship with my heavenly Father. Whenever things didn't go right, this miniature Job would plead his case before God. Since I knew God wasn't unfair, I assumed he didn't have all the facts he needed, and I was always happy to share some of mine with him. Even though I knew God, I did not trust him *as* God.

I have seen God do many things that defy my reasonable expectations, extending grace to others in ways that didn't seem fair in light of what I had gone through. I have resisted his work, complained at my perceptions of his inactivity, and railed at his judgments.

There have been times when I have spent the bulk of my prayer life trying to counsel God to resolve my situation in the only way I could imagine a loving God doing. But that only shows the limits of my imagination, not evidence that God lacks power, compassion, or fairness.

When I told my dad about such conversations with the Almighty he would shake his head in disbelief. "Who are you to talk to God that way?" he would ask.

He knew something about God that I have only since come to fully appreciate. God is over all; he is not to be *challenged* but *followed*. Though we can always ask him for more insight, charging him with dereliction of duty will get us nowhere.

We will not always understand why God does what he does, but we must learn to trust him enough to endorse his plans for us instead of trying to get him to fulfill ours. If we're not willing to let God extend his grace in ways more marvelous than we understand, we risk disqualifying ourselves from his joy.

I have since come to trust God as the owner of the vineyard in which I am planted. Rare are the moments now that my prayers challenge God's working in my life. Letting my Father be the owner of the vineyard brings rest inside even when circumstances rage without. I always note how much God has changed my heart when I'm caught in a crisis with someone who hasn't yet learned that we are only branches in his vineyard.

They say things like "Why didn't God prevent this?" or "How could he just sit by and watch it happen?" Who's to say he did? Why do we trust our personal limited perspective in a situation more than we trust that God is at work by means other than we would perceive or prefer?

The problem with persistently demanding that God's actions satisfy our own desires is that it will eventually destroy the trust so essential to our relationship with him. The people of Israel did the same thing, and were chastised for it strongly: "Woe to him who quarrels with his Maker. . . . Does the clay say to the potter, 'What are you making?' " (Isaiah 45:9).

Most people don't carry this frustration with God all the time. I see it mostly when crises and confusing circumstances hit. Then I can more clearly see the anguish that hides beneath the surface of their otherwise-contented spiritual lives. At that point they can tick off a list of their disappointments with God that stretches back over many years. If an unwillingness to trust God is present in a crisis, you can be sure it adversely impacts your relationship with him at many other times as well.

Precisely at moments of crisis is where our trust is needed most. If we can hold on to it then, it will give us the peace and security we need to draw close to God. Without it, we'll shove him away at arm's length and the resulting circumstances will only seem to confirm our conclusion that he is not treating us fairly.

Trusting God unquestioningly is a choice of faith that we all must make. What are you going to believe: your interpretation of events, or God's revealed character attested to by thousands of his people throughout history? In any situation you can know instantly what you're trusting. Our own perspectives will leave us frustrated and discouraged, eventually trapping us in despair. In contrast, whenever we choose to trust God, our hearts will fill with peace and security. I am in his hands and therefore I am safe.

In the advantage of hindsight, I can look back even to those moments when I was disappointed with God's working in my life and fully affirm that God had something better in mind. He has always been faithful to me, seeking the highest good for my life even when it was beyond my ability to understand.

"Don't I have the right to do what I want with my own money?" The conclusion of the parable of the generous landlord is haunting in its simplicity: Let God be God. A marvelous moment occurs in the life of a believer when he finally realizes that he cannot judge God by his present circumstances.

Instead, we judge our circumstances by what we know to be true of God. What I'm going through may not look like God is involved, but I know he is, because he is always loving and faithful. He has always taken me through before, and I know he will do it again.

3

THE TENDER CARETAKER

*Sing about a fruitful vineyard: I, the Lord,
watch over it; I water it continually. I guard it
day and night so that no one may harm it.*
ISAIAH 27:2,3

In the last chapter I risked confirming what many people fear most about cultivating a personal relationship with God: The thought of God lording over the vineyard as its owner didn't stir in them blissful thoughts of trust. Instead, it only sounded like a common refrain—might makes right! God is just bigger than we are, so all we can do is blindly trust him even when he seems unfair.

Such thoughts are particularly common to people who have felt powerless in the face of someone else's demands on their life. A school bully—or even more painful, a domineering father or other authority figure—can teach this lesson all too well. They have not known authority apart from its misuse, taking advantage of people for their own gain, and discarding them when they are no longer a source of pleasure. "Might makes right" to them means that the strong get their way because everyone else is helpless against them. But nothing could be more wrong when applied to the Master of the vineyard.

A young couple I know have a chronically ill child who has been that way since birth. They may never see him grow to adulthood. Despite their earnest pleadings, God has not as yet done one visible thing to improve the health of this child. Day after day they watch him suffer in pain and in the limitations that his condition forces upon him, waiting for what they perceive to be his impending death, confused about God's intentions for them.

I hurt every time I pray for them because in my own limited way I understand their feelings. Our own firstborn child had a severe case of jaundice. Every day we bundled up our fragile infant against winter's penetrating cold and took her back to the hospital, where they drew blood from her tender feet. Our days-old daughter screamed in pain.

We watched those first five days as her blood count continued to climb. The doctor told us that if the count didn't drop tomorrow, we would have to put her back in the hospital. Even though her condition wasn't life-threatening and relatively speaking her pain was minimal, I remember how frustrated I was driving back from the hospital that afternoon wondering why we couldn't just take our daughter home and enjoy her like everyone else.

The next day her count was down, and soon our trips to the hospital ended. I can't tell you how grateful we were to God. When I think of this other couple, and multiply my five-day frustration by eight years, I begin to get a glimpse of their distress. To them, hearing that God needs to be trusted because he is bigger than anyone else may not be all that comforting.

For them to walk in the fullness of the kingdom, they must come to know God at a deeper level than just beholding his awesome command over the affairs of the vineyard. As the landowner we can understand his authority and our accountability to him. He is God, after all, and we certainly can expect no less.

To stop there, however, will lead us to a severely distorted picture of God. We not only need to see the authority he holds, but how he *exercises* that authority. This landowner is also the gardener—one who takes care of his own vineyard. Isaiah paints a touching portrait of God as he cares for his vineyard with great compassion. He watches over it. He waters it continually. He guards it day and night so no one can harm it.

The word translated "gardener" or "husbandman" in John 15 carries the meaning of one intimately involved in the growth and nurturing of the vines. This, Jesus said, depicts the Father's role in the garden. He is not just the awesome, majestic Creator of all, but also a God of gentle tenderness who treats the objects of his creation with overwhelming love. The picture of the vineyard draws together both aspects of God's nature and presents them to us in a dynamic tension that makes God wholly attractive. He cares for each branch with intimate care.

I have seen the reflection of that care in my earthly father's eyes toward his own vineyard. He was part of a passing generation of family farmers. He cared for his own vines, refusing to buy more land than he could farm himself. He could never have been a manager of a farming conglomerate. If you were to pass by his farm, he (or his children) would be the ones you would see out in the morning frost—pruning the vines, or driving his tractor through a moving cloud of dust.

He has just retired and sold his farm because he would not stay on the land beyond his ability to farm it. Many farmers hire out the work to others, or even rent out the entire vineyard to someone else's care. They still live on the farm, but only as landlords. But not my father. He did not relish hired hands in his vineyard. He only hired others for the work he could not possibly do himself, and that with great apprehension.

No one he ever hired met his exacting standards. That wasn't because he thought of himself as the world's greatest farmer, but because he knew that no one else would care for his vineyard as much as he did. When he did have to hire, he preferred his family and friends. Maybe they would share his concern.

I've seen the disappointed look in his eye when he saw raisins carelessly strewn on the ground after someone had turned the trays or rolled them. The person paid by the number of trays doesn't care whether a bunch falls off or not.

His wages will be affected if he stops his momentum to pick it up.

I've also felt his pain when he gazed at a vine I had carelessly pruned. In my haste to race my brothers to the end of the row, I had cut off too many good canes. There were not enough left for the vine to reach its full potential in the year ahead. I remember my father's patience in telling us to slow down, training us to do a better job.

But no lesson was more powerful than the fact that I had let him down. Somehow my treatment of that vine had hurt him. I could see it in his eyes, even though he demonstrated no anger. I looked at the good canes lying useless on the ground at my feet. If only I could have glued them back on. . . .

Let me risk mixing metaphors because Jesus illustrates this exact point with a different agricultural analogy. Perhaps he knew that we could understand care directed to animals more easily than grapevines. Even in this day, when scientists tell us our plants will grow better if we talk nice to them, we still don't see people weeping over the death of their favorite houseplant. But if you've ever had a pet you deeply loved, you'll understand the shepherd's love for his sheep.

> *I am the good shepherd. The good shepherd lays down his life for the sheep. The hired hand is not the shepherd who owns the sheep. So when he sees the wolf coming, he abandons the sheep and runs away. Then the wolf attacks the flock and scatters it. The man runs away because he is a hired hand and cares nothing for the sheep.*
>
> JOHN 10:11-13

Here's an interesting shepherd. In the midst of danger he willingly lays down his life for the sheep, risking his own life to keep them safe. That's how deeply Christ loves his own. No hired hand would show the same care; he will labor only until the pain or risk exceeds the quantity of his paycheck—then he's off to find safer pastures.

David risked his own life against a bear and a lion on two separate occasions to rescue his sheep. Farming with an eye only to the bottom line would never even consider such a sacrifice. How could anyone think to risk a human life for a sheep? How about a God who would trade his life for yours?

This is the gardener in whose vineyard you have been planted. His vine is his own Son, and each branch another son or daughter. He loves them more than any other ever could. When I ask someone to surrender to the landlord of the vineyard, this is the one to whom they surrender—the God of tender lovingkindness and compassion, whose mercies never fail.

I can't explain to the young couple why their son suffers so; and though I understand their pain, it is truly misdirected if God is the source of it. He loves them and their son, and though I can't explain his seeming inactivity of the past, I know it is not complicity.

If I understand their pain, how much more does he? God has not hung back indifferent to their prayers or their pain, but has labored over the suffering as well. God wants to redeem their situation, bringing glory out of pain, but to see it they will have to let go of their mistaken conclusions and trust him.

Certainly it won't be easy. Disappointment and hurt can be difficult obstacles to overcome. God knows that. That's why he pictures himself coming to us with such tenderness. Maybe, just maybe, it will sink through one day, and we'll give up fighting just long enough to see the incredible love of the one who holds us in his hands.

The gardener is fully capable of taking any branch, no matter how wounded, and putting it back together again. This may not mean a quick fix. It may take awhile, but God has grace enough to forgive our failures, and strength enough to transform any crisis.

Even when other laborers worked for my father, he kept a sharp eye on their work. Long after they had gone home to rest for the day, my father would walk the rows. He was always the last one out of the vineyard. He would pick grapes that others had missed, scoop up raisins that had been spilled on the ground, and find canes that had come unwrapped from the wire (and tie them up again).

I have seen God do the same thing in the lives of his people. No matter what we endure, no matter how much others might have failed us, he wants to be the last one to touch every area of our lives. Cleaning up from our mistakes and the abuses of others, he can bring fruitfulness out of the most dire circumstances.

The story of Joseph is not meant to be a unique one in God's kingdom. It reveals God's heart for all of his children. The envy of Joseph's brothers led him to be sold as a slave in Egypt. There we still find God, working to fulfill his plan for Joseph even though others meant him great harm. Later, when Joseph was falsely accused because of the integrity of his heart, God even used his jail sentence as a stepping-stone to Pharaoh's court.

Can you believe him to do the same in your own life? It is this kind of trust that allows me to release so much significant ministry to people in the congregation where I serve. I used to worry about people making mistakes. Not every need would be met perfectly; often the wrong thing would be said or the right thing left unsaid. How greatly someone could be damaged, I would think. But not any longer. If they are looking to the Father, he will always be the last one to move through their lives. He will heal hurts and override failures, using both as greater stepping-stones to growth.

Now that's a gardener you can trust completely!

THE FAITHFUL PROVIDER

Then the Father will give you . . .
JOHN 15:16

In many ways my father's care for his vineyard mirrors the way God cares for us. But there is one aspect of the Father's care for the vineyard that my father could never duplicate.

God can superintend every detail of his vineyard, monitor every circumstance, and overcome any enemy of growth. Though my father did as much as he could for his vines—irrigating when the rains were insufficient and fertilizing to enrich the soil—he was not always able to overcome all the forces of nature. He was as much a victim of the elements as each vine in his vineyard.

One day I watched him as rain fell on his freshly picked crop, bringing total destruction to a year's worth of labor. It's not supposed to rain in September, and if he could have stopped it, he would have. I've seen other vineyards wiped out by a late freeze in spring. If the vines have already budded, a freeze will destroy the grapes. Though the vine will grow and look as lush as ever, it will be completely bare of grapes.

Paul recognized that in both vineyards, physical and spiritual, though our own efforts are limited, God's are not: "Neither he who plants nor he who waters is anything, but only God, who makes things grow" (1 Corinthians 3:7). He is not only the caretaker of the vineyard, but he is also Master over all creation and the force behind every stage of our growth.

He not only cares for us, but he has the power to change any circumstance we face. He can give us whatever we need to flourish, and he has power enough to overcome obstacles set against us. Throughout Jesus' story of the vineyard the Father continually hovers in the background. He is not just the gardener who prunes, but the loving Father who provides everything his children need.

That connection would have been especially meaningful to Jesus' hearers in that upper room because of the role that vineyards played in the Old Testament. In Genesis, God called Joseph a fruitful vine, and from that point on the vineyards of Israel acted as special symbols of God's provision and care.

Why a vineyard? Why not a wheat field?

Remember that the Israelites began as a nomadic people. Vines to them were unthinkable. Unlike wheat, vines aren't planted in the spring and harvested a few months later; it takes five years to bring a new vine into full production. When God promised his people vineyards he was telling them he would settle them down in safety long enough to partake of their fruit. His work in them was not just for the moment. His perspective encompassed not just the present, but the whole of their lives.

Israel's vineyards became the symbol of God's provision and care, his promise to allow them to settle in one place and be at rest. When they settled in Canaan they became the beneficiary even of vineyards they hadn't planted—a sign of God's abundance:

> *When the Lord your God brings you into the land he swore to your fathers, to Abraham, Isaac and Jacob, to give you—a land with large, flourishing cities you did not build, houses filled with all kinds of good things you did not provide, wells you did not dig, and vineyards and olive groves you did not plant.*
>
> DEUTERONOMY 6:10,11

When they returned from the exile in Babylon, God reassured them that they would once again be planted in Canaan and have the chance to plant vineyards again, a sign of the enduring protection God would extend to them:

> *They will live there in safety and will build houses and plant vineyards; they will live in safety when I inflict punishment on all their neighbors who maligned them. Then they will know that I am the Lord their God.*
>
> EZEKIEL 28:26

When God blessed his people you could see it in their vineyards. He promised them weather tailor-made for their crops if they would keep him first in their hearts: "I will send rain on your land in its season, both autumn and spring rains, so that you may gather in your grain, new wine and oil" (Deuteronomy 11:14).

Conversely, when God removed his provision as an act of judgment against those who had forsaken him, that too was reflected in their vineyards. Without his involvement their security was lost, and along with it their provision and their joy:

> *You trample on the poor and force him to give you grain. Therefore, though you have built stone mansions, you will not live in them; though you have planted lush vineyards, you will not drink their wine.*
>
> AMOS 5:11

> *The earth is defiled by its people; they have disobeyed the laws, violated the statutes and broken the everlasting covenant. Therefore a curse consumes the earth; its people must bear their guilt. Therefore earth's inhabitants are burned up, and very few are left. The new wine dries up and the vine withers; all the merrymakers groan.*
>
> ISAIAH 24:5-7

There are not many things so desperate-looking as a withered vineyard. When vines die it is not like a corn crop falling victim to a drought. No matter how great the damage to the corn, it is still only one year's loss. Next year's corn can be replanted and a full crop harvested. Not so with the vine. If it is destroyed, crops are wiped out for years to come. No sight is more forlorn than rows and rows of vines, shriveled and withered, the leaves blackened and the canes drooping to the ground.

But even after such days of judgment God promised to restore his people, bringing them back to the security and provision that he had always desired them to have. Once again, their grape crop specifically was signaled out as a sign of this restoration:

> *The Lord has sworn by his right hand and by his mighty arm: "Never again will I give your grain as food for your enemies, and never again will foreigners drink the new wine for which you have toiled; but those who harvest it will eat it and praise the Lord, and those who gather the grapes will drink it in the courts of my sanctuary."*
> ISAIAH 62:8,9

Even in his prophecies of coming destruction, Isaiah promised Israel she would once again be a fruitful vineyard:

> *In the days to come Jacob will take root, Israel will bud and blossom and fill all the world with fruit.*
> ISAIAH 27:6

So it goes through much of the Old Testament. Firmly set in the minds of the disciples as they gathered around Jesus in that vineyard on their last night together was the significance of the grapevine as a symbol of God's provision. The Lord's blessing and discipline were measured in Israel's vineyards and so was his withholding of that provision when their hearts wandered after false gods.

The disciples already knew God as more than a farmer at the whim of rogue storms and swarms of leaf-eating insects. He is God, behind the scenes in every situation.

But this wouldn't mean to them that just because God is able to control circumstances he correspondingly does so to ensure for us a life of ease. You don't have to walk with God long to see that even though he could do so, he does not override every adverse or painful circumstance in our lives.

Some people, not understanding this, see every moment of need or disease as proof that God either doesn't care for them or is powerless to change their circumstances. The connection between righteousness and external provision seems to be far closer in the Old Testament than in the New. God used that connection as a demonstration of the spiritual realities that exist. When we seek God, he gives us life. When we turn away from him, the death caused by our sin is released to work against us.

But even in the Old Testament this relationship was not absolute. Consider the story of Job, whose great calamities are depicted not as punishment for any unrighteousness, but only as an onslaught of Satan to try to destroy Job's faith. Such things happen in a world entangled in sin and hostile to the God who created it, where Satan himself is the prince of this age.

In the New Testament the priority of spiritual life is shown to be inside us. Peace and joy abound for the believer, often in defiance of the circumstances they face and not because of them. While the message of the Old Testament could easily be misunderstood as "Follow God and avoid trouble," the New Testament makes it clear that to follow God will *bring* you adversity.

"We must go through many hardships to enter the kingdom of God" was a word of encouragement that Paul and Barnabus brought to the early church. How many of us would consider that much of an encouragement?

It would only be such if those hearing it were already encountering great difficulties and pain. Instead of using hardships as evidence that God cannot be trusted, they discover that without such hardships access to the kingdom is denied. This doesn't mean we have to suffer to earn access, but rather that our fleshly nature is often confronted and overcome only in moments of adversity.

Two streams of understanding must flow together here. Though God often chooses to be our provider *through* difficulties and not *from* them, that in no way diminishes his power to override them when he so desires. The New Testament shows God doing both.

Jesus submitted to the hostility of those who nailed him to a cross, but only days earlier he had confronted the false religion of the Pharisees. Once he suspended the storm that threatened the disciples on the Sea of Galilee, but there's no indication that he did the same with any other storm they faced.

The early church seemed to see no difference in God's provision whether he was transporting Philip supernaturally to Azotus after speaking to the Ethiopian or riding the waves with Paul adrift in the open seas because of a shipwreck. The ·same God works in different ways.

Certainly God is able to change any of our circumstances and even invites our requests to do so. But if he chooses not to remove our adversity, we are to rest in knowing that adversity is as much a part of our growing as is rest. It is not the most enjoyable part certainly, but it is almost always the most effective part.

In the second section of this book we'll walk through a year of growth in the vineyard. Through spring, summer, fall, and winter we'll look at the different aspects of growth and circumstance that affect the fruitfulness of the vine. One thing we'll see that is common to all four seasons is the necessity of *hardship* to promote fruitfulness. In each season the vine encounters hostile forces. These have the potential to destroy the vine, but they also provide the vine with the opportunity to respond to them in ways that actually enhance the vine's fruitfulness.

As we grow in the vineyard we can trust God as our provider. Regardless of the circumstances, he is as able to change *them*, as he is to change *us* through them. The choice is his, not ours. Our response should not be, "If God loved me this wouldn't be happening," but rather, "Because he loves me even in this, what does he want from me?"

A poignant line from David is a good encouragement to us all: "Those who know your name will trust in you, for you, Lord, have never forsaken those who seek you" (Psalm 9:10). To know God's name is to know the faithfulness of his character and the endless depths of his love. Those who know that fact will put their trust in him.

If you're having a difficult time trusting God in the circumstances you face today, it's only because you need to know him better. And he wants nothing more.

5

A PEEK AT GOD'S PRIORITY

He cuts off every branch in me that bears no
fruit, while every branch that does bear fruit he
prunes so that it will be even more fruitful.
JOHN 15:2

There's nothing a farmer likes to do more than peek.

Throughout the development of his crop, he's always peeking to see how it's coming along and how big he can anticipate the harvest to be.

To this day, anytime between the first budding and the final day of harvest, I can ask my father, "How does the crop look?" and without hesitation he always has an answer.

"About average," or, "Looks like 15 percent above normal."

Even when the grape bunches are smaller than the eraser on my pencil, he's already seen them, looked at how many grapes fill those bunches and how many bunches hang from each vine. That all takes some serious peeking.

So when I think of a grape farmer the image that comes most quickly to mind is when he reaches into a vine with both hands, pulling back the leaves and peeking into every nook and cranny. He is as delighted by every bunch he sees as a child under a Christmas tree finding brightly wrapped packages with his name on them.

This peeking continues even in days after the harvest—just in case one of his gifts has been missed by the harvesters.

There is nothing more important to a farmer than the fruit growing in his field. After all, why else plant a vineyard?

In Jesus' lesson on the vineyard he tells us that his Father is no different. Nine times in his brief sermon reference is made to fruit or fruitfulness (John 15:1-17). Everything the Father does in his vineyard is geared to making each branch on the vine fruitful.

If a branch doesn't bear fruit he cuts it off. No sense wasting the vine's energy on that which will not bear fruit. If a branch *does* bear fruit he cuts it too—not *off*, but he prunes it *up* so that it can be even more fruitful.

Fruit, fruit, fruit! That is the Father's priority, and unless we come to share it we will be forever frustrated with the Lord's dealing in our lives. Unfortunately, we haven't all come to the kingdom of God with that same priority.

Some of us came to the kingdom because we were scared. God offered us security in the face of our fears. Surely, we think, there is nothing more important to God than making sure my circumstances never again make me feel insecure.

Some of us came to God in a moment of crisis. He offered answers to rescue us. Surely, we think, there is nothing more important to God than making sure I am never in need again.

Some of us came to God out of great anguish and guilt for our own sins. He forgave us and promised cleansing. Surely, we think, there is nothing more important to God than protecting me from any temptation that will cause me to sin.

Some of us came to God brokenhearted by the misery of circumstances we had endured. He was a strong tower and healed the hurts that raged in our souls. Surely, we think, there is nothing more important to God than making sure I am happy and never hurt again.

Think again! Is God's greatest priority our feelings of security, safety, or happiness? Many people, confident that it is, find themselves in great confusion when those expectations are not satisfied.

Here is the cause: God has one priority in your life—to make you fruitful. Our priority, however, is often not so noble. We would much rather be happy or at the very least comfortable. Since God's priority will carry the day, as long as we hold to any objective but fruitfulness we'll find ourselves in continual conflict with God's work in us.

For some this talk of fruitfulness may seem a far cry from our early discussion of fulfillment. "That your joy may be full" may seem to have little in common with "that you bear fruit," but a farmer knows that they are directly linked. Fruit only results from fullness. And God knows that only out of fruitfulness do we find true joy.

What is best for the vine's life is also best for its fruitfulness, for fruit is simply the overflow of life. Healthy vines produce fruit; stressed vines do not. A vine poorly pruned, poorly nourished, or encountering a severe lack of water will cast off its fruit in order to keep itself alive for future seasons.

On the other hand, no vine left to itself will be fruitful; it will instead become a sprawling mass of fruitless leaves and branches. Attacked by insects and weakened by lack of care, there will not be enough life to bear any fruit. Neither would we be able to bear fruit if God allowed us every one of our ambitions and every quest for comfort.

That's why the Father trains and disciplines his vines. Though it causes some rough going in the short term, he wants them to know the fullness of joy that comes from being fruitful.

To accept the Father's priority of fruitfulness we have to be willing to endure temporal difficulties at times. Jesus demonstrated that to his disciples when he approached Jerusalem for the last time. Though his disciples didn't understand, he told them that the hour for his death had come. Then in what appears to be a spontaneous burst of emotion, we see the battle Jesus fought.

"Now my heart is troubled, and what shall I say? 'Father, save me from this hour'?" Isn't that the cry that springs most easily to mind when we encounter trouble? It also did for him. Should he pray that way, he asked his disciples? Certainly our Lord wanted to forgo the pain, but he chose something better.

"No, it was for this very reason I came to this hour. Father, glorify your name!" (John 12:23-28). Wonderfully for us he chose the better response. Instead of crying out for his own salvation, he put God's glory first. He sought God's glory over his own comfort, and in so doing showed us the way to be fruitful.

In a study which our fellowship shared through the book of John, we came to this very passage on one of the most painful Sunday mornings I've known. The day before a mother of four young children, the wife of one of the leaders in our congregation, died most unexpectedly on her thirty-fifth birthday. She seemed perfectly healthy up to a week before, when she suddenly had a convulsion. What doctors originally thought was an aneurysm turned out to be a very rare blood disease that brought her life to a swift conclusion. Many in our congregation were only finding out that morning.

And what shall we say? "Father save us from this hour"? Wouldn't we all want to pray just that? Don't let bad things happen to us. But our prayer must be, "Father, be glorified even in this moment." That prayer releases God to take the most painful of our circumstances and use them for his glory.

That does not mean he orchestrates our pain, or delights in our suffering. Nothing could be further from the truth. I don't think God killed that young mother, any more than he killed his Son on the cross. Though both events were in the context of his will, the acts of destruction are the work of darkness. God chose to use them for his purposes. I cannot tell you why the woman died, but I can tell you that even from her husband's own lips God's faithfulness has been affirmed again and again. As we shared earlier, his love is big enough to contain even a horrible circumstance such as this.

A God who is preoccupied with our personal convenience would never have allowed persecution to scatter the church in Judea, or Paul to battle a thorn in the flesh, or James to die by Herod's sword. Obviously God is motivated at a level far higher than our personal convenience. Through all of our adversities he seeks a deeper fruitfulness and uses our circumstances for greater redemption.

He has not promised us circumstances that promote our comfort. Instead he has chosen us to be *fruitful*, and the greatest fruit is often born of struggle. Great promises in

God's kingdom come with great responsibility. Too often we emphasize the former and try to ignore the latter.

As much as God delights in blessing his children, the intent of that blessing is so that we might be a blessing to others. From Abraham on down God invites people to blessing so that through them he might make his blessings available to all the nations of the earth.

Israel had a difficult time keeping that perspective. They misunderstood God's blessing as privilege alone and not as a responsibility to share God's goodness with those around them. Let us not make the same mistake. We should always be looking for ways God wants to use us as a means to bless others.

The only priority that drives the Master of the vineyard is to bring us to fruitfulness. He will do whatever it takes to make that happen. That's also why the farmer peeks so often. He is not just estimating the crop, but also assessing how that crop is doing. Is it maturing? Are there any pests, mildew, or diseases attempting to destroy that harvest? Is there anything he can do to help the fruit?

Everything a farmer does is linked to this peeking. You don't grow grapes in the same way you build a bookcase. It's not a matter of following well-prescribed steps within a controlled environment: Cut this, glue that, sand here. Growing a crop is a dynamic process, demanding constant adjustment to an ever-changing environment. There is no schedule to follow that will work successfully each year. You have to observe the vine and its needs in light of the current weather and circumstances that impact the vineyard.

During the year the vines will need pruning and training. Weeds will need to be pulled and pests sprayed. At the right time the vines will need to be irrigated. No fixed schedule suffices; each year is too different, too unique. So it is with God and us: He watches over the fruit growing in our lives, carefully tending to its development and thereby ensuring the harvest that is to come. Nothing delights his heart more than finding his vines spilling over with fruit. That's the reason he plants them and nourishes them. Consequently, there is no greater demonstration of worship or honor than finding our way into a fruitful Christian life.

This requires that we follow the same path Jesus blazed. In whatever circumstances you face, pray as Jesus did. Forsake your desire for personal comfort and submit each moment to God's design: "Father, glorify your name."

In God's vineyard, fruitfulness is not optional. It will take us to some dark valleys, but even in our most difficult moments he will still be there, giving us abundance in the midst of our sacrifice, healing for our hurts, courage in the face of fear, and joy and peace that can flourish even in crisis.

Being fruitful will also lead us to some impressive peaks. There is no greater exhilaration in a believer's life than sensing God's delight when he pulls back the leaves and sees his fruit growing from our branch.

6

WHAT DO YOU MEAN, FRUITFUL?

This is to my Father's glory, that you bear much fruit, showing yourselves to be my disciples.

JOHN 15:8

Imagine you've arrived at my father's ranch during the high days of harvest. "Sit here," my father tells you, "while I get you some of the fruit of my vineyard." Immediately you picture a bulging bunch of vine-ripened grapes, their green color dusted with the faintest touch of gold from the sugar packed inside. You can almost taste the sweet juice exploding in your mouth with each bite.

What if, however, when he returns he brings you a bowl of boiled grape leaves, or a plate of stir-fried vine bark?

You would be shocked! Everyone knows that you don't grow a grapevine for leaves or bark. Though a local ethnic dish is prepared in cooked grape leaves, no one around here has any doubt about the fruit of the grapevine: It is those round succulent grapes that hang in bunches from the vine. Chew on some leaves if you like, or even the canes. But after you've bitten into the grapes you'll be satisfied by nothing else on the vine.

With the same simplicity let us be sure what fruitfulness actually is in the kingdom of God. Throughout the last chapter I talked of fruitfulness—how it is God's one driving passion

49

for his vineyard—but I never precisely defined what that fruit is. Before I do, let me ask you, What do you think spiritual fruit is?

Did you come away from the last chapter having defined with a certainty that you are in fact bearing that fruit to God? If you did and you were right, great! But I find that most people define fruitfulness by the very thing they lack. There's almost a mindset among believers reminiscent of an abused child: Whatever I do isn't good enough!

If I'm effective in leading a Bible study, I'm sure that real fruitfulness lies in bringing new converts to the kingdom. If I'm evangelistically successful, then I'm sure that real fruit lies in practically serving people in need. If I'm serving people in need, I only do it because I can't do the "real" work of the kingdom, which is teaching great numbers of people.

On and on the cycle goes, few of us ever hearing God's delight, "Well done!" We're just not quite sure what it is he really wants of us.

Part of our confusion about fruitfulness stems from our bent to *quantify* everything as a measure of success—number of converts, bodies in pews, churches in the denomination. Certainly our society's penchant for focusing on the bottom line is no help here. Add to that an incomplete view of Scripture's use of fruitfulness and it's no wonder our view is blurred.

The Old Testament uses fruitfulness almost exclusively to refer to having babies—progeny. "Fruitful" is used 13 times in Genesis, and 12 of those times specifically refer to increasing in number, mostly through bearing offspring. From God's first instructions to the animals he created to his promises to the patriarchs, fruitfulness was specifically linked with an increase of numbers.

Only a few references hint at God's deeper view of what it means for us to be fruitful in his kingdom. Psalm 72:3 links fruit with righteousness and Isaiah 32:17 extends that application: "The fruit of righteousness will be peace; the effect of righteousness will be quietness and confidence forever." But perhaps the clearest reference comes in Hosea 10:12: "Sow for yourselves righteousness, reap the fruit of unfailing love, and break up your unplowed ground; for it is time to seek the Lord, until he comes and showers righteousness on you."

Fruit here is seen as an expression of righteousness that comes from the unfailing love of the Father. Here Scripture's definition of fruitfulness deepens beyond a simplistic increase of numbers and deals with the depth of our character.

In the New Testament the tables turn completely. There is only one reference to fruitfulness as expanded numbers (Colossians 1:6), and that passage deals with the fruitfulness of the gospel. When the fruitfulness of *individual* lives is addressed, however, only one definition is used: Fruitfulness is the demonstration of God's transforming power in the character of his people.

John the Baptist encourages us to "produce fruit in keeping with repentance." In Philippians 1:11 Paul exhorts believers to be "filled with the fruit of righteousness that comes through Jesus Christ—to the glory and praise of God." In Ephesians 5 he contrasts the difference between the fruit of the light (goodness, righteousness, and truth) with the fruitlessness of darkness.

Finally, in Galatians 5:22,23, a passage long revered for its profound simplicity and clarity, he lists the fruits that God desires from his people:

> *The fruit of the Spirit is love, joy, peace, patience, kindness, goodness, faithfulness, gentleness and self-control. Against such things there is no law.*

The first three fruits—love, joy, and peace—are often referred to as blessings that God bestows on his children. He gives us the capacity to love, fills our life with his joy, and gives peace that goes beyond anything we can understand.

The second three fruits define our relationships to other people. Scripture encourages us to be patient with all, to demonstrate kindness in every opportunity we have, and to be a reflection of God's goodness and justice in our actions.

Finally, the last three fruits mark the demeanor of someone who is being transformed by God's kingdom. They are faithful through good times and bad; are gentle in spirit, rather than forcing their own way; and have self under control, living only to please the one who redeemed them.

There is no need to define these fruits further. Even a child understands what love is, or joy, or what it means to be kind. These are not difficult concepts to understand. They are only difficult to live out daily.

But let's take all these traits together. What would someone look like who could demonstrate love, joy, peace, patience, kindness, goodness, faithfulness, gentleness, and self-control in each situation he or she encountered? Why, I think he would look just like . . . Christ. He would reveal Christ's nature to everyone around him. What greater fruit could there possibly be?

Fruitfulness has nothing to do with how many Bible studies I've taught or how many people I've led to Christ, nor has it any attachment to any other religious activity. *Fruit is borne in our character.* It is the transformation of our lives so that we reflect God's nature to the culture around us. In John 15 the call to fruitfulness and the commnad to love one another are one and the same.

When we love the way God loves, we bear the fruit of his kingdom. It's what he wants to work into us through the long process of growth and maturity. The fruits of the Spirit are not what we can make ourselves be for a moment, but what God produces in us for a lifetime. At its fulfillment this fruit is how we freely respond to people and situations. Obviously, this kind of fruit is not produced overnight. Learning to respond like Christ is fashioned in us over time as God walks us through our joys and disappointments, all the while transforming us from the very depths of our being.

Our ability to reveal God's image to the people around us is more important than our worship, our prayers, our religious deeds, our devotions, our spiritual gifts, even our acts of evangelism. For without this fruitfulness there is no spiritual work that counts, no evangelism that succeeds, and no gift that prevails. All of these other aspects are valuable in our growth in God's kingdom, but these are not the fruit that God seeks in our lives. If the objective of our time in worship or

Bible study is not to allow God to transform us into his image with ever-increasing glory, then it means nothing!

Who hasn't seen people who have done great things for God, or been used in tremendous ways by the Lord, but whose lack of love, gentleness, or self-control rears its ugly head to mar all else that has been accomplished. First Corinthians 13 is right: Without love we're just a loud crashing sound, regardless of the successes.

How is the world to know we are his disciples? Is it by our ornate church edifices? Is it by the breadth of our TV or radio ministries? Is it by the expensive musical productions or complicated children's programs? Is it through our sharp advertisements or overplanned worship services?

No! None of these are wrong in themselves, but we've got to recognize that what the world waits to see is a people who demonstrate God's character by the way we treat one another, by whether we are laying down our lives for each other in the same way Jesus did for us. They watch to see if we're serving each other, giving up our comfort for one another, forgiving each other—in short, loving each other deeply. If not, why should they believe? The only image of God the world will see is what he stamps on our lives.

Jesus said so—right in the midst of all his instructions about the vineyard: "This is to my Father's glory, that you bear much fruit, showing yourselves to be my disciples" (John 15:8). Notice that Jesus didn't spend much time teaching his disciples to plan crusades or door-to-door campaigns. He had already told them earlier that evening what the fruit was that both the Father and the world were looking for: "By this all men will know that you are my disciples, if you love one another" (John 13:35).

This is Jesus' model for evangelism. For all our technical expertise, we are sorely lacking in our ability to demonstrate to the world a self-sacrificing community where there is love and honor instead of backbiting, manipulating, and complaining.

They witness church split after church split. Consider this: In December of 1989 our congregation helped plant a new congregation in a village in central Mexico that had no church of any kind. When some of our team returned to Mexico three months later they found two churches, split apart by a dispute about eternal security—both believing that members of the other congregation were no longer Christians.

Our first thoughts were, Where did they learn such nonsense? They hadn't known salvation long enough to even contemplate such matters. Then we learned that outside people had come in to exploit what God was doing for their own gain.

No wonder the world rejects the gospel! Why shouldn't it? If love does not fill the house of God, how will people know that he is real? Without intimate love overflowing through his church we are only a loud noise that the world will never comprehend. The quality of our lives is the only platform on which we can ever stand as far as the world is concerned. What we say of God's nature is far less important than what we demonstrate.

Each time we lay down our lives for another person we allow this world to see what happened 2000 years ago at Calvary. Our sacrifices make the cross and God's love visible to people around us.

This is the fruit of the vineyard. All the Father's efforts toward us are to see his character replanted and spilling out of our lives like grape bunches from an overloaded vine. As it is his passion, so it must be ours.

7

WHAT OF UNPRODUCTIVE VINES?

*If anyone does not remain in me, he is
like a branch that is thrown away and withers;
such branches are picked up, thrown into
the fire and burned.*
JOHN 15:6

Fruitless branches are obvious. The branch itself may look fine, but the canes that spring from it are withered and sickly. Few if any of them will even reach up to the wire intended to support them.

I've seen it happen a thousand times and each time it seems such a waste. It takes many years for a branch to develop, and each branch holds the potential for bearing much fruit. But when it becomes obvious that a branch was not fruitful, there was nothing else to do but cut it off.

I'd fall to my knees beside the vine and pull the pruning saw from my back pocket. I'd unfold the blade and saw off the fruitless branch, tossing the dead wood into the middle of the row. Because branches were too big to be churned into the soil as canes are, they would be collected later.

So it is in God's vineyard. He is so passionate about fruitfulness that the consequences of not bearing fruit are dire indeed. Jesus didn't want that warning to escape us. After describing himself as the vine and the Father as the gardener he drives home this point. The Father cuts off every branch that doesn't bear fruit.

He goes on to describe five other things that happen to that branch. It is thrown away and it withers. Then it is picked up, thrown into the fire, and burned. Of all the things that happen to the branch the only one that ultimately matters is the first.

Once a branch is cut off its life ends. What happens after that only describes what is left to be done with a dead branch. Without the life-giving connection to the rest of the vine, the sap spills out and the branch dries up. What else can you do with that branch now but burn it?

When Ezekiel confronted Israel with her continuing rebellion against God, he reminded the people of just that fact. Did they really have any other purpose than to please God?

> *Son of man, how is the wood of a vine better than that of a branch on any of the trees in the forest? Is wood ever taken from it to make anything useful? Do they make pegs from it to hang things on?*
>
> EZEKIEL 15:2,3

Certainly not! Grapevines are not all-purpose plants; they are good only for producing grapes. If the vine doesn't do that its wood isn't useful for anything else. You can't eat it, build with it, or make tools of it.

Some people in our section of the country do use grape canes for craft projects. They twist the canes together to form a wreath and then decorate it with dried flowers, wooden geese, and billowy ribbons. Actually, I've never gotten used to these wreaths. No matter how you dress up dead vines, I've lived too long on a grape ranch to think of them as anything other than fire fuel or fertilizer for next year's crop.

The gardener prunes away those branches that do not bear fruit. This was not specifically directed at the disciples. Jesus reassured them in the very same breath that they were not in danger of this pruning since he already made them clean. He wanted them, however, to understand the Father's passion for fruitfulness. God, it seems, has as little use for unfruitful branches as farmers do. No matter how large or well-developed the branch is, it must be removed, for God is not looking for lovely brances but ripening fruit.

Some of the stories from Jesus' life that have bothered me the most were of the times Jesus turned away seemingly promising candidates for the kingdom. A man wants to follow Jesus, but he wants to go bury his father first. Jesus' response is harsh: "Let the dead bury their own dead, but you go and proclaim the kingdom of God" (Luke 9:60).

Or what of the time when the rich young ruler wanted to follow Jesus, but Jesus was only going to let him do so if he would sell everything he owned and give it to the poor? The young man left discouraged because he wasn't willing to do this.

Once Jesus even chased off a crowd of more than 5000 who had eaten of the miraculous lunch of multiplied bread and fish, and then pursued Jesus around the Sea of Galilee. To these he said, "Eat my flesh and drink my blood." The crowd didn't understand his cryptic words and went away confused and disillusioned. What bothers me is that Jesus didn't stop them. He didn't call out, "Hey, you misunderstood. I was talking about communion."

These people seemed far more serious about pursuing the Lord than many I have seen who hang around our churches today. Why did he eliminate these people with challenges certainly too difficult for new converts to bear?

Or was Jesus looking at something far deeper? Could he see that these were branches that were not going to plant deep enough to bear fruit? The first man would always cater to his family at the expense of the kingdom. The money of the young ruler would always be his real god, and trying to have both would only provide endless frustration. Was the crowd with satisfied bellies looking only for a free lunch, while lacking the faith that would endure the many other times when God's activity would supersede their reason?

Perhaps Jesus realized that without some choice for change these people would not be fruitful and would need to be cut off anyway. There is an accountability to the kingdom that grace does not mask. Grace does not cover our slovenly lack of response to the presence of God in our lives. We cannot hide behind it as an excuse not to bear fruit. To make us fruitful is the very reason grace has been extended to us:

> *So, my brothers, you also died to the law through the body of Christ, that you might belong to another, to him who was raised from the dead, in order that we might bear fruit to God.*
>
> ROMANS 7:4

I am constantly amazed by those people who want the smallest bite of salvation they can take and still feel confident they can escape hell. God has opened to us a glorious kingdom where we can live in him and know the fullest of joy. Why settle for less?

But maybe you have. Maybe you've spent years near the kingdom of God, yet you do not see fruitfulness flowing from your life. Is there hope for you? Will God cut you off, or has he already?

Though God's judgment concerning our fruitlessness is certain, it is not always swift. Jesus tells another parable to illustrate his Father's heart for the vineyard that bears repeating. Though the vineyard that Jesus used in this parable is full of figs, the application of his teaching is no less vital to our understanding. Here we see that though the Father yearns for fruitfulness, his patience far exceeds that of any farmer I know.

> *A man had a fig tree, planted in his vineyard, and he went to look for fruit on it, but did not find any. So he said to the man who took care of the vineyard, "For three years now I've been coming to look for fruit on this fig tree and haven't found any. Cut it down! Why should it use up the soil?"*

*"Sir," the man replied, "leave it alone for one more year,
and I'll dig around it and fertilize it. If it bears fruit next
year, fine! If not, then cut it down."*

LUKE 13:6-9

In this brief parable the farmer comes to the vineyard disappointed at the fruitlessness of one of the vines. He had planted it three years ago, but it had not yet borne any fruit. Now no farmer would expect a vine to be in full production in three years, but it is extremely unusual for a vine to grow that long without any fruit at all appearing.

He is ready to cut it down and replace it with a new vine that will bear fruit, but the gardener here has a better hope: Let's give it another chance; I'll do everything I can to encourage its fruitfulness, and then if it still doesn't bear fruit we'll cut it down.

Jesus tells the parable to let the gardener's heart reveal the Father's. Here again he differs from the farmer who only looks at the bottom line. Yes, the track record may not be good, but we still have three years' worth of roots here. Let's try one more year, doing all we can to coax fruitfulness out of the vine.

Behold the immense patience of our God! He sees potential where we often miss it and is willing to invest all his resources in one more attempt at fruitfulness. Cutting off the unfruitful is never God's first choice; it is only his last resort after he has pressed every other possibility.

God still has hope for fruitfulness from your life even if it feels as though you've squandered the preceding years. If you are still hungry and willing to respond to the gardener, your time is not up yet, though I would encourage you not to keep testing his patience.

Those who hunger after God's priority will want to bear fruit. It is not so tricky a path for he does not ask us to *produce* it. Only Jesus can make us fruitful as he lives his life through us. As we'll see, the branch's concern is not with producing fruit, but in staying joined to the true vine. Do this and you'll have more fruit than you know what to do with.

8

WON'T YOU BE MY FRIEND?

Greater love has no one than this, that he lay down his life for his friends. You are my friends if you do what I command.

JOHN 15:13,14

"I am the vine; you are the branches." Almost poetic in its simplicity, Jesus comes to the crowning theme of his lesson. For one who has grown up around grapevines, it is a jarring statement.

Few plants come in as many fascinating shapes as grapevines. Their trunks twist up from the ground in a myriad of shapes and forms. Two feet or so above the ground the trunk separates into craggy arms that continue the seemingly random twisting and turning as they reach toward the wires above. One of the games we played as children was to challenge each other to impersonate a chosen grapevine by contorting our own trunk and limbs to match it.

Thinking back I can't ever remember making much of a distinction between the vine and the branches. The same rough, flaky bark that starts just above the ground continues out through the branches where the canes emerge. I think of a vine as one unit made up of both trunk and branches. The disciples, who had seen thousands of vines, would have thought similarly.

If you asked me to go out today and saw off a branch for you, I could do it easily enough. But in looking at a grapevine up close there is nothing about the makeup of a branch that distinguishes it from a trunk. There is no fixed line that says the vine ends here and the branch begins. I could saw from the point at which it separates from another branch, but the cut line would only be arbitrary. You would not know when I was done if I had all branch, or sawed part of the vine in the process.

When Jesus called himself the vine and us the branches, he could have chosen no better illustration of the intimate bond he seeks with his followers. He desires that we identify so closely with him that others cannot tell where he leaves off and where we begin.

Earlier he had already described what kind of vine he is. He is the true vine—solid, firm, reliable. The phrasing itself assumes there are other vines that promise fulfillment and fruitfulness. But they are imposters. While promising life, they only draw life from us, leaving us empty and isolated.

Jesus is the only vine that really gives life. That's how exclusive Jesus' terminology is. I am the true vine and there is no other.

This picture takes us to the heart of salvation. For Jesus, salvation was not merely our reprieve from hell, but a doorway through which we could enter into the fullness of his life. Those who regard salvation only as an escape from eternal punishment develop a maintenance mentality about their lives. They hold on to God just enough to ensure that they don't lose their salvation.

But Jesus invites his followers to plunge in deeply and bear the fruit of his kingdom. No mere maintenance mentality here; he has launched us on an adventure into the depths of Christ that the ancients could only long for.

Then he defines the exact nature of the incredible link that joins a branch to the vine: "I have called you friends."

Few things are more marvelous than a good friendship. What a joy whenever we find someone who reciprocates our pleasure at being with him or her, respects our ideas, gets involved in our struggles and successes and offers us the safety of always being honest and genuine. Good friendships are filled with spontaneity and warmth.

Take all that you know of a good friendship, pick the best you've ever known, and you'll understand the wonder of Jesus' words to us as branches. He wants to be the best friend you ever had—sharing every moment of your life. And, unlike any other friend you've ever had, this one will never fail you.

One winter afternoon not so long ago I blazed up the field following the kickoff, maneuvering myself to get a sure tackle on the receiver. As he approached he made a move toward the sideline. I turned toward him to shove him out-of-bounds when suddenly he cut back to the left. I tried to cut with him, but my feet slipped out from under me on the wet grass. I reached out to grab him in one last desperate attempt, but went sliding by hopelessly as he cut up the middle and scored a touchdown.

My ten-year-old came trotting back up the field laughing so hard that he crumpled on the ground next to me. "You should have seen your face!" Andy cackled.

I laughed with him there on the grass. We had been playing for half an hour, and I was exhausted. We talked about some of the best plays and laughed together. All the while we were being constantly pestered by our yellow Labrador, who kept dropping a tennis ball on various parts of our anatomy, hoping we would hurl it across the lawn for her to chase.

Catching my wind, I devised a plan. "I'll throw her tennis ball toward the end of the lawn, then let's both go after her like she's returning a kickoff." Andy was excited at the prospect.

I tossed the ball and off went the dog in full stride. We jumped to our feet and pursued her. She never knew we were coming until she picked up the tennis ball, wheeled around, and saw the two of us running at her screaming. The shocked look on her face was worth the whole exercise as she bolted around us, unable to figure out what we were doing. Again we collapsed to the ground laughing at the dog and each other. As our laughter slowly drained we lingered awhile, talking of Andy's day at school, news he had heard on the TV that evening, and a variety of other things.

Of such moments intimacy is created. I am responsible to train Andy in the ways of God, but I do that best only to the degree that I am his friend. My friendship with him does not demean my fatherhood, but defines it. This friendship allows me the difficult moments of demanding his obedience without compromising our relationship or his self-respect.

In no less a way does Jesus invite us to friendship with him. He wants us to know him with the same kind of warmth, to laugh with him through our slips and spills; he wants to relax with us in our weariness, to commune with us on the issues that affect us most. Though most believers are comfortable speaking of "personal relationship with Jesus," few concepts are so personally inexperienced as that of true friendship with him.

Some people shy away from intimacy with Jesus, preferring instead to concentrate on his transcendence: He is the great Lord who by a word spoke worlds into existence. They have seen the imbalance of people who feign a chumminess with Jesus that isn't quite real and often not respectful of his greatness. But sometimes that is only an excuse.

Often what lies beneath the theology of a distant God is frustration at God's seeming inactivity. Prayers go unanswered. Requests for wisdom seem caught in a backlog of celestial red tape. In our darkest moments he did not come and change our circumstances. To allay disappointment we may prefer the simplistic explanation that friendship with God is an abstract thing, and then find some measure of comfort in resignation that his ways are higher than ours.

But God's awesomeness and his nearness are not conflicting images. His nearness only makes his greatness that much more awesome. What so-called god in any other religion or legend has ever displayed such greatness of power and such warm tenderness toward people? Who else has subjected himself to the sin of his own creation by suffering such unjust punishment against himself for its salvation?

Such intimacy does not diminish his lordship, but brings it to our lives in the most powerful way possible: In the tenderness of a warm friendship. That tenderness is no better demonstrated than the way Jesus loved his worried followers the night before he was to be crucified.

They begged him for alternatives to his impending departure. Surely you won't leave us. We'll stay with you no matter what. Can't we go with you?

He was not deaf to their cries, but little did they realize that if he fulfilled their limited expectations it would deny them the greater joy he had in store for them. So he sat down and ate with them, took them for a walk in a garden, and taught them how to pray in moments of conflict in a way that invites God closer and does not push him away.

Jesus was being their friend *through* the circumstances he wouldn't change. He promised them another Counselor who would be with them forever. He makes clear his invitation: I want to be your friend. Will you be mine?

The offer of friendship is the point of the tale of the vineyard. Jesus offered his disciples fullness of joy and challenged them to be fruitful for the Father, but neither of these were to be the object of their pursuit. Seek fulfillment and you will only find hollow days of temporal satisfaction that fade as fast as a snowflake on a warm car. Try to make yourself fruitful and you'll only know the endless frustration of good deeds that never fulfill their intentions, and effort that never seems enough for God.

The fulfillment and fruitfulness Jesus offered is only found in our friendship with him. That's what he told us to seek. How we develop that friendship and remain in it daily will occupy the chapters ahead. It is the essence of life in God's vineyard, defining how we as branches are joined to the one true vine.

Don't ever let your relationship with Jesus become overgrown with anything other than the simplicity of friendship. He wants you to enjoy him. Marriages begin to fail the day husbands and wives become so concerned about the work of survival that they forget how to enjoy each other. So does our relationship with God. We can be so absorbed in religious activity we forget to enjoy him.

Nothing could be more tragic, for he wants to go with you everywhere—not only to church and ministry outreaches but also to a camping trip with your family, a round of golf with friends, and even a backyard football game with your children.

9

I'VE BEEN CHOSEN

You did not choose me, but I chose you.

JOHN 15:16

What gives any of us the right to presume such intimacy with one so magnificent? The answer is found in how we came to be a branch on the Lord's vine to begin with.

At first glance over Jesus' words about the vineyard it is easy to miss. He didn't describe it in detail, since those he talked to were already firmly implanted in the vine, but he did remind them how it all began.

"I chose you." It was that simple. They had not come to him by their own determination or because they just happened to be at the right place at the right time. Their participation in his life was not a random act of nature. He had chosen them.

I wonder how much those words meant to Peter on this treacherous night. Circumstances were tumbling downhill with increasing velocity. Danger and confusion swirled in the darkness. He must have thought, How did I get myself into this?

"I chose you." The words must have leapt out at him. I remember now; that's exactly the way it happened. How vividly that day would have remained in Peter's memory: Exhausted from a long and unsuccessful night at sea, he had just finished cleaning the nets when Jesus approached him. What Peter knew about Jesus before that moment is unclear.

We do know that even after his discouraging night of fishing, he consented to Jesus' request to use his boat to speak to the crowd.

Evidently impressed to some degree, Peter calls Jesus "Master" shortly after he is finished, and even follows another odd request from Jesus. Yes, he'll put out the nets again—even though they caught nothing the night before and were now lying at his feet cleaned and folded.

He had hardly slipped them overboard when the water began to boil with fish leaping into his net. The load was too big for one man, and he called for help. Though Peter's eyes may have been on the net, his heart was fixed on this incredible man. "Go away from me, Lord; I am a sinful man."

Jesus didn't honor Peter's request, but instead invited him to go fishing with him; this time for people. That was all it took. Peter left the greatest catch of his life for others to sell.

I've met two kinds of people who are disappointed by the lack of reality they have found in their relationship with the Savior. The first I have described in previous chapters—those who blame God for not caring enough to help them. Peter is an example of the other type—those who feel like damaged goods. They are too filthy, too ugly to tolerate God's presence. They will tell him to leave them alone, and if he doesn't they'll run away themselves.

But Peter had been chosen, and by that simple act his fears were dispelled. Here is an amazing attribute of this vine, unlike any I've ever seen: Jesus chooses the branches that will draw life from him. This was not Peter's doing. He had not earned it.

What a difference from anything else in his culture. "If you want something, go out and get it. No one is going to walk up and hand it over to you." This was especially true of religion. The religious leaders were a select class; they had to have money or connections to surface at the top of the ladder. But in one moment on a makeshift dock Jesus short-circuits the process. Reaching past those who had completed the religious obstacle course of the day he simply chooses Peter. "I want you; will you come?"

Jesus makes the same invitation to us, because branches in his vineyard don't just grow naturally out of his vine, like they did in my father's field. Jesus harkens back to a far more special process called grafting.

The most detailed picture of how grafting works is painted by Paul in Romans 11:17-24. Though he writes of olive trees, the same process was also used in vineyards. And though he writes in generalities of the Jewish and Gentile nations, it is what we all go through on a personal level before we can become partakers of Jesus' life.

Grafting is a nearly-miraculous process in which one new plant is made out of two different ones. There are various methods for doing this, but all involve a branch cut from one vine and inserted into a cut on another vine. The two are then bound together with an adhesive compound or tape (or in ancient days mud or clay). As the wound heals, the two plants become one, the new branch drawing sap from the roots of the established vine.

Notice that grafting demands a wound in both parties. Jesus, as our vine, was cut open on the cross to make room for us. For us to be grafted into him we must also be wounded in complementary fashion so that we will fit into the place prepared. That's why we have to identify with the death of Christ. Unless we are cut away from our roots in the past we cannot be placed in him.

As Israel was "broken off because of unbelief," the only way we can be grafted in is by believing in him. Believing in Jesus means that we will surrender our life to his control and trust his word about everything.

This reaches to the very heart of Paul's analogy. He points out that grafting is "contrary to nature" and as such superbly illustrates our new Christian life. We can no longer trust the natural ways of our flesh since we've become part of something so wonderfully new.

Usually cultivated branches were grafted onto wild roots, which were more vigorous, but Paul turns the analogy here. We are the wild shoots because of the hostile and ignorant ways of our flesh. Jesus is the cultivated vine. If we are going to experience God's life we're going to have to draw from his roots.

The reason this is so important for us to settle at the outset is not only because of the confidence it gives us to pursue Jesus with hope and joy, but because it sets a serious precedent for everything about the Father's vineyard.

He is my total resource for strength, nourishment, comfort, and direction. Everything to the branch flows through the trunk. Moisture and nutrients from the soil are delivered to the branches on the vine's timetable. As that vine, Jesus sets the direction for my life. He chooses my portion today, my ministry, my feeding. I am to become totally dependent upon him, a responder in the life of the kingdom, not an initiator. Nothing happens by my choice unless it was first his.

Grafting is a process that can only be done one branch at a time. It requires the personal attention of the gardener as he cuts and fits us into Christ, and a personal response from us. Each of us must respond to his work, because God has no second-generation disciples.

My wife and I are getting to watch that process right now in our 12-year-old daughter. Sara and I are actively helping Julie develop her own relationship with God and find an accountability to him that does not run through her parents. We began on her twelfth birthday to release an increasing number of decisions into Julie's hand so that we can help her through the sometimes painful process of learning to hear and believe God's voice.

And it's paying off. Recently she was invited to a birthday party of a good friend. This was to be a sleep-over event, and since this friend lives out of town, Julie would be the only one not from her friend's school. The last few years when she has attended daytime parties for this girl, she has felt left out because all the other girls were such good friends.

"Do I have to go, Dad?" she asked with a disgusted whine. She knew from plenty of past times that we made them go to the parties of children whom they have invited to their own.

"Julie, you're 12 now and the decision is yours. I'm not going to make you go. You need to decide for yourself what is right to do."

Immediately her countenance changed. "Should I go?" the whine was now gone. I wasn't going to make her and by that simple act I had become someone who could now help her with the decision.

"She came to your last party."

"I know, but, Dad, everyone leaves me out." The whine had returned.

"I'm not saying you have to go. I'm only helping you see what to consider. Have you prayed about it yet?" This time I got a scrunched-up nose and that look of "whatever for?" "Why don't you go up to your room and ask God what he wants you to do? If he wants you to go, then go. If not, then don't."

She did exactly that, and 20 minutes later she came back out on the landing. "I'm going to go to the party," she said with a broad smile. It's so much harder to be accountable to God than it is to manipulate a parent, but so much more joyful.

It was a small matter, but my relationship to my daughter is changing. God now needs the place I have had in her life for her first years. Julie has a heart for God and a desire to please him, and I need to release her to be grafted into that vine as well. Though I risk letting her make mistakes, I would much rather have her make them in small things like birthday parties when I'm close enough to walk her through them than when she's choosing a mate for life a thousand miles away.

Without being personally grafted in, our life in God will always be empty and irrelevant. We cannot afford to let a parent, pastor, or Bible study leader be grafted in for us. We dare not try to draw our life from them—only from Jesus himself.

What about you? Jesus not only chose those first disciples, he continues to choose his followers today. *He* is the one who guarantees our place alongside him. He wants *us*, not our abilities or talents. Whatever excuses we think might prevent that grafting must dissolve along with Peter's, because it was Jesus' choice before it was ever ours.

Anyone who has ever waited in line, only to be the last chosen for a team, knows the terrifying humiliation of not being wanted. Regrettably, many of us carry that same feeling into Christianity. "Whosoever will" has come to mean that God *has* to take everybody. So when God says, "You are a chosen people, a royal priesthood, a holy nation, a people belonging to God . . ." it doesn't mean anything to us. Yet there is no greater assurance than knowing that Jesus has chosen us to be planted in him.

What is especially magnificent about the Lord's choosing is that *his choosing me does not exclude anyone else*. When five people compete for a new position in the company, the joy of the person selected is purchased at the severe disappointment of the other four. In the Father's vineyard, however, there is a time (even numerous times) in every life when God extends his hand to choose each person. Not all walk over to join his team, however. Many walk away unwilling to give up their life to gain his.

But why do I pursue abiding in the vine with such fervor? Because no matter how unloved I've felt in the past, no matter how filthy I feel in my sin, God knew all of that when he chose me to be on his team. He wanted *me*, and he also wants *you*. Hope for finding fulfillment in his kingdom springs from that simple truth. You can have fulfillment in his kingdom specifically because *he wants to give it to you*.

I don't know if this was a source of comfort to Peter the morning after he denied Jesus. If it had been me, I'd have come back to Jesus' simple words the night before. Jesus knew well how weak Peter's flesh would be in this trial. Yet to him and the others he still said, "I have chosen you."

When it comes down to our relationship with Jesus, what else really matters?

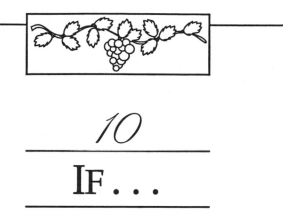

10

IF . . .

If a man remains in me and I in him,
he will bear much fruit; apart from me you can
do nothing.
JOHN 15:5

In the vineyards of this world, branches don't have freedom of choice. They are silent victims of whatever the farmer or his workers decide to be their lot.

Each winter as I pruned vines in my father's vineyard, I had total freedom to shape the vine any way I chose. It was my decision which branches should remain and which would be cut off. I was master of that vine, and I chose at times almost on a whim which branches might be robust enough to promise a good harvest ahead.

The branches had nothing to say about it, no volition of their own. Branches are unthinking objects. They had no ability to prune themselves even if they wanted to, or stick themselves back on the vine after I had cut them off. They were victims pure and simple, without any voice or choice in the matter.

But here the Father's vineyard takes another major departure from our earthly ones, for in his vineyard the branches have their own will. No one compels them to grow here. The Father has set the stage, but it is their choice whether or not they want to be part of the drama of life in the vineyard.

Jesus conveyed that truth to his own followers with a simple two-letter word: "if." Five times in these short 16 verses Jesus

uses *if*. Each time it is followed by a simple statement high-
lighting the role that the branch plays in being part of this
vineyard.

- *If* a man remains in me and I in him, he will
  bear much fruit.

- *If* anyone does not remain in me, he is like a
  branch that is thrown away and withers.

- *If* you remain in me and my words remain in
  you, ask whatever you wish, and it will be
  given you.

- *If* you obey my commands, you will remain in
  my love.

- You are my friends *if* you do what I command.

If. A simple word to state simple realities. Do this and that
will happen. Don't do it and something else will. Cause and
effect, quick and clean. The apostle John, perhaps better than
anyone else, picked up the stark contrast of this simple word.
He uses "if" 74 times in his gospel and 21 times in his first
brief epistle.

"If" allows no room for maybes, as if Jesus' words were
mere wishful thinking or statements of probability. These are
simple facts, simply stated, without loopholes or mitigating
circumstances. This is the way God has set things up. Choose
to come along, or choose not to. The decision is ours.

There is no better way to define the balance between God's
sovereignty and our free will. For our free will does not mean,
cannot mean, that the branches have the run of the vineyard.
This is *God's* vineyard. He made it and he determined how it
will function. We are free to choose whether or not we want to
be part of it, but we cannot change the way God's vineyard
functions in order to suit ourselves.

If we do not choose to remain in the vine and be fruitful, we
cannot also choose to hang around the vineyard anyway; he
will cut us away. Certainly many people want God's favor and
blessing on their lives. Who would resist that? But even with

that desire, many persist in living life by their own wisdom, following the appetites of their own flesh.

Somehow, they hope, grace will extend beyond their own selfishness and failure to submit to God's ways. I'm not talking here about those who war against their flesh as they fall victim to it, but those who willingly give in to their appetites hoping that God will somehow override the consequences of their choices.

While growing up I always wanted the money that Dad paid us for working in the vineyard, but I never wanted to do the work to get it. What a dilemma! I wanted to play all the time, but still have the rewards of those who work. I face the same attitude in my children today. They like being the beneficiaries of the work that needs to be done around the house—clean clothes and dishes—but they struggle with being participants in the process of gaining them.

For a branch in God's vineyard this simply cannot be. The "if" clauses of this passage compel us to make a choice. That choice is not whether we want to be fulfilled in God's life, or whether we want to be fruitful for his kingdom. The choice is whether or not we want to remain in him, to accept his offer of friendship.

If we do, an array of dazzling opportunities are offered to each of us. If not, we are confronted with certain judgment. The branch dries up and is thrown away. Why? Because one powerful reality lies behind all of Jesus' teaching on the vineyard: "Apart from me you can do nothing." When we cut ourselves off from relationship with Jesus, we are incapable of doing anything in God's kingdom. This doesn't mean we won't be busy in any number of religious activities on his behalf, but simply that none of these will bear the fruit of his kingdom.

How I wish this were as clear in the spiritual vineyard as it is in the earthly one! The moment a branch cuts itself off from the life-giving nourishment of the vine it begins to wither. The leaves wither almost immediately, and though they're still green, their limpness tells you that death has already come.

With us, however, we can become distracted from Jesus'
involvement in our lives and hardly even notice it. We can still
be engrossed in a wide variety of spiritual activities. His
blessing still seems to accompany us even as we get by on our
own strength, unaware of the creeping death that has been
unleashed. Then one day we wake up feeling empty or
stressed by the demands on our lives. We wonder why God
doesn't seem as close to us as before, never recognizing that
we have drawn back from the vine.

Simple neglect of our friendship with Jesus is the biggest
danger any of us will face. It happens so easily, because like
vines we are easily distracted from his presence by the challenges and opportunities of our culture.

Vines are crafty plants, always looking for nourishment
wherever they can find it. They are notorious for rooting
wherever they are given the chance. All a cane has to do is fall
to the ground and if the dirt covers it the same buds that are
meant to produce fruit and leaves are just as happy to produce
roots instead. These roots can become so strong that they
draw their own nourishment from the soil and if cut off from
the vine these branches will become their own vine. It happens so simply that it is one of the chief ways vines are
propagated on earth, but not in God's kingdom!

Listen to Jeremiah's lament: "I had planted you like a choice
vine of sound and reliable stock. How then did you turn
against me into a corrupt, wild vine?" (Jeremiah 2:21). How
indeed! It happens when branches themselves sink roots into
the ground to develop their own roots and seek their own
nourishment. Branches are not supposed to have roots—just
canes, leaves, and fruit.

What a picture of our own lives! Even while we seek to
follow Jesus, the enemy lures us with opportunities to sink
our roots into the simplest things. About every six months
one family in our congregation banishes their television set to
the garage for a few weeks. They don't do that because they
consider it evil, but because they recognize at times how
much it dominates their attention. At some point it crosses
the line from being a tool they can rightly use for information
and entertainment and instead becomes a resource for coping

with boredom and a distraction to their relationship with God. It begins to control them, and they are sensitive enough when that happens to cut it off before their roots sink into it.

Many people struggle with other things. Eating is a natural and delightful gift of God, but the enemy has tempted many people to sink their roots into it as a way to deal with pain and misery. Other people deal with their anxieties by shopping, abusing drugs or alcohol, or overdosing on their chosen form of recreation. When our roots sink into these as a means to live our lives, our life in Christ is cut off.

Why do we do it? Because there are so many things that can at least temporarily make us feel good. They do provide temporary relief, and often far more easily than we can find it in the cross of Christ. But these things only *cover* pain, they don't actually heal it. In time the pain returns in ever-haunting ways, demanding even more degrading attempts to mask it.

The result of rooting in anything but Jesus is bondage and destruction. Promising instant gratification, the devices of this world offer no true healing. Apart from him we will not find any joy or fruit in any way that counts.

In him, however, is life full and abundant. The next few chapters will cover the implications of each of these "if" statements as we look at the qualities of friendship Jesus defined to teach us how to remain in him and be a thriving branch on the vine. The way of the vineyard calls us not just to understand or even agree with Jesus' instructions, but to follow them.

In recent decades of Christianity our approach to God's life has been mostly centered on creeds and confessions—the words of our mouth. Do you want to know Jesus? Pray this sinner's prayer with me. We ask people to confess to God what they want of him, without putting enough focus on the lifestyle we must embrace.

When we wander away from the faith disillusioned that God's promises didn't meet our expectations we need to be honest enough to probe whether or not our walk fulfilled the promises we made to him. In God's kingdom it matters less what we tell him we want to do than what we actually do.

Walter Wangerin in his book on marriage, *As for Me and My House*, illustrates this problem. A couple is planning to have a baby, and the husband promises that when they have it, he will cut back at work and help out more around the house. When the baby comes, however, he has been promoted, or has forgotten the intensity of his feelings, or has now realized that the home is less pleasant to be around than he imagined. Listen to his conclusion:

> *There are people who, to escape the burden of today, make wondrous promises against tomorrow. These people live in their words alone; they are infants in responsibility. More than their bond they think their words themselves are deeds! In fact, they are pleased to believe that by promising something they have already accomplished something.*

Too many of us make the promises and never get around to fulfilling them. No wonder our relationship remains lifeless and empty, because the quality of our friendship to Jesus hinges upon our active choice to remain in him.

That's what he has asked of us. Don't mistake responsive actions for outward efforts to earn God's grace through legalistic efforts. The responses given in this passage are first demonstrated in the heart and then reflected in actions. Jesus did not ask for perfection in our conduct, observance of religious rituals or laws, or sacrifices to demonstrate our sincerity—only for hearts that will stay in his presence no matter what!

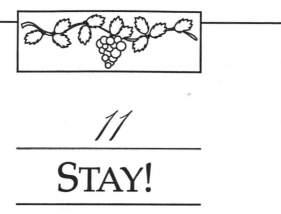

11

STAY!

If a man remains in me and I in him,
he will bear much fruit.

JOHN 15:5

My prayer closet these days is a cotton field and plum orchard behind our home. I don't own them, but borrow them for a few moments most mornings. My dog is my faithful companion to these prayer times. She loves dashing through the fields hoping for a rabbit to chase or a pheasant to flush.

But having her that far out without a leash makes for some interesting moments, especially when we meet other dogs. Buffy has walked these fields ever since she was a puppy and assumes, I think, that they all belong to her. She will chase after anything that comes near, from Dobermans to horses. She even chased off a wild coyote that had taken up residence here.

Her only protection against the dangers of other animals and the roadways we walk near is her ability to understand one simple command: Stay!

Buffy knows it well enough, but I'll have to admit that whether or not she obeys it depends on how close she is to me when I call it. If she's too far away and the temptation is too great, lured by an aggressive dog intruding on "her" territory, she's off, and no amount of yelling will bring her back until the chase is spent. Then she returns with great remorse in her eyes. Even a dog knows it is easier to ask for forgiveness than permission!

So far she's always returned, because the object of her pursuit has always fled at her approach. I regret the day she meets an animal that stands its ground. I'll call her back, but it will work only if she will listen. If she'll just stay with me, I can keep her safe.

That same response is all Jesus asks of the branches in his vineyard. "Remain," he repeats throughout his lesson ten times to be exact, most of the time in the simple call to remain *in him*. His command should not be difficult to understand. It's the same as commanding a dog to stay, or giving instructions to your child as you plunge together into the midday crowd at the local mall. It's what I've said a thousand times to my children when they were younger as we set up our campsites in the mountains. "Stay nearby. If you wander so far that you can't see our camp, you've gone too far."

What Jesus intends here is just that simple, though admittedly far more powerful. On two fronts my analogy is too weak to convey the depth of our opportunity. First of all, when I call my dog to stay, or encourage it of my children, I mean it only for the moment when the situation is tenuous. When Jesus invites us to remain, however, it is no temporary request.

His word speaks of a persistent remaining, as in taking up residence. That's why some translations prefer the word "abide." This perhaps more aptly conveys the permanence of our relationship with Jesus. We don't just hang around his presence when trouble strikes, but we are called to remain in him all the time.

Unlike a wild animal that will only drink when it is thirsty, the branch drinks from the vine all day every day. It never goes out on its own and never gets thirsty and comes back for a drink. It is there all the time. We cannot compartmentalize our spiritual life, making time for God like we do our work or play. Life in Christ permeates everything we do.

The second difference lies in the construction Jesus uses as he invites us to remain *in* him. Though it sounds fine when we speak of vines it is a bit jarring when we refer to people. We naturally think of remaining *with* someone, not *in* them. But the level of intimacy that a branch has with the vine is the standard by which Jesus measures our relationship with him. This is an intimate link. We are not just staying *with* him, standing nearby, watching what's going on; we are linked *to* him. Our identity and existence are bound up in the vine.

It's no wonder that the phrase "in Christ" became a popular definition of the Christian life in the epistles. The early church understood the depth of intimacy that Jesus invited them to discover. They weren't just born-again Christians, as if they had joined a new club. They were people "in Christ," daily drawing his life and daily reflecting his glory.

"Remain." The same thing Jesus asks of us he offers to us as well. Two times in this very passage he tells us that *he* will remain *in us*. Not only will we *live in him*, but he will *live in us*.

Jesus compares the depth of our relationship with him to the fellowship he shared with the Father. "You will remain in my love, just as I . . . remain in his love." We can know Jesus in the same way he knew his Father. The same intimacy that brought strength, wisdom, and comfort is available to us. What a marvelous promise; what a fantastic relationship to pursue! Growing in it will be a lifetime adventure. All we have to do is stay in the vine where the Father planted us.

What a contrast to everything this world teaches us. If we want anything in this life we have to *achieve* it, vesting our energies to somehow gain the thing we desire. But this is not true in God's vineyard. We don't have to achieve anything. When God established us in Christ he gave us a gift of friendship, regenerating our hearts, making us sensitive to his presence and his voice. All we need to do now is continue to embrace that friendship and not run off at every distraction or be pulled away by every temptation.

Stay attached—in the vineyard it's the only assignment a branch has. If nothing is allowed to sever it from the vine, it will be all it needs to be. The same is true of our life in God. If we'll remain in the vine, fruitfulness and fulfillment will accompany us wherever we go. If we fail to do that, it matters little what else we do, for we will inevitably end up empty and frustrated.

Remaining in him is as simple as regularly being where he is. Jesus doesn't hide from his followers, but clearly tells us

where to find him. He has invested his presence in some very
simple things—in his Word, in prayer, in our surrender, in
the lives of other believers, and in serving people who are in
need. Staying in his presence is as simple as meeting him
regularly in these places.

What transforms any of these things from religious routine
to life-giving nourishment from the vine is our own heart of
worship. It's Jesus we're looking for in all of these places, and
worship is the key to sensitive hearts that will come to his
presence.

"Enter his gates with thanksgiving and his courts with
praise; give thanks to him and praise his name" (Psalm 100:4).
Our access to his presence rises out of praise and thanksgiving. God is worthy, and by affirming that in my own heart I
am drawn away from my critical and complaining nature that
serves only to separate myself from him. The Scriptures encourage us to cultivate moments throughout our days where
we pause, if sometimes only for a few moments, to heighten
our awareness of Jesus' presence with us.

We remain in the vine to the extent that we share these
special and intimate moments of friendship with Jesus. We
withdraw from the frenetic demands of our culture and steal
away to our prayer closet, wherever and whatever that may
be.

There we focus our attention on him, express our affection
to him, and let him draw near to us. There he soothes our
demanding fears, exposes our seductive flesh, or gives us his
insights in the midst of our day. Sometimes his touch comes
almost before we even turn our attention toward him, at
others it comes after we have lingered, waiting on him and
bringing our hearts to rest in his presence.

I have often been in my office lost in the latest project
demanding my attention only to be buzzed by my secretary
and told that an appointment has arrived. I look at my watch
in shock. Already! I'll push away from my desk, but before I
go for my door, I'll bow my head before my Lord. My prayer at
such times may be nothing more than, "Jesus, help me." But
often, wonderfully often, in just such a moment he drops in

my mind a nugget of wisdom into my heart that shapes my heart toward that appointment.

That's how real he wants your moments with him to be. Being with him is not a religious duty, but a time for us to enjoy our friendship with him. He is faithful to those moments and by them transforms us ever more into his image, producing in us the fruit we so desire to offer him.

But remaining in him has a twofold meaning. Not only does it mean to stay in his presence by our daily responses to him, but it also stirs us to long-term faithfulness, an attitude that will carry us through anything that comes our way.

12

FRIENDSHIP FOR THE LONG HAUL

[I] appointed you to go and bear fruit—
fruit that will last.
JOHN 15:16

The only difference on a grapevine between a cane and a branch is longevity. A branch has been there for a long time. It's ability to transform the nourishment of the vine into a harvest of grapes results from its years of continued attachment to the vine.

Some of the branches in my father's vineyard are more than 40 years old, and yet they keep on yielding one harvest after another. Vineyards are long-term crops with mature vines producing far more than young ones.

As Jesus looked across those young men in the garden he wanted them to know he wasn't inviting them to any short-term flash of brilliance. He had no desire to use them up, allowing their zealous lifestyles to burn out in a few short months or years. He challenged them to cultivate a relationship with him that would look to the long haul, that would still be there through the doubts and fears this age would hurl at them.

He wanted fruitfulness from them that would last all of their lives. For the better fruit comes from the greater depth that the passing of time affords. He invited them to a friendship that time would only make more glorious.

Unfortunately our society knows so little of the beauty of long-term friendships. We are a transient culture, moving so frequently that lifelong friendships are indeed rare. Advertising preys on our penchant to become quickly bored with anything that becomes too familiar and lures us with the excitement of something new or different.

I sat across from a newlywed couple who had encountered their first seemingly insurmountable conflict. They were at an impasse and deeply concerned about the future of their relationship. "And the first year is supposed to be our best one," the wife said hopelessly.

No comment riles me more.

My wife and I have developed a friendship through three years of dating and 17 years of marriage. Sara and I have had that much practice loving each other and we are getting pretty good at it. We've let God shape us alongside each other so that we complement each other far more now than when we were first married.

We are now reaping the glorious benefits of long-term friendship: private jokes no one else can understand, thinking the same thing at almost the same moment, saying more to each other with a glance and a wink across a crowded room than less-practiced couples can say in a night of conversation. We laugh harder than we've ever laughed and hold each other more tenderly through difficult moments than we ever could a few years before. I can't wait to find out what this friendship will be like another 20 years from now.

The first year of marriage was never meant to be anyone's best. Our first year we were just rookies, and though it was fun, every year since has gotten even better.

Jesus wants the same for us. Every year is meant to be better than the one before, because we've grown to know him better and have been changed more into his likeness. We've tasted of his faithfulness in the heat of battle and found it far more real than we ever dreamed.

Only long-termers discover that depth, those who've not allowed their trust to be compromised by the challenges in their life. You'll find there is nothing the enemy works harder to destroy than your trust in Jesus. He does it best in times of crisis. Why should a loving God let this happen to me?

As Jesus told the tale of the vineyard he was preparing his followers for the traumatic days they were about to face, days that could make them question everything Jesus had ever said to them. He didn't want their pain and confusion to destroy their trust. "In this world you will have trouble." But they would also have him if their mistrust didn't cause them to push him away.

Mistrust comes far more easily than any of us care to admit. I saw it one day in my then three-year-old son, Andy. It was early summer in the Sierra Nevada Mountains where my family had come to camp. As we prepared our evening meal we could hear the distant rumble of thunder move ever closer to our camp. A late-afternoon thunderstorm was building in around us.

We began our dinner to the sound of raindrops popping the blue tarp spread out over our table. Flashes of lightning photographed our little camp as the storm grew closer. The thunder grew louder, our children increasingly nervous. "Is it coming here?" Andy asked. The edges of his lips curled upward, expecting the answer he didn't want to hear.

"It's on its way," I said, hoping my flippant attitude would reassure him. Just to be safe I added, "But there's nothing to be afraid of." The scowl on his face told me I had not succeeded.

I kept my eye on Andy as he continued to eat halfheartedly. He listened to every thunder roll as the storm approached. Each time he would grimace until the rumbles finally dissipated into the forest around us.

FLASH! Our camp lit up as if a thousand flashbulbs had suddenly gone off.

CRACK! KA-BOOM! Instantly the thunder exploded. The concussion was so loud you could feel it. A lightning bolt had hit a rock on the hill behind us.

No one moved as we listened to the thunder chase down the nearby valleys. The rain fell harder now against the tarp. The eyes of our five-year-old daughter stood wide open, her mouth agape. I don't think she blinked for five minutes, but she looked more surprised than afraid, and I wasn't nearly so worried about her. Andy, however, slowly looked up from his plate, his eyes full of fear and his shoulders hunched up to his ears.

"What was that?"

"That noise?" I feigned surprise that he would even ask. I knew my next few words were critical. This was one of those brief but tenuous moments where the right words will save a flood of tears. I groped to find them. "It's just the storm. Lightning hit the hill behind us."

He thought about it for a minute. "Who did that?" His mouth tightened with anger. Andy is a lot like his dad; he finds any crisis easier to weather if he can find someone to blame it on—a most unfortunate inheritance.

But maybe this was my out. In our three short years with Andy we had taught him about God's love. Even if he didn't fully understand, he did know that God had created all things, that he loved us enough to send his own Son to die on the cross, and that he cares about the challenges we face.

"God did!" I smiled, hopeful that if he knew God was involved, his security in God's love would redefine his fear of the storm. God is good. He made the storm. Andy need not be afraid. Looking back, I don't know what possessed me to make such an assumption.

Immediately Andy's mind began to churn. We watched as he tried to bring these new facts together, like a computer trying to correlate conflicting data. After what must have been an entire 30 seconds, he looked up from under his forehead and announced between gritted teeth, "I don't want him to do it anymore."

Sara and I caved in with laughter, and that set him at ease. We at least avoided the crying spell that usually puts more focus on fear. But the price hadn't been cheap.

We could argue as to whether or not God had put that exact lightning bolt into the rock behind our camp, and whether my attempts to reassure my son were well-placed, but the upshot of the day was simple: This was the first time the simplicity of Andy's faith lost to the reality of his circumstances. Until now it was enough for him to accept that God loved him and could be trusted with his life. That had won us battles over swimming lessons and dark nights.

This time his fear was too great. Instead of viewing his circumstances through God's character, he judged God's character by his circumstances. Maybe God can't be trusted. Maybe his intentions are not all good. The unknown produced the same mistrust in him that it did in Adam and Eve in the Garden. He could only express his displeasure at God and the desire to control any future actions that might result in his discomfort.

That evening we watched our little boy begin a journey on which we've all embarked, and over which our faith must win. Certainly it is only part of growing up, but when the flesh begins to serve up cause for unbelief it's one of the worst parts, for those who define God's love by what happens to them in this age will for the most part be wrong. It is only an attempt to measure God's love by human wisdom.

"Remain in my love." How much more simply could Jesus have said it? No matter what the challenge, no matter how right our perspective might appear. Invest your trust in him for the long haul.

It was only lightning that day for our son, and he has long since moved past it. But what of his future and ours? Will our security in God's love win over misunderstood suffering, unanswered prayers, months of unemployment, or the abuse of friends? This is the essence of fire-tested faith. It endures even the events we cannot understand, and finds its resolve in knowing that God is wholly good and that he can be trusted with our lives. It is only out of this trust that we can discover that the mystery of God's grace and wisdom will always be enough to help us overcome in any situation.

At the end of his life, alone in a prison cell in Rome, realizing that the churches in Asia were quickly deserting the true gospel for cheap imitations, Paul declared with absolute certainty, "I have kept the faith."

Maybe that's all we're asked to do. Amidst the struggles and fears, the confusions and doubts, don't let go of faith no matter what. Jesus is the only thing solid enough to cling to in all the universe.

Everything else is just passing thunder.

13

LIFE-GIVING
NOURISHMENT

If you remain in me and
my words remain in you . . .
JOHN 15:7

Tying vines is potentially the most painful of farm duties. Each cane remaining on a freshly pruned vine must be wrapped around the wire before the sap begins to flow. Often that put us out in the vineyard while frost still clung to the canes. Since we were paid for tying by how many vines we completed, speed was of the essence.

Every once in a while, however, in my haste I wouldn't get all the canes tightly secured. One of them would slip off the wire, pick up speed as it uncoiled itself, and smack me on my frozen cheek. I don't know if you've ever been slapped in the face on a subfreezing morning, but I can only commend it as an excellent form of torture.

For me, pain is almost always followed by anger, and often before rationality set in I would rip the cane out of the vine for its vile deed. Only then would the destruction I had caused sink home. Not wanting to be caught tying a vine with four canes when they're all supposed to have five, I would shove the base of the cane back into a cranny in the vine and tie it back on the wire. No one would be the wiser.

At least not until the sap flowed. And though it still might be stuck into the vine, we've already seen that if it is not attached to the vine, nothing will happen. Not one bud will swell, not one leaf will sprout.

The most significant contribution the vine makes to the branch can't even be seen by someone walking through the vineyard. It goes on deep beneath the scraggly bark. Through small capillary tubes, nutrients and water flow up through the roots, travel through the trunk, and spread out through every branch until they reach every leaf and maturing grape bunch. This life-giving sap makes the difference between a branch that is fruitful and one that is fit only for destruction.

The only time you get to see this flow of sap is early in the spring, before the vine fully shoots. Hanging on the end of each trimmed cane is often a small drop of sap. In the low-lined morning light these drops reflect like diamonds, a sure sign that spring is at hand and the sap is once again flowing in the vines.

That sap is what the vine gives to the branch to make it fruitful. Like the branches in the vine it is not enough that we are just near the presence of Jesus, we must be linked to him in a way that nourishes our lives. We are not transformed by just having read the Bible or having gone to church, but only to the extent that those things have allowed the life of Jesus to flow into ours.

How can we know if that is happening? Jesus gave his disciples one sure test. "If you remain in me *and my words remain in you.*" The nourishment he gives us is in the words he speaks to us. If we are remaining in him, his words will fill our lives.

This is the first of four distinct qualities of our relationship with Jesus that he specifically highlights in the parable of the vineyard. Each one demonstrates not only what the vine provides to the branches, but also how the branches respond so as to remain in the vine. Here and in the next three chapters we'll take each of these in turn:

- Our friendship with Jesus is built on revelation, as he makes clear to us the ways of the Father.

- Our friendship with Jesus allows us to make requests of him with a reasonable certainty that he will give us what we ask.
- Our friendship with Jesus grows only as we obey him.
- Our friendship with Jesus calls for sacrifice; not only his for us, but ours on his behalf as well.

Let's begin with the first—our friendship is built on revelation. Your closest friends know the most about you, and you about them. Throughout the lesson of the vineyard this theme keeps popping up. At its beginning Jesus told the disciples that they were clean, or freshly pruned, by the *words* he'd spoken to them. At its end he told them that his words of revelation define the nature of their relationship. He didn't want them to be his servants, but his friends:

> *"I no longer call you servants, because a servant does not know his master's business. Instead, I have called you friends, for everything that I learned from my Father I have made known to you."*
>
> JOHN 15:15

Servants know only what they need to know to get their work done and are not invited in on the whole panorama of family life. Jesus, however, invites his followers to a far more intimate relationship based on greater communication. These are the words he wants us to live in.

There are two important ways this revelation takes place in our lives. The first should be most obvious—Scripture itself. Those who desire to be linked to the vine will be students of Scripture. Here is God's full revelation, recorded so that at any moment we can pick it up and know his mind.

Like worship, this is one of those places where Jesus has invested his presence. He inhabits Scripture and every bit of it speaks of him. On the way to Emmaus the resurrected Lord began with Moses and all the prophets explaining to his unsuspecting companions "what was said in all the Scriptures concerning himself."

If we want God's fullness of joy and fruitfulness in all situations, we must cultivate a daily time in the Word that allows Jesus to teach us his ways and by it transform us. We need to learn how to read it, study it, reflect on it and interpret it accurately.

Recently a friend of my copastor was going through a very difficult time. He had been laid off work with what appeared to be incredible underhandedness by his employer. Frustrated over a situation suddenly gone bad, and unsure of what else God would have in mind for his future income, he was desperately seeking direction.

"What have you been hearing in your Bible readings these days?" my copastor asked him.

"What?"

"Haven't you been having some time in the Word?"

"Well, to be honest, this work stuff has been so distracting I haven't gotten to it."

As my copastor related this conversation he shook his head in disbelief, "The time someone needs the Word the most, they give it up." We all need to have God's Word filling our lives. Even Jesus used the power of Scripture to turn back the temptations of Satan.

The "words" Jesus referred to that night with his disciples are not completely fulfilled by Scripture alone. The force of his encouragement goes beyond that to a believer's *ongoing perception of his words*. The second place we find his words then is in his voice. He still speaks today, and we can walk in the full glory of his friendship as we learn to recognize that voice.

I realize I'm sailing into deep and dangerous waters here. The mere mention of God speaking to people today incites a host of responses. Some jump at the idea, ready to fulfill their most bizarre or selfish dreams while proclaiming that God told them to do so. Others reject it out of their own inexperience, mistakenly assuming that because they haven't learned to recognize God's voice, others can't either. Many see it as a threat to Scripture's authority, because some people claim revelations equal to the authority of Scripture, and usually superseding it if the two conflict.

These deceptions notwithstanding, our God is a God of revelation. He delights in making himself known to his people and leading them in his ways. He has a long history of doing exactly that, from his personal appearances to Enoch, Noah, Abraham, and others, to the revelation of his law and his counsel through his prophets.

Finally, God spoke again in the greatest revelation of all—his own Son, the exact representation of God himself. Did God's revealing nature end there? Of course not.

Jesus himself told his disciples just after his tale of the vineyard that he had much more to tell them. But because they were unable to hear it he entrusted that revelation to the work of the Holy Spirit (John 16:12). Though the Spirit does not appear in our passage concerning the vineyard, he is the primary character in the context from which it springs. From John 14 through John 16 the major theme of Jesus' words center on the coming Comforter who would take Jesus' place in teaching, leading, and guiding his followers daily.

Jesus wanted his disciples to know that they wouldn't have to go on alone, trying to make do with the best applications of all he had said to them. When the Holy Spirit came on the day of Pentecost Peter announced that this was the fulfillment of God's promise to reveal himself to all people who follow him. The result, demonstrated throughout the early church, was a people empowered by God's presence and sensitive to his voice.

This promise was extended to everyone God would call to himself from then on (Acts 2:39). His revelation continues even to the present. God's activity among his people didn't stop just because Scripture was completed.

Whenever God condemns idol worship, he expresses his incredulity that people would want to worship anything they could make themselves that cannot speak or act on their behalf. Isaiah taunted Israel with the sheer contradiction of building an idol out of the same piece of wood from which they had cut kindling to cook supper. Silent gods are false gods. People prefer them because they would rather follow their own idea of a god than serve the awesome, transcendent God of the ages.

To embrace God's revealing nature, however, doesn't de-value Scripture one bit. In fact it does just the opposite. The Scriptures are the *complete* revelation of all that God is and all that he comes to do in behalf of men. Anything the Spirit speaks today will only apply the truths of Scripture to the immediacy of our circumstances. But that continued disclosure is exactly what Jesus offered us.

Scripture is the only place where we can develop sensitivity to God's voice. These are God's words absolutely, and learning to hear him there will help us recognize his thoughts when he breathes them into our hearts.

Measuring our thoughts against Scripture is also the only objective test we have to distinguish the difference between our thoughts and God's. The apostle Paul warned us that our perception of God's voice in this life would not come with absolute clarity. He compared it to a poor reflection in a mirror (1 Corinthians 13:12). Though it is still a valuable vantage point we have to recognize that we will not see perfectly until we are transformed at his coming. Therefore we respect how easily colored our discernment is by our own preferences and desires. If our perceptions of God's voice don't square with Scripture, whether in content or intent, they can be soundly rejected. God will always be faithful to his written revelation.

The friendship Jesus offered his followers hinges on intimate communication. Jesus wants you to know what the Father is doing in your life and in situations around you. He doesn't want you to grope around in uncertainty, and has offered you his ever-present voice.

But there are times when, despite our best efforts in prayer or study, we remain confused, unsure what God's will might be. We usually cycle through feelings of condemnation that Jesus isn't being clear to us because we've done something wrong, to anger that he won't communicate with us, to a mistaken conclusion that God doesn't speak today so we just ought to make do without it.

It's too bad that the very words Jesus spoke to comfort us in difficult moments are the ones that leave us most frustrated. I can't always tell you why at times it is more difficult to hear his voice. I do know he's promised to disclose to us what the Father is doing so that we don't have to guess what he's up to or resign ourselves to fatalism. That's a depth of communication I keep pressing toward because he's offered it.

Developing this discernment is a lifelong venture for a branch. I've no doubt God speaks to all of his followers daily; it's just that we don't always recognize his voice. It is easily drowned out by the clamor of circumstances, our fears, or our own desires.

But if we will continue to immerse ourselves in his Word and listen quietly for his voice we will learn to hear his voice with increasing clarity. Where is Jesus leading me today? What is he teaching me? What attitude or appetite is he dealing with, and how do I cooperate with him to see that work completed?

Remaining in those words is how we draw the nourishment of the vine. There is no greater treasure in our friendship with Jesus than this.

14

WHATEVER
I ASK?

*Ask whatever you wish, and
it will be given you.*
JOHN 15:7

In our understanding of the vineyard the contrasts between my father's and God's have been as significant as the similarities. Now we come to the most incredible contrast of all, for which there is not even a remote example in the vineyards of this earth.

In God's vineyard the branches themselves can make requests of the gardener that he promises to fulfill! What an awesome thought! I never heard a branch on any of the thousands of vines dotting my father's land ever make a request, much less get it answered.

The second quality of friendship Jesus pressed on his disciples was the open door to pursue our requests with him with a certainty that he will give us what we ask. It reveals yet another place where we go to remain in his presence—prayer. Not only does he want to speak to us, but he also invites us to speak to him, disclosing ourselves to him. Everyone who follows him needs a prayer closet, a time and place to regularly draw away to prayer. Why? Because the Almighty God who spoke worlds into existence invites you to ask whatever you wish from him *and* promises that he will give it.

Regretfully, however, instead of being awed by this promise, it is too often a source of frustration. Such a promise is
only credible if God actually backs it up, and most believers
have a backlog of unanswered prayers that seems to make
mockery of it. *Whatever* we ask we can have? Who is he trying
to fool?

I read this passage to my children this morning as part of
breakfast devotions. When I got done reading it, Andy, my
ten-year-old son (who rarely makes comments about anything from the Bible), immediately responded, "That isn't
true." His tone wasn't accusing or frustrated, just matter-of-
fact.

"What do you mean?"

"What you just read: It doesn't really happen."

I was sure what he meant, but I asked him which part
anyway so I could hear from his own lips what lurked in his
young mind.

"It says whatever you wish for you can have. I have wished
for a big-screen TV and I don't have one." Case closed.

"It doesn't say we can have what we *wish* for, but what we
ask for. Have you ever asked for one?" Don't worry, I knew I
was on thin ice here.

"Dad, can I have a big-screen TV?"

"It doesn't say to ask me." I asked Andy if he had ever
prayed about this, and he honestly said he hadn't. Then we
talked about whether we should ask God for something like
that, and his response was, "It says 'whatever you ask.'"

I'll grant you that the promise Jesus makes in this passage
appears all-inclusive. At face value it suggests a 100-percent
return on any request we make. Who, however, has an answered prayer list that reflects that standard of success?
Anything less can become a source of frustration and disappointment.

How easy it is to overlook all the times God has answered
our prayers when our latest request is seemingly on the back
burner, if it made it to the kitchen at all. It is no wonder people
eventually give up on prayer, either convinced that God
doesn't really answer prayers today or at least won't for someone like me.

Our prayer theology is finally reduced to nothing more than throwing up a request and hoping for the best, like filling out a requisition form. Ship it upstairs and maybe if you're good enough, or if your request is pure enough, you might get what you ask for. But most times you don't, so don't expect much. After all, God knows what's best.

On the surface, such thinking sounds wonderfully biblical and wholly submitted to the Master's desires, but it flies in the face of the very certainty about our prayers that Jesus put forth to the branches in his vineyard. There is a place in him, he said, where we can ask for anything and *know* that we will get it.

Don't let the disappointments and imperfections of the past rob you of this hope and therefore short-circuit the process for getting there. Like almost every other promise in Scripture, it is not intended to frustrate you but designed to stimulate your growth until it is fulfilled.

Let us apply the same patience to growing in effective prayer that we do breaking free of the sins that entangle us. Both mandate a process that God invites us to embrace with hope. We would do far better growing in this process if we would shift our focus away from the frustration that accompanies unanswered prayers to being awed every time God *does* move in response to our prayers. That puts the focus in the right place and encourages our further growth.

Jesus' promise of answered prayer is not without precondition. We can have whatever we ask, "*if*," as he already said, "you remain in me and my words remain in you." Jesus isn't hiding anything here. Our effectiveness in prayer flows out of the depth of intimacy we have established with the vine. If we're drawing our life from him, and allowing his words to have access to every corner of our lives, then (and only then) we can expect our prayers to be answered.

One of the things that most baffles me is when believers miss this connection between intimate relationship and answered prayer. Those who plow into their jobs or recreations with a fervor, leaving no time to cultivate the presence of Jesus, will be the first to complain when God doesn't meet their expectations. How can we fairly expect Jesus to respond to our requests if we are blatantly ignoring his?

I know such talk smacks of earning God's favor by our own sacrifice. Nothing could be further from the truth—not for our salvation nor for prayer. This is not a trade-off turning in Bible-reading credits for answered prayer. Something far deeper is at stake when we learn to remain in him and his words. By staying close enough to Jesus to know what he desires, we will find our desires being transformed to match his.

In C.S. Lewis' fourth book of the Narnia series, *The Silver Chair*, Prince Caspian arrives in heaven and expresses one of his desires to Aslan, the Christ-symbol. "Is that wrong?" he asked.

"You cannot want wrong things anymore, now that you have died, my son!" We can experience that same reality here as we die to our own desires. Jesus wants us to find a place in prayer where every request can be answered, because every request is a godly one.

It is impossible for us to remain in him and use prayer for our own gain or convenience. Not only do wrong prayers reinforce the wrong motives, answering them just isn't possible from God's perspective. How often do you think prayers by well-meaning believers motivated by selfish desires would conflict with the prayers of others?

What if God only let it rain in the San Joaquin Valley when someone prayed for it? That would be fine if there were just one person to contend with, but when you add many people, who would he listen to? No matter when it rains in our part of the San Joaquin Valley, someone's crop is hurt by it. During our recent five-year drought we had what even our media termed a "Miracle March." Seven inches of rain fell in that month, almost two-thirds of our normal yearly total.

As elated as most people were with the rain, the media was still able to find farmers for whom the rain brought suffering. Fruit trees with tender blossoms were most at risk. Some trees the hail stripped, while others couldn't be pollinated normally because the bees were grounded in the inclement weather. Cotton farmers lamented that they couldn't get into the fields to plant.

Can you imagine God trying to respond to those varied requests? Even if he could get all the farmers to agree on rain at the same time, someone else would have planned a church picnic for the same day, and a whole flock of believers would pray against it. Regardless of what happened, some people would be overjoyed that their prayers were answered because they got what they wanted, while those who didn't would wonder why God doesn't love them. If we're going to get serious about answered prayer we're going to have to stop trying to use God for our own trivial convenience. Jesus only interfered with the weather one time and it wasn't to save a church picnic. The promise of John 15 was not intended to be a tool for our own comfort.

Neither can it be taken apart from Jesus' other instructions about prayer. Remember when James and John asked for fire to come down from heaven to consume the Samaritans for not welcoming Jesus? Far from answering their request, Jesus rebuked the spirit from which it came. And Jesus could not grant Peter's desire to derail him from going to the cross without circumventing a higher plan of God.

Scripture gives many other reasons why our prayers go unanswered, and it is well for us to search them out. They are not intended to rob us of the certainty of God answering our prayers. Rather they are to show us why he sometimes doesn't, so that we can dispense with those kinds of prayers.

When Jesus promised his disciples around that grapevine that he wanted to answer whatever request they would make of him, his purpose was not centered in them at all, but in God and his mission: "This is to my Father's glory, that you bear much fruit, showing yourselves to be my disciples" (John 15:8). God moving in response to our prayers accomplishes three things:

First, it brings glory to the Father. When God's power moves in our lives beyond our own abilities or plans, it testifies to his presence. People's attentions are drawn to the Father and not to our skills. God is glorified by answering the godly requests of his people.

Second, God's answers are a key ingredient to our bearing fruit. Developing an intimacy of relationship with the vine does demand confidence that we can draw from him what we need. Without that active involvement we won't be able to produce anything fruitful in his kingdom, any more than a branch can produce fruit if it doesn't receive nourishment consistently from the vine. This also hints at the direction of our prayers. Instead of praying for God to save us out of difficult circumstances we will instead pray for that which will bring the greatest glory to God, which as we said earlier will produce in us the fruits of his Spirit.

Finally, God's answers demonstrate an intimacy of friendship that testifies to God's reality in our lives and gives others hope of finding the same relationship as well.

How often the disciples were enamored by Jesus' prayers! They could see how the Father immediately responded to his requests for a storm to be stilled, blind eyes healed, and sinful people forgiven. "Teach us to pray" was not an attempt to learn a spiritual discipline, but to find out how to effectively tap the Father's resource. They wanted that same relationship, and so will others as we demonstrate a flow of God's power in our lives.

For all these reasons God wants to respond to our prayers with complete fulfillment, even more than we want him to. When he doesn't, this should signal us that perhaps our request was wrong or that some wrong motives have twisted their way into our prayer. If we don't go on to probe why not, we'll never become more effective in prayer and merely consign ourselves to sending requests and settling for whatever we're fortunate enough to get.

In the same way we should never get smug about the prayers he does answer, as if we in our goodness somehow deserve them. Nothing we've covered in this chapter is intended to communicate that answered prayers are to be worn as merit badges. Though unanswered prayer is a good indicator of how much more deeply we can grow in the vine, answered prayers are not something to boast in. Sometimes God moves in spite of us as much as because of us, and any boasting runs counter to the fruit he wants to produce in us.

God wants to teach us through our praying how to zero in on his will, and how to bring it into reality through prayer. His goal is unchanged: He wants to give us *whatever* we ask. If we'll remain in him he will teach us. It's one of the lessons he wants all of his branches to learn well.

GOING
MY WAY?

*If you obey my commands, you will
remain in my love.... You are my friends
if you do what I command.*
JOHN 15:10,14

A certain farmer had two sons. One morning he went to the first and told him he needed him to work in the vineyard that day. "I will not!" the son answered.

How I can relate to that! Every time my dad wanted me in the vineyard, I didn't want to go. My three brothers and I spent Christmas vacations pruning vines, Easter breaks hoeing weeds, and the last weeks before school picking grapes. Our Saturdays also brought further opportunities to tie vines, pick up discarded branches, or box raisins. I got sick of working in the vineyard. I guess we all did, since none of us ended up back on the farm.

So I relate to this poor son (at least his desire), although I'm not so sure I would have seriously answered my father the way he did. My father was very fond of that "when-I-say-jump-you-only-ask-how-high" philosophy of parenting. I rarely rebelled so openly, though it did cross my mind.

Afterward, however, the son repented of his attitude and left whatever else he was doing to begin work in the vineyard (Matthew 21:28-32). What might have triggered his change of heart we're not told. Jesus doesn't say the father argued with him or punished him for his insolence. He just went on to the second son and made the same request.

"I will, sir!" was the second son's response. Our hearts are warmed by his quick choice of obedience, and by the words of respect with which he answers his father. This is the kind of son anyone would want—ready for obedience at a moment's notice.

Well, not quite. Ready to *talk* obedience at any moment was closer to the truth. Again we're not told why, but this son never made it to the vineyard. Perhaps he had no intent to obey, only dismissing his father by telling him what he wanted to hear. The vineyard could have been large enough that his father would not have known anyway. Or maybe he wanted to obey, but in the going was distracted by a better offer—by a friend to go swimming at the creek, perhaps.

Having told this simple story, Jesus asked an even simpler question, which no one would have hesitated to answer correctly. "Which of the two did what his father wanted?"

"The first," they answered.

This was one of my favorite parables growing up because it had great value in keeping my parents off-balance. I'm pretty sure Jesus didn't teach this parable for the reason I used it, but when my parents told me to work for them, I would often respond like the first brother: "I will not." I could see their jaws set and their eyes squint, but before they could say anything I was off to the task they had asked of me. What could they say? It drove them nuts. No one likes to be told no, but I would refer them to this parable and they would only shake their heads in frustration.

Even though my application was selfishly motivated, this parable intends to make exactly that point. What matters in the kingdom of God is obedience—not the intent to obey, or the promise to, but the actual act, even if it comes after initial resistance. He would prefer both, of course, the expression of obedience and the act, but the parable makes clear the act is the most important.

This parable was not told to Jesus' disciples, but to the chief priests and elders who had interrupted him in their latest attempt to trap him into offending the adoring crowds around him. They were the ones who answered his question so easily and the ones to suffer the full force of the parable's conclusion. "I tell you the truth, the tax collectors and the prostitutes are entering the kingdom of God ahead of you."

These leaders gave the appearance of pursuing God, but somehow never got to the task. While their mouths said "I will," their lives said "Sorry, not now." Sinners, on the other hand, whose lives started out with a great big no, ended up in the Father's vineyard.

It is always easier to follow God with our mouths than with our lives, and the danger doesn't diminish with our longevity on the vine. Religious forms and traditions are easier to follow than simply doing the things God asks of us each day.

Jesus didn't want his disciples to meet a similar end. The third quality of friendship that Jesus highlighted in his parable of the vineyard is incredibly special. It is true in no other friendship they would ever have. "If you obey my commands, you will remain in my love, just as I have obeyed my Father's commands and remain in his love."

Our participation in the vineyard is not a merging of two branches. Quite the contrary, our lives are planted onto the one, true vine. Even though that relationship is defined by the tenderness of intimate friendship, we must never forget that this is not a friendship between equals. The branch draws from the vine, not the other way around.

Jesus hangs the continued development of our friendship *with* him on our obedience *to* him. In case they missed it the first time, he says it again a bit differently four sentences later: "You are my friends if you do what I command."

Who else could ever make such a statement? Try it with your spouse or one of your friends, and see where it gets you. When you think the mood is just right lean over to them and say, "I'll always be your friend if you do everything I want you to do."

Sounds absurd, doesn't it? We understand that friendships grow through give-and-take, each person offering something to it and drawing value from it. When disagreements emerge we seek to incorporate the best insights of both in finding a solution that will best address all concerns.

Apply those same ideas to your relationship with Jesus, however, and you will find yourself drying up on the vine. There is only one way to go in this vineyard and it is his. Why is it different with Jesus? Because he has all wisdom and power. His judgments are not clouded with favoritism or selfish pursuits. He knows what is best for us, and for the development of our friendship with him.

Even in our passionate campaigns to get God to understand our concerns and insights, we can't lose sight of who he is. We don't ever have to battle him, but instead cultivate a heart of surrender and obedience. Nothing will affect the growth of your life with him more than this simple heart of submission.

Our friendship with him is marvelously one-sided, but that certainly doesn't mean it has to be any less intimate. He tenderly wants to share his presence with us and disclose to us all that the Father is doing around us. But this is not a place we come to *talk about* the things of God but to *give ourselves to them*. What he asks in return is that we not just hear his words but obey them.

Note the priority here. Obedience is one of the last things the branch is asked for, not the first. Many people try to cultivate their friendship with God by being obedient to some expectation they think God holds for them. They put off their pursuit of the Lord until they start going to church, give up smoking, or in some other way become a "better" person.

Obedience does not earn our acceptance, it flows out of it. Only as we have accepted Jesus' offer of friendship and been cleansed and nourished by the power of his words, do we have any understanding of what obedience means for us or any capacity to follow through with it. Remember, without him we can do nothing, absolutely nothing!

Out of friendship and learning to clearly hear him we begin to understand what obedience means. Many people mistake obedience for perfection. It is not. Our struggle against the flesh is a lifelong war and more than any of us would like we'll fall prey to its appetites and deceptions. Jesus

knows full well the weaknesses of our flesh, and the obedience he invites us to is not living up to a list of rules or
expectations, but direction as timely as the circumstances of
each day.

Jesus demonstrated this in Peter, who in a few hours from
this instruction would deny Jesus. Though Jesus clearly did
not want Peter to fail, he knew how weak he was and how easy
it would be for him to succumb to his fears. It's interesting
that Jesus didn't tell him not to deny him. Instead he told him
how to rebound from his failure by returning to strengthen
his brothers. Jesus knew that was all the obedience Peter
could live up to that day.

Obedience, Jesus said, was the secret to remaining in his
love. It had been no different between Jesus and his father:
"Just as I have obeyed my Father's commands and remain in
his love." Jesus had already set the example for the disciples.
He had done everything the Father had asked him to do.

In the next few hours he would do it yet again. From this
garden he would be thrust into the mockery, torture, and
death that would procure our salvation. His strength through
it came only as he surrendered to God, "Not as I will, but as
you will." If Jesus wanted to remain in the Father's love he had
to obey him in the midst of those dark hours.

What if Jesus had called a legion of angels to rescue him?
Would God have loved him less? Of course not. But in his
disobedience he would have removed himself from the care
and protection of God's love. That's where many misunderstand the nature of God's love.

Yes, it is unconditional. He will love us no matter what, but
Jesus isn't talking here about how much he loves us, but
whether or not we'll receive that love and share in its power.
I've sat with parents anguished by the rebellion of their own
children. Though the parents still love them deeply, unless
these children turn away from trouble and return to that love,
they will not share in it.

It's a lesson I teach every couple who comes to my office
wanting to get married. As much as I teach them the necessity
of loving their partner without demanding that they meet
certain expectations, I teach them that the quality of their

marriage will hinge on obedience to the vows they will take. The depth of their friendship will depend upon how well they learn to cherish each other, care for each other, and endure the troubles of this age with each other *every* day.

The day we repented and were grafted into his vine our commitment was to forsake our own way and go his. Only by doing that will we continue to grow.

It's what the branch does to stay linked to the vine, and if we do this one thing Jesus will make us fruitful in every circumstance and draw us to even greater depths of intimacy with him.

16

DIE
TO IT!

*Greater love has no one than this, that he lay
down his life for his friends.*
JOHN 15:13

Caring for a vineyard is hard work.

Not a season goes by that there isn't something the farmer
has to do if he is going to have a fruitful vineyard. Many plants
will at least bear some fruit in the wild, but not the grapevine.
It cannot even support its own branches. They must be pains-
takingly tied on a wire to keep the fruit and canes off of the
ground. If it is not pruned every year all the energy of the vine
will be spent producing leaves and none producing fruit. So
month after month the farmer is in the vineyard.

He prunes.

He ties.

He waters.

He shovels.

He sprays.

He picks.

He cleans.

None of these tasks require a great deal of talent or offer
back any deep sense of accomplishment. They are menial,
dirty tasks often demanding to be done even in the harshest
conditions—the blazing heat of summer or the biting cold of
winter.

Some people even consider the work demeaning, similar to how the disciples felt about a different task a few hours before their trip to the vineyard. They had come to the upper room with feet soiled from dusty lanes of the city. Since their room was rented there was no designated host to make sure the guests' feet were washed.

How awkward those first moments in the room must have been! Lots of dirty feet and no one willing to wash them. They must have thought about it, certain that someone else was supposed to do it. Let Judas, he paid for the room. What about Bartholomew? He was the last one chosen wasn't he? They ultimately decided to skip it altogether and pretend their feet weren't dirty, because dinner was already being served and no one had volunteered to wash the others' feet.

That is until Jesus tied a towel around his waist. Though some obviously didn't want *him* to do it, no one else offered. So he washed their feet. Some have suggested that Jesus did so to teach them humility. John disagreed. He said Jesus washed their feet expressly to show them "the full extent of his love" (John 13:1). This was not a show. It was a photograph of love in its most complete form. Jesus cared about them enough to do the most menial task for them.

"Greater love has no one than this, that he lay down his life for his friends." The fourth and final quality of friendship that Jesus delineates in the vineyard is that our friendship with him calls for sacrifice. Friends give up their lives for each other.

Jesus was that kind of friend. Though he would prove it again in a few hours on a brutal cross, he'd already shown them the extent of his love when he didn't consider it beneath his dignity to wash dirty feet. He loved them, even the one who would betray him.

When we consider his call to absolute obedience, remember who it is that asks it of us. This is one who will not use our obedience for his own gain. We are compelled to trust someone like that, no matter what adversity we face. The apostle Paul reflected on it time and again when he was tempted in the midst of crisis to believe Jesus didn't care for him. If Jesus would go to such lengths to save me when I was a sinner, would he really deny me anything I need to find my way into His life now that I'm seeking to follow him? (compare Romans 8:32).

But there is a larger lesson here. The love Jesus demonstrated is the love he asked from the disciples. I want you to lay down your lives for me as well. How? By dying on a cross?

No, he had something else in mind. Even though most if not all of the disciples in that circle would eventually die for him, their death was not the sacrifice he sought. "Love each other as I have loved you." He instead called them to lay down their lives for him by laying it down for each other. Perhaps this is the harder of the two. Sometimes it is easier to die for someone than to live alongside them.

Except for the call to remain in him, this is the only other lesson of the vineyard that Jesus repeats. He follows his call to obedience by his one command: Love one another. This is the obedience upon which all our other obediences hang.

It is a familiar call to anyone who has been a Christian for very long, but don't let that distract from the power of his simple statement. This was not an abstract call to love all of God's people. There were only 12 people in that vineyard. I wonder if Jesus even gestured around the circle as he spoke the words. For the love he asked of them couldn't be hidden in generalities. These men knew each other, weaknesses and all. Surely he doesn't mean the power-grabbing Zebedee boys. Or Peter, the man who would be our leader except that he can't get his foot out of his mouth long enough to be of much use. Certainly he doesn't mean Thomas whose incessant questioning drives us all nuts.

Here is where love is tested, and here is where the lesson of the vineyard reaches its conclusion. For we have arrived back at the beginning. The fruit that God is coaxing out of each of us is his love. This is the testimony the world cannot refuse.

This is the fruit of our remaining in him and the command that fulfills all others:

> *You, my brothers, were called to be free. But do not use*
> *your freedom to indulge the sinful nature; rather, serve one*

*another in love. The entire law is summed up in a single
command: "Love your neighbor as yourself." If you keep on
biting and devouring each other, watch out or you will be
destroyed by each other.*

GALATIANS 5:13,14

Nothing will destroy our flesh faster than learning to love
the people around us through the most menial forms of
service. The world teaches us to be preoccupied with our own
needs and ambitions. Jesus, however, offered us the opportunity to lay down our lives for him by being a blessing to
others. Learning to love that way is part of God's plan to
reverse the world's agenda. No longer preoccupied with our
own desires, we become part of God's work to touch others.

Recently our church sponsored a youth outreach to three
unreached villages in central Mexico. Thirty-two people went
down over Easter break, a prime opportunity to learn the
depths of love. Dan, one of the leaders of the outreach, came
back with an amazing story that became a powerful lesson for
me.

Everything does not always run smoothly on such trips,
and it's easy for people to get on your nerves. Virtually every
time Dan got frustrated by someone else, God saw to it that a
missionary we worked with in that area was nearby. Seeing
Dan's frustration begin to build, he would quietly sneak behind Dan and whisper in his ear, "Dan, die to it!" That was
all, nothing more. But a gentle smile would sneak past Dan's
lips as he would give in to the vital message it held.

Not all wars are meant to be fought, not all preferences
have to be championed, not all hurts need to be ironed out.
Some things we can just die to, giving up what's in it for us
and going on, washing the feet of others in a practical way.
Dan's testimony of that lesson was like a splash of cool water
on a hot face. What freedom! It reminded me about so many
things I face in the fellowship here at home. I don't have to
vent every frustration. Sometimes I can just die to it, trusting
God to work his will without me pushing for my own way.

Don't get me wrong; honesty and justice are valuable vir-
tues for a body of believers growing in unity, but so also is the
freedom to die to our wants.

What a testimony to others when believers love with such grace and deference to one another! What results is the deep fulfillment we spoke of earlier, joy as we've never known it because it rests in things far more eternal than our latest purchase or career achievement. We do not touch eternity any closer in this age than by sharing God's love for people.

Throughout the last few chapters I've emphasized that we remain in Jesus by being where he is. We've talked already about his presence in worship, prayer, and Scripture, and about his voice and our obedience. Now Jesus' command to love one another brings us to the last two places where we regularly confront the presence of Jesus: the community of believers, and people in need.

"For where two or three come together in my name, there am I with them" (Matthew 18:20). Jesus is present where believers come together to share his life. I'm talking way beyond church membership or attendance. Sitting in a large gathering watching all the action happen onstage doesn't even begin to approach the power of Jesus' call here.

Body life in the New Testament was not primarily centered in meetings, but relationships. Though I find great joy in gathering with large groups for worship and hearing the Word taught, it alone is not the community God desires. The early believers lived out their faith through intimate and mutually supportive contact with other believers. The house church movement of this century is far closer to the biblical example. At least three or four times a week our paths should cross those of other believers in ways that we can share his presence together.

We really do need each other. This is an interesting vineyard Jesus talked about. It is a one-vine vineyard. Every branch grows from the same vine, Jesus.

On a grapevine, no branch lives independent of the others. When one is besieged, they all are. When one is in need, the others can help make up the difference. I've seen entire branches stripped of their leaves by voracious insects. Not a leaf left on the branch, and without leaves grapes won't

sweeten. But these still did. Why? Because the sugar produced by the other branches on that vine found its way to the
grapes on the denuded branch.

Anyone who tries to go it alone does so at his own peril. It's
like trying to be a one-person softball team. No matter how
good you are, there's no way you can win a ball game by
yourself. How can you cover the whole field on defense? Who
are you going to throw to? And when you're at bat you have to
hit a home run every time or you're out, and who's capable of
that?

Neither can we win alone in the kingdom of God, though I
see many people try it. They'll come to church on Sunday and
then to my office on Wednesday wanting help with some
struggle. I tell them that to overcome, part of what they'll
need to do is get involved in the lives of other believers. It's
amazing. Those who do, get healed. Those who think they
can make it on their own never overcome and never seem to
figure out why.

We need the other believers who are linked to the same
vine we are. We need the supportive, intimate friendships,
the opportunities to serve, the added wisdom and strength,
the lessons of forgiveness, and a place to be held accountable.
If we will not be obedient to Jesus at this point, we will lose
our place in the vine.

The last place Jesus clearly said he invested his presence is
in ministry to the needy. "Whatever you did for one of the
least of these brothers of mine, you did for me" (Matthew
25:40). He affirms his presence in the needs of his creation
and tells us that our response to people in need, not just
believers, is a response to him. We have been blessed by God
to be a blessing to others.

Everyone who wants to grow in Jesus' presence needs to
find regular ways to serve others in the daily course of their
lives. Find outreach opportunities to go into another person's
world and serve. You don't have to go out of the country for
these opportunities. Serving in a soup kitchen or tutoring an
underprivileged child at your neighborhood school can be
every bit as powerful as going on outreach in Asia. In my own

city, Asia has already come to us in the form of refugees from Laos.

True Christlike love is foreign to our flesh and in the beginning it will be difficult learning to lay our lives down. But learning to live in love's freedom is one of the great pleasures of being a branch in this vineyard. It is always deeply fulfilling and full of surprises. We'll find ourselves doing and saying things to others that will astound us. "That's not me" and "I've never felt like that before" will become common expressions under our breath.

That's fruitfulness, and it will only arise as we lay our lives down for others, regardless of the resistance of our flesh. "Die to it!" is the battle cry of a fruitful branch.

17

A WIDER VIEW: WORKERS IN THE VINEYARD

Listen to another parable: There was a landowner who planted a vineyard. He put a wall around it, dug a winepress in it and built a watchtower. Then he rented the vineyard to some farmers and went away on a journey.
MATTHEW 21:33

It was a conspiracy, plain and simple.

The vineyard workers huddled together against the wall at the property's edge. For some time they had been watching a lonely figure making his way up the road to the vineyard, the dust of his feet billowing behind him in the still morning air. He was close enough now for all to recognize him. It was who they thought it was—the owner's son. For weeks they had been badgered by the master's servants coming to collect the fruit of the vineyard.

But they had already decided to keep the fruit for themselves, no matter the cost. Their final plan took shape quickly. "This is the heir. Come, let's kill him and take his inheritance."

Before we begin our study through the seasons of the vineyard, let's expand our view of the vineyard. To this moment we have primarily focused on the lesson of the vineyard as Jesus taught it on the way to Gethsemane. As he taught the disciples how to find fullness of joy and fruitfulness in his kingdom, he talked about himself as the vine and his followers as branches.

But there is another analogy that Jesus used on numerous occasions in the vineyard. Not only are we branches, but we are also workers in the vineyard. We've already seen this reflected in the parable of the workers who were hired throughout the day, and two brothers who were told to work in the vineyard. Now we'll examine one other story that prepares us for a wider view of the vineyard.

As the picture of us as branches focused on our personal growth, the analogy of us as workers highlights our responsibility in ministry to other believers. The vineyard then not only teaches us personal discipleship, but also practical ministry. What can we do to promote growth in other believers around us; and almost more importantly, where do we overstep our bounds to the detriment of others?

Interestingly enough, the parable that begins our chapter comes directly on the heels of the short parable we examined two chapters ago about the two brothers.

From that story, Jesus launches into this one with the same priests and elders who worked so hard to thwart his ministry. Instead of exercising their role as leaders to help people into the life of God, they were doing all they could to make sure others were kept out. Jesus' story cuts to the heart of their motives, and in so doing serves as timely warning to any who labor in God's vineyard.

Let's go back to the beginning of Jesus' parable. A landowner planted a vineyard on his land and dressed it with a wall to protect it, a winepress to process its fruits, and a watchtower to keep it safe. This was a first-class vineyard.

Then he rented out his vineyard to his laborers. Leaving it to their care, he went on a journey. Harvest time came and went. The landlord sent his servants to collect the fruit. But these were not only greedy but vicious men. Instead of meeting their obligation they mistreated the landlord's servants. Some they beat, some they killed, and some they stoned.

Their treason did not form overnight. For a long time the landowner sought their attention and could not get it. The same is true of us. Rejecting God's words almost never happens overnight, but over a long process of refusing those God sends to call us back to himself. The first time is always the hardest; then it gets easier and easier even as God makes more impressive overtures. We can even come to the point, like the workers in this parable, where we turn on Jesus himself.

Israel's long history of abusing God's messengers should be a clear warning for us. A similar phenomena exists in the history of the church. No one resists the fresh working of God in any age of the church quite like the church itself as it grows sluggish and institutionalized following previous times of renewal.

This should give us pause. Are we today listening to the voices we want to hear, or are we hearing those that God is sending today to call us to change? Have our institutions grown rigid? God always holds people in leadership accountable as to whether they make it easy for people to respond to God or difficult by their cumbersome rules and personal refusal to submit to the life of Jesus as he intended.

The landlord sent his son as the last resort. "They will respect my son."

But they did not. They had already decided to usurp the landlord's place in the vineyard and assume control by treason. They wanted all the fruit for themselves. Instead of serving God in his vineyard, they wanted the vineyard to serve them. So when they saw his son coming unprotected they knew how to secure final ownership of the land they craved. They threw the landlord's son out of the vineyard and killed him, thinking that now all would belong to them.

Here Jesus stops the parable and asks a question: "When the owner of the vineyard comes, what will he do to those tenants?" He waits for their answer. "He will bring those wretches to a wretched end and he will rent the vineyard to other tenants who will give him his share of the crop at harvest time" (Matthew 21:33-44).

Matthew thought it important enough to note that the chief priests and Pharisees knew that Jesus was talking about them. Most of the time they didn't understand his parables at all. He was accusing them of using God's work for their own gain, even to the point of committing murder to steal his vineyard.

Though this parable was especially directed at the leadership of Jesus' day, its application extends to all of us under the New Covenant. For we are all called to minister Jesus' life to other believers around us. The church Jesus sought to plant was not one dependent upon leadership, but one that creates an interdependence among those who are sharing his life.

Paul minces no words about our calling: "In Christ we who are many form one body, and each member belongs to all the others" (Romans 12:5). I am not alone. I belong to other believers, and they to me. We do not have the luxury of being preoccupied with our own growth alone, but as his workers to labor on behalf of others as well.

Though many of us will think first of "ministry" tasks we can carry out to help others, the primary biblical application of ministry grows out of deep and personal friendships with other believers around us. Though this friendship should be grounded in a local fellowship of believers, it is by no means limited to it. We are to seek out fellowship and service to other believers regardless of whether they gather behind the same four walls we do on Sunday morning.

All that we have discussed in the previous chapters of the work God is accomplishing in us to make us fruitful and fulfilled in his kingdom he is also doing in others around us. It is a responsibility we cannot shirk, but one that must be applied with great care.

As a worker in his vineyard, take heed to the warning Jesus passed to the Pharisees in this passage. At some point they shifted from just being workers in God's vineyards, to wanting something more—ownership of God's work for themselves. They would benefit from its fruit instead of giving it back to God.

As branches we can never forget in whose vineyard we are growing; as workers that becomes even more critical. No matter how God chooses to use us, we cannot ever allow ourselves to think that his work in others is meant for our gain or pleasure. We can only serve well as we remember that all the fruit belongs to God.

If history is any teacher at all, we know how easy it is for us to lose sight of how *we can benefit the vineyard* and to think instead of how *the vineyard can benefit us*. The prophets in the Old Testament chided Israel's shepherds who misused the sheep for their own gain. Instead of risking their lives to keep the sheep happy, they butchered the sheep to fill their own bellies. In this same mixed metaphor Jeremiah showed us how we can abuse God's vineyard:

> *Many shepherds will ruin my vineyard and trample down my field; they will turn my pleasant field into a desolate wasteland. It will be made a wasteland, parched and desolate before me; the whole land will be laid waste because there is no one who cares.*
>
> JEREMIAH 12:10,11

This is God's vineyard. Everything we do in it must flow from *his* desires, and every produce of it belongs to *him*. He must receive what is due him, freely given from our hand. If not, the vineyard will waste away and he will have to remove us.

Jesus concludes his parable by identifying himself as the rejected cornerstone. Those who do not accept him will have the vineyard taken away from them and "given to a people who will produce its fruit" (Matthew 21:43).

I told you fruitfulness was God's passion, as much in our service to others as it is in our personal lives. As we've seen throughout the vineyard, that fruit is only produced where Jesus remains the central focus. That's as true for workers as it is for branches. He is the line of demarcation in all things spiritual. Are we following his voice and his desires, or are we only trying to do things for him for our own gain or blessing?

As we move now through the seasons of the year, keep in mind this wider view of the vineyard. All that we will learn to help us embrace God's work at varying seasons of our lives will also be true of other believers around us. Not only will we discover how to find our own way to fruitfulness and fulfillment, but we will also learn how we can better assist other believers in finding theirs.

The two are inseparably linked. It is the way of God's vineyard, and a beacon for us if we want to live in God's fullness.

PART TWO

The Seasons

18

SEASONS OF THE VINEYARD

There is a time for everything, and a
season for every activity under heaven:
a time to be born and a time to die, a time to
plant and a time to uproot.

ECCLESIASTES 3:1

What must it have been like, that first dawn over God's creation? Where did those first rays of the brand-new sun strike this planet as God spun it into place in the heavens? We don't know, for no one was there except God alone.

But it must have been an awesome moment as the sun launched into the morning sky and stretched its rays over the barren land beneath. What promise it held for creativity yet unleashed as God set about gathering waters into oceans, and with his finger perhaps separating it from the dry land! In days ahead God would fill it with flora and fauna of immense diversity and beauty.

Ever since that first day, nothing except God himself has had more impact over creation than this sun of the first dawn. Around it our globe spins in an orbit with a spectacular tilt that lets the sun be shared in the course of a year over the widest possible area of the globe.

This carefully chosen orbit produces in each hemisphere an unending cycle of seasons. As the sun spreads its beams over most of the Northern Hemisphere we experience the hot days of summer, while the southern part of our globe endures their winter. Our days are longer, theirs shorter. But in June the sun begins its retreat southward. Our days diminish in length as theirs grow longer, until in December and January the roles are reversed.

And so it continues, year in and year out. Winter gives way to an explosion of spring, spring to the overbearing summer, summer to the gentle autumn, autumn to winter's chill. It has been so since that first dawn. It will continue so until the last.

We have God's word on that, in a promise he made to Noah after the flood:

> *As long as the earth endures, seedtime and harvest, cold and heat, summer and winter, day and night will never cease.*
>
> GENESIS 8:22

You cannot understand the growth of any plant apart from the changes in weather and sunlight brought on by these ever-changing seasons. The vineyard is no different: At every moment what the farmer does in the vineyard is dependent upon these seasons. If he tries to gather grapes in spring he will find only the smallest beginnings of a harvest still to come. No one will want them. If he tries to prune in summer he will only destroy the vine he is committed to care for. The seasons control everything a farmer does in the vineyard.

Would it be fair for us to also assume there are seasons in the Father's vineyard? Often God's creation is not only an expression of God's awesome beauty and creativity, but it is also a tool by which God can demonstrate to us his marvelous ways.

So it is here as well. Jesus' own analogy hints at those seasons when he speaks of the father's pruning, for that can only be done in winter unless the farmer wants to destroy the vine. David in Psalm 1 much more clearly attaches seasons to our spiritual life. He compares the righteous to a tree planted by a river, which "yields its fruit in season." There is a time for fruitfulness in our lives, which also indicates that there are seasons for other things as well.

Ecclesiastes simply states it: "There is a time for everything, and a season for every activity under heaven."

Solomon is not writing about plants and crops, but human endeavors. God has mirrored in his seasons the way he works with his people.

As we will see in this section, a myriad of Scriptures refer to appropriate times and moments of God's working that can be analogous to our four seasons. Anyone who has walked with God for any length of time recognizes that God works with us at different times in different ways. At some moments our lives seem to bubble over with joy. At every turn we see God's hand moving, and every time we open the Scriptures the words seem to leap off the page with application to specific situations we're facing.

At other times the joy we experience is far deeper as we endure painful or distressing circumstances. During such times God's Word has to be mined more fervently and at greater depth. Need presses us from all sides. During these times we find ourselves repenting far more often than rejoicing.

If we don't understand God's working in seasons, we'll make the mistake of assuming that the moments of euphoria are what Christianity is meant to be, and that anything less is a source of continual condemnation.

Look at the life of Jesus. His life was marked by seasons when he was overjoyed and by those when he was deeply troubled, only able to offer up "prayers and petitions with loud cries and tears." We see him in crowded moments with great numbers of people clamoring for his favors, and at others alone on the hillside taking time to be with the Father. We see him making wine for a young couple's wedding, and later driving out money-changers in the temple.

Jesus was not afraid to embrace the changing spiritual seasons of his life. He didn't try to find a rigid code to live by that would meet the expectations of each day. Rather, he flowed with God's moving, responsive in each season.

We would do well to follow his lead. Our spiritual growth demands an ever-changing climate, various seasons where God's work is tailor-made to the circumstances in which we find ourselves. These seasons are not controlled by the sun overhead, but by the Father's design as he stirs us toward fruitfulness. As we shall see, these seasons will bring us a healthy balance of joyful moments and challenging ones, of diligent effort and renewing rest.

Without the changing seasons, vineyards would never bear fruit. Each season offers something that the vine needs for its continued growth. Spring brings the needed rain and softened days to help stimulate growth without crushing it in the searing heat. Summer offers enough sun to bring the grapes to maturity. Autumn offers the opportunity for harvest undaunted by rain and a chance for the vine to restore itself before winter. Finally, winter brings a much-needed rest and restaging to the vine. Without it, the vine would not be able to cycle again to harvest.

As we recognize four seasons of God's working in our life, we'll also see that from each we will receive something we need for continued growth. We'll see that even if we could, to remain in any one season forever would abort our fruitfulness in days to come. So we must not only learn to embrace the season we're in, but to let it go when it changes.

We'll also find each season producing its own source of danger and challenge. The dangers, from weeds and invading insects, need to be recognized and avoided. The challenges, however, must not be resisted. Without the cutting of winter and the discipline of spring, nothing would grow from our lives. The same is true of learning to endure the long, hot days of fruit-ripening. In each season we must not only enjoy the resources which our Father makes available to us, but learn to rejoice in the challenges as well.

That's what the cross is all about: Life can be celebrated in the midst of pain. Not all suffering is harmful, for much of it produces the very fruit in our lives that brings great pleasure to the Father. Though he never delights in those things that hurt us, he does realize how necessary some of them are to bring us into the fullness of his glory.

Let us be aware of God's working in us. Let us learn to recognize the various seasons of God's work in us, and then cooperate accordingly. How is God using the current challenges which I'm facing to produce his greater glory in me? At such moments I don't have to blindly resign myself to my circumstances, or to sit in frustration when they don't meet my expectations. Instead, I can know what the Father is doing through them and give myself wholeheartedly to that work.

We will begin in spring and walk the vineyard through its various seasons. As I describe what the vine is going through, we'll look for parallels in our spiritual lives. Seeing God's hand through these moments will leave us more equipped to anticipate his working in us and more prepared for the seasons yet to come.

Before we begin however, let me highlight one important distinction between seasons in the vineyard and seasons in our lives. In the vineyard, all vines endure the same climatic realities together. They are all pruned in winter, cultivated in the spring and summer, and harvested in the fall.

This does not seem to be true of our spiritual lives. Though sweeping generalities can be made at times about what God might be doing in a specific congregation or even geographical area, such observations may not hold true for everyone. God deals with each branch on the vine individually, giving special care to its own unique growth. And since our seasons are not controlled by external elements of environment alone, they may not line up with anyone else around us. I may be enduring the restoration of winter while someone near me is enjoying the fun of harvest.

That is exactly why Scripture warns us repeatedly not to compare ourselves to other believers, and why, when we do, we will end up confused.

> *We do not dare to classify or compare ourselves with some who commend themselves. When they measure themselves by themselves and compare themselves with themselves, they are not wise.*
>
> 2 CORINTHIANS 10:12

To make matters worse, whenever we compare ourselves with someone else we almost always compare the *best* thing going on in their life, with the *worst* going on in ours. Instead of looking at the rest and refreshing which God brings through our spiritual winters, I will instead focus on the circumstances that surround it—the diminished activity and fresh wounds from the recent pruning. When looking at the person who is in the middle of a fruitful harvest, I will highlight their joy and acclaim, forgetting the risk and cutting that go on in those days as well. As much as we might want to see some fruit in winter, it won't happen. It is a fact that vines can't produce fruit in the winter. Take comfort in this, however, for it is also a fact that branches cannot bear fruit *without* winter. Without the rest and restoration that comes from the dormancy and the pruning, fruit would not appear again.

What is even more ironic in this scenario is that while a wintered branch may covet the harvest, branches in the harvest will covet the peace and serenity of winter! All of God's branches would be far better served by doing less looking around for something better and instead enjoying the work that God is doing right now. We do ourselves and God no service when we are always frustrated by what God is *not* doing in our lives instead of participating in what he *is* doing.

For he is always working. It may not seem like it sometimes, since we may have missed his hand in the distractions or challenges we're facing, or because he isn't doing what we think he should be doing. God is always working. Jesus took great comfort in this simple fact: "My Father is always at his work to this very day" (John 5:17).

Instead of complaining, I am better off looking for the way God is working in my life at any given moment. That's the key to walking with God. *We* are not the initiators, *he* is. He determines the seasons of our lives—when to prune, when to feed or when to harvest our fruit. We are just his followers, free to follow his perfect plans for us.

Spring

NEW LIFE BEGINS

*See! The winter is past; the rains are over
and gone. Flowers appear on the earth; the
season of singing has come, the cooing of doves
is heard in our land. The fig tree forms its
early fruit; the blossoming vines spread their
fragrance. Arise, come, my darling; my
beautiful one, come with me.*

SONG OF SONGS 2:11-13

Slowly at first, and imperceptibly, the vines stir to life. The warming afternoon air signals the return of spring, and the vine responds with a flow of sap up from the roots out into the branches. Open wounds from the winter's pruning may even drip some, but for nearly a month nothing else is evident.

But vines are not the first to signal the return of spring. The white blossoms of the almond tree and the vivid pink of the peaches break out much sooner. The vine takes its time, not willing to send out its tender buds until the danger of frost is far past. While other fruit trees trumpet their glory, the only change observed on the vine (and for this you would have to look closely) are the swelling of its buds.

Then one day, as if on cue, they all explode together. Looking down the vineyard row you can see the faintest tint of

green as the leaves curl out of the broken bud and aim skyward. The tender shoots are an iridescent green, almost
transparent against the low-lying sunbeams of dawn. They
are soft and pliable. In ensuing days the growth is rapid as a
bright green laurel crowns the row of grapevines.

Spring heralds the days of romance and beauty. The flowers
bloom and their fragrance covers the land. Is there any time
more beautiful or glorious, especially out in the countryside,
where you can look for miles over blooming orchards and
wildflower-strewn hillsides?

I don't know if more people fall in love in springtime than
at any other time, but ever since man's earliest poetry love has
been connected with spring. Even Solomon immortalized in
his own poetry the fresh resurgence of life after the winter as
a celebration of his desire for his lover—and he wanted to
celebrate that love in the vineyard.

> *I belong to my lover, and his desire is for me. Come, my
> lover, let us go to the countryside, let us spend the night in
> the villages. Let us go early to the vineyards to see if the
> vines have budded, if their blossoms have opened, and if the
> pomegranates are in bloom—there I will give you my love.*
> SONG OF SONGS 7:10-12

Spring comes to the vineyard, and the forces of fruitfulness
begin their long and steady process. Every leaf is fresh and
clean, spreading out to catch the sunshine. Underneath them
the blossoms emerge, promising a future day of harvest many
months away. Though vines warm to the spring slowly, once
begun they grow rapidly, watered by the spring rains and
coaxed out by the ever-warming sun.

Love, joy, beauty and promise are all synonymous with
spring, and so it is in our spiritual lives. We have all known
times when we touch the presence of God at every turn, hear
his voice with clarity and find no circumstance too daunting
for our faith. We look to the future with hope and vision,
blossoming with promise and confidence in God's ability to
bring our hopes to pass. Following on the heels of the colder
and more difficult days of winter, spring is always welcome

indeed. No season is more glorious, with the exception of the harvest. Each day is a fresh adventure in God's grace.

But as glorious as the days of spring are, they are also a time of extreme danger. In fact there is more danger in spring for the maturing vine than in any other season, for life begun is life most fragile. The delicate young leaves and blossom bunches will never be more vulnerable. The simplest of things can bring a swift end to the fruitfulness, or at least diminish the quality of it. A late frost, a mad hailstorm, or an assault of weeds or insects can spell a quick end to a promised harvest.

Even in times of joy and beauty, we must not forget how precious our faith is—and how much the prince of this age would like to snuff it out. Like a lighted match in the wind, it needs protection. How many times when we have felt the most secure has the enemy come to snatch away our newfound joy?

It is easy to give into his distractions and find the promises of God aborted because we became preoccupied with the things of this age. It has happened to us all. God prepares us to bear his fruit, but just when he's ready to set it we allow it to be stolen by other affections of our heart.

It doesn't take much. A lingering need, a persistent sin, a major disappointment, or some unkind words from another believer can destroy our joy if we let it. Such destruction does not even demand evil events. Many are those who stand distracted from the promise by an unhealthy preoccupation with what might even be God's own gifts to them—an effective ministry, a promotion at work, or a new child or home.

Our branch begins to send its own canes into the soil to develop its own roots, away from the vine that has brought us such joy. Months later we look back nostalgically at these days of promise with frustration. We imagine how it used to be and wonder why God never accomplished what he promised us. Maybe we were wrong; maybe God changed his mind.

Yet all the time the Father's heart has not changed. Instead, we didn't follow through to fruitfulness. We must learn in the spring how to cultivate God's work deeply in our hearts, so that when the blossoms fade, we'll stay with his work until those weak nubs at the end of our branches become the glorious bunches of grapes the gardener desires.

19

YOU ARE
ALREADY CLEAN

*You are already clean because of the word
I have spoken to you.*
JOHN 15:3

Nothing is cleaner than when it is new, and that is especially true in the natural environment of the San Joaquin Valley.

This is a desert, though not as you might imagine filled with cactus and snakes. Left to itself our ten inches of rain a year would produce only some brief scrub brush that would swiftly melt into the dust that is such a staple in our valley between May and October, when virtually no rain falls.

Nothing of value would grow here if it were not for the abundant aquifer beneath the ground and the yearly runoff from the magnificent Sierra Nevada mountains to the east. These two resources have turned this desert into a garden, one of the most productive regions on the planet.

But that doesn't mean it eliminates all the dust. Whenever the fields dry up for even a few days, the ever-present dust returns. It clings to the leaves and is stirred by the slightest movements. Plowing on a tractor, especially downwind, can keep you in a cloud of gagging dust all day long. Even in sealed-up homes, dust is the constant challenge of any homemaker in this valley. It is everywhere!

There is one time, however, when the vineyard is clean: the early days of springtime. At no other time of the year does it look better. The labor of winter has left the vineyard neatly trimmed and perfectly tied to the long, straight rows of glistening wire. The field is freshly plowed and every weed is shoveled away from the vines. The flexible new canes and miniature leaves are a vivid light green, and spotless. The spring rains have kept the dust at bay.

This is the vineyard at its best, tidy and uniform. All is under control. The farmer looks across his vineyard with a deep satisfaction at its beauty and order. It's not unlike the feeling I get now looking over my freshly mowed lawn, only far greater. Everything is clean, ready for the fruitful season ahead.

That's exactly how Jesus described his disciples as he told them the story of his Father's vineyard. It comes at an interesting moment, too. Jesus has just warned them of his impending departure, though they didn't understand the cross to come. His first words to them about the vineyard were how the Father cuts off unfruitful branches and prunes those that are fruitful.

They, like us, must have wondered where they fit in. What does he think of me? Am I about to be cut off? So gently, Jesus pronounces their safety: You are already clean! Don't worry about the pruner's shears; it is not time for that. You are already neatly trimmed and fit for the season ahead.

Though we miss it in our translations, Jesus' pronouncement is an interesting word play. The word he uses for "clean" comes from the same root as the word he used for *pruning* in the sentence before. He demonstrates by his usage exactly what pruning is meant to accomplish: It makes the vine clean in the fullest sense of the word—not just dust-free, but trimmed and ready for growth. But Jesus doesn't seem to indicate that they had been freshly pruned. No, in their spiritual life this was their first spring. They had enjoyed it throughout the ministry of Jesus, and now he was preparing them for days to come. And even though the theme of John 15 is a call to bear fruit, Jesus wasn't asking that of them today. This was spring, not harvest. They were ready for the process of fruitfulness to *begin*; they had not yet completed the cycle. Our growth in God's kingdom does not aim ultimately for cleanliness; it *begins* there.

How was this accomplished in the disciples? By the word that Jesus spoke to them. He made them ready with the truth of the gospel that he had expounded to them these past three years. As they responded to that gospel it had washed them and made them clean. Paul uses the same image in his marriage counseling:

> *Christ loved the church and gave himself up for her to make her holy, cleansing her by the washing with water through the word, and to present her to himself as a radiant church, without stain or wrinkle or any other blemish, but holy and blameless.*
>
> EPHESIANS 5:25-27

Christ's word makes us clean and able to stand before God beautifully adorned and blameless. There is no more foundational work than this for fruitfulness. Since fruitfulness arises only out of the depths of our friendship with Jesus, it cannot begin until we are comfortable in his presence, confident that we belong there.

So Jesus made a way for us to come to the Father as freshly cleaned as a spring vine. The same word that Jesus used for clean, the writer of Hebrews takes up when he talks about the cleansed conscience of a believer under the New Covenant. Our conscience is made perfect by the work of Christ, and the writer goes to great pains to show us that this is not mere mental gymnastics. It is not an assumption of forgiveness by someone who has traversed the proper theological steps.

That was the limitation of the sacrifices which the Old Covenant provided. One had to believe in his forgiveness because he had made the sacrifice. But his consciousness of sin did not depart. From one who seemed to know the difference firsthand, having served God under both covenants, the writer of Hebrews extols the marvelous cleansing of the New Covenant that leads us to God's presence with a perfect conscience. No pang of guilt endures, no fear of punishment remains. His word of forgiveness buries the past at the foot of the cross, removing all stain of our sin and rebellion.

We are exhorted to come to God's presence with confidence and boldness; we belong there. Intimacy demands that kind of confidence. What child is comfortable with his father or mother still feeling the guilt of one of his failures? Only when atonement is made can friendship ensue. Our sins have been forgiven, and we can approach God assured of our welcome.

All we have to do to embrace this cleansing is repent—to turn from living life our own way and choose to live it his. This is the door into his cleansing. That is not only true the first time we come to know him, but true every day we walk in him.

This call to cleanliness also sets our priority in coming to God's kingdom. When first we come in the door, his desire is to clean us up from the forces of sin that have raged against us. Spiritually that happens in the blink of an eye as he justifies us in God's presence the moment we call to him in repentance. But practically walking in the freedom of that cleansing may take some time.

I'm not talking here about becoming perfect in every area of conduct, but being free of every past failure and degradation of sin. Particularly people who come from abused or neglected backgrounds struggle greatly here, as do those who have been deeply involved in major expressions of sin. These give the enemy an opportunity to plant patterns of thinking that will, if not dealt with, leave you feeling like a second-class citizen of God's vineyard.

Don't ever settle for second-class status. God wants to heal all the wounds of your past so that you can go on to know the full joy of his kingdom. If you still feel stained by your past, let God deal with it. Seek out the prayer and ministry of others who can help you fully appropriate the cleansing that God has already given you.

Once again walking in repentance will be a key here. Even where you have felt the most victimized by others your freedom lies in being able to accept responsibility for how you reacted to their sin. The enemy's agenda here will be to get you to blame others, or even God, but this will not lead you to freedom. Instead, submit your ungodly responses to him in repentance, turning from the false conceptions of yourself and God which the enemy has planted in your mind.

You'll know this is accomplished when you can rise to each day confident of your lovability and acceptability to God. Then for the rest of your life guard that cleanliness. Keep it fresh by continued repentance and surrender to God. Don't get defensive at the things God might expose in you, for he only wants to forgive and transform you.

Jesus declared his disciples already clean, and by so doing declared springtime in their hearts. Conversion is always our first spring. Nothing more aptly describes those who embark on a new walk in Christ! For each of us our first days in God's kingdom are just like spring. We begin in his kingdom newly made, fresh and clean. Our friendship with Jesus is established and his voice and his power begin to evidence themselves in our lives.

But this is not the only spring we get in the kingdom. Periodically we will note times when God freshens his presence and renews us with promise and vision. These may not recur yearly or at regular intervals, but remember that the calendar doesn't control our spiritual seasons. Yet come they will on the heels of our spiritual winter, when our lives are pruned and prepared for the next work that God wants to do in us.

This spring cleaning is the key to everything in God's kingdom. Here is where we differ greatly from the physical vines we're discussing. Though they are only clean during one season of the year, we are called to be clean at all times. Each day through our repentance we can receive God's cleansing work. Each moment we can be confident of our access to God as we keep turning from our own ways to follow obediently his desires for us. As we do this we will continue to know cleansing. Otherwise our spiritual life will only accumulate the dirt of this world until we can no longer see that we are welcome in his presence.

20

TRAINING UP
A VINE

*No discipline seems pleasant at the time, but
painful. Later on, however, it produces a
harvest of righteousness and peace for those
who have been trained by it.*
HEBREWS 12:11

They're called suckers, and that aptly describes what they
do.

They are new canes that sprout from the base of a vine. If
left there, they would suck life out of the vine that would
otherwise be directed at the fruit.

New growth in spring is so prolific that left to itself it will
sprawl out everywhere. Not all of that growth is good, for
some of it will siphon off the strength of the vine instead of
adding to it. One of the most important tasks the farmer
accomplishes in the spring is to direct growth on the vine for
maximum fruitfulness.

Some of these tasks are performed on even the most mature
branches. Suckers, for instance, need to be pulled off. Sometimes even beginning grape bunches are plucked off, either
because the crop is too large or else to make sure that those
bunches that do mature are far larger and sweeter than they
would be otherwise. Some table-grape farmers girdle their
vines, cutting a trough around the trunk itself to direct more
nutrients to the grape bunches.

Perhaps the best place, however, to see the farmer train his vines is in the work done with those vines just entering their first growing seasons. How these new vines are trained will have impact years down the road. To get this training started the farmer tears off every shoot that grows from the new vine, and this growth tends to happen at every joint where a leaf emerges. What the farmer wants, however, is for the young vine to have only one long branch, diverting all the energy to strengthen that part of the vine. This will help it move faster toward production.

The following winter the farmer prunes that branch at the height he wants the vine to be, in order to allow next year's shoots to branch off from the top. Branches lower down on the trunk will again be plucked off to force the strength of the vine into the branches that will ultimately bear the fruit. Every year after that the farmer still has to pull off those branches that grow too low on the vine.

Part of the tidiness of the vineyard in springtime comes from this trimming and training. For us it represents a second aspect of cleanliness so vital to our spiritual growth. During our spring seasons, when growth is profuse, the gardener comes to align us with his intentions for the growth of the year to come. This training is known as *discipline*. Those whom God loves, Hebrews 12 tells us, he disciplines or trains. Without this training there will be no fruitfulness, and yet there's nothing more we resist from God's hand than his training.

First of all, it is uncomfortable. We don't like being channeled, preferring to let ourselves grow naturally. After all, haven't we been set free in Christ? So most attempts by God to bring discipline to our lives usually meet with screams of "legalism!" We rationalize that any restriction in our lives can't be God, because he wants us to be free!

How wrong we are, and how much of our growth is swallowed up by our refusal to submit to the Lord's discipline. All restriction is not legalism. Two types of evidence can easily identify legalism so we don't confuse it with discipline. Legalism results either from meeting the rules or expectations of another person or else from attempting to achieve acceptance and status from God. From those two restrictions we have indeed been set free.

Discipline, however, is *obedience to God as he directs our growth.* Obedience is not legalism, nor an optional component of salvation. Jesus said that if we're not ready to obey him, we had best not come near the kingdom. Our freedom in Christ is the freedom to obey his wishes, not to live the way we think is most natural for us.

Second, discipline should not be confused with punishment. Someone is punished when he is repaid for something he has done wrong. It may have deterrence in mind, but primarily punishment is *retribution.* The Lord's discipline, however, has our *training* in mind. Though it may be hurtful at times, that is not its intent. It is meant to *shape us according to God's desires*, even at the cost of temporal discomfort.

Jack Hayford once defined discipline as the process in which God narrows the flow to increase the force. That's exactly what happens as a young vine is trained up. By narrowing the flow of sap into a few good branches, you ensure the fruitfulness of the vine as a whole. By restricting our lives to God's intentions, we allow his Spirit to bring us to fruitfulness and fulfillment in God's kingdom.

If, on the other hand, we resist God's efforts at training, we will forever be frustrated that our lives never come to match the full promise of God's salvation. Indeed, far too many of us have found a niche beneath God's promises and have made ourselves comfortable there. We rationalize away the promises of God we're not living in, precisely because we've refused his hand of training.

The best time for discipline is before we need it. The tender shoots of a young vine can be plucked off or tied up to the vine with a minimal amount of effort. At this stage they are as flexible as boiled spaghetti. The longer they grow, however, the more rigid they become. Within a year they will break if bent too far. A young vine can be trained to grow straight up the pole if it is carefully tied as it grows.

When God calls you to an act of obedience, act quickly and such acts will grow more easy to do each time. The longer you resist, however, the more difficult it becomes to obey. That understanding helps me resist procrastination in my obedience. It will not get any easier, only more difficult. Any thought that it will actually get easier is the trick of the enemy to justify our own independence.

That's also why the first few months of a new convert's life are so crucial. Charles Finney observed that most converts live for a lifetime on the patterns and doctrine they learn within the first three months of their conversion. He saw it as the key time for training, since they are most pliable and receptive at this time. That should encourage us to take seriously the task of equipping new converts, but it should also give us pause to reflect on the things we learned ourselves during our first few months of salvation, verifying their biblical accuracy, and being willing to change those things that need correcting. Too many people are rigidly committed to either false or incomplete perceptions of what it really means to follow Christ.

God takes our discipline seriously. He trains us not by tying us to poles and wires, but by calling us to obey his voice. He speaks through a message from Scripture, through a comment from a friend, or in our hearts as we sit before him. In shaping us to his image, often what he asks of us runs counter to our personal interest or independence. Simply put, he asks us to lay down our lives for him, and that's why obedience is difficult and risky.

Like a vine being trained, we prefer to go our own way, and we often rationalize our interpretation of God's voice to better fit our own ambitions. When we resist God's gentle urgings, he uses our circumstances to bring greater clarity to his direction. Often these are painful because our selfish pursuits and self-sufficiency are revealed for what they are—vain attempts to find life ourselves. Consider Psalm 32:8,9:

> I will instruct you and teach you in the way you should go;
> I will counsel you and watch over you. Do not be like the
> horse or the mule, which have no understanding but must
> be controlled by bit and bridle or they will not come to you.

God doesn't want to use the bit and bridle—those painful circumstances that prod us to God's will—when we are willing to respond to the gentle call of his voice. I've seen horses trained well enough that the slightest touch on the side of the neck, or a single word from the master is all it needs. God would prefer the same of us. But God will still use the confines of circumstances for those who have prayed, "Whatever it takes, Father, lead me to your will."

I appreciate wholeheartedly the honesty of Hebrews 12: "No discipline seems pleasant at the time, but painful." How true! The training of a grapevine breaks the natural inclinations of a branch's growth, as does our obedience. Sometimes we feel as if we're being bent the wrong way. If we respond, however, it will produce God's fruit in our lives.

"Endure all hardship as discipline," Hebrews continues. He is seeking to mold us after himself. But who ever admits to such things? Every time I hear someone going through trials it is always the enemy's doing: "Satan has really been after me this week!" More than we know we should be saying, "I have been through some difficult moments these past weeks, because God has been training me to be more like him."

Hardships cause us to change more than hearing God's voice in times of ease. So when difficult things begin to happen don't always rebuke the enemy; sometimes you need to submit to God more deeply. Let him have that false crutch you hang onto so tightly.

Most of this training has to do with the most important priority of the branch—remaining in the vine: learning how to spend daily time in the Lord's presence that tunes us to his voice and purifies our heart from the dust of this age. There's nothing more important for a believer to learn than drawing life from the vine.

Establishing a healthy growth configuration for a vine is more important to the farmer in the early years than producing fruit. No vine will produce fruit the first year anyway, nor enough in the second and third to make any difference. Those farmers who are farsighted enough to forfeit the small crop of those earlier years will pick off the bunches just after they have bloomed so that all the energy of the vine will go into rooting deeply and developing branches from which abundant fruit can grow later on.

I've often wondered if that's why God asked the Israelites to consider all fruit forbidden in the first three years, and in the fourth year to give it as holy to the Lord (Leviticus 19:23-25). "In this way your harvest will be increased." Their obedience would be a point of trust in the Lord, with the practical implication that it would be more healthy for the vine. Not only would that obedience receive God's blessing, but it also would create a better vine. The Father does indeed know best.

Before we move on, there is one interesting sidelight to this kind of training. Sometimes a vine gets so old or its branches so weakened that it doesn't bear fruit well. The farmer then chops it off close to the ground and lets one new shoot grow out of the old stump to make a new vine.

God can do the same with our lives. Maybe your perception of Christianity has grown too complex or confusing. Perhaps you can no longer separate God's desires from your own. If so, let God start you fresh again with the simplicity of what it means to love him. That won't discount everything good he has already taught you, but it will allow a new branch to form that has not gotten so confused and disoriented.

That's exactly what God did with his plan of salvation. After the law demonstrated our inability to live to God by our own strength, he cut it off in order to let a new vine of grace emerge. Listen to these words of Isaiah 11:1: "A shoot will come up from the stump of Jesse; from his roots a Branch will bear fruit."

That new shoot was Jesus, who implemented a plan of salvation that could encompass us all based on God's doing and not our own. That's the vine to which our lives can be joined to bear the joyful fruit of God's amazing kingdom.

21

THE BLOOMS
OF PROMISE

*In days to come Jacob will take root,
Israel will bud and blossom and fill all the
world with fruit.*
ISAIAH 27:6

What are blossoms if not promises—a springtime reflection of the harvest to come?

It's easy to be confused when you look at a peach orchard in bloom. The brilliant pink sea they suspend above the landscape is one of the most breathtaking scenes of spring. Blossoms contain not only some of the most beautiful colors in nature, but many of the most pleasing aromas as well. The overpowering scent of an orange grove or lilac tree in blossom is a sweet pleasure indeed.

These floral displays would be worth it if their only purpose were to lend aesthetic beauty to our world. But God made flowers for something so much more spectacular: Blossoms celebrate the promise of fruitfulness. A new generation is formed; the future is secured.

It's not as easy to lose sight of that fact on a grapevine, since its blooms are not spectacular. Tiny white flowers pop open beneath the leaf cover. You can't even see them from a distance. Neither is their fragrance overpowering. The sweet aroma is subtle and can only be enjoyed if you are trained to

153

pick it up. It's no wonder that no one picks grape blossoms for flower arrangements.

There's no mistaking a grape bloom; it is a promise of fruit to come, nothing more.

Blossoms are the glory of spring, emerging at the very beginning of the growth cycle. It doesn't take a strong vine or a mature tree to bear blossoms—even the youngest will put forth blooms. The same is true of God's promises of fruitfulness in our lives. Spiritual springtime in our own lives is marked by fresh vision and promise from Jesus himself. At a time when we're exploding with the renewal of his life, he allows us to catch a glimpse of the glory that awaits us.

In inklings that grow ever-clearer in our minds until we can no longer ignore them, God makes his promises to his people: "I'm going to use your depth of compassion to help heal broken lives." "I'm going to use your gift of music to break the enemy's hold, just like David's worship soothed Saul." "I'm going to free you from your bondage to other people's expectations." "I'm going to make you as patient as the little brook wearing its way through a huge boulder."

Talk to almost any believer, and in the deepest recesses of his heart, if he has not already had them buried beneath disillusionment and false modesty, you will find that he carries meaningful and significant promises that Jesus has given him. If you can get him to talk about it without feeling silly, he will tell you of promises God has made to him.

Almost always you will find that these promises came in spiritual springtime, when the person's relationship with God was undergoing a season of renewal. What a joy that God has a future and a hope for each of our lives, and is willing to disclose it to us! A believer carrying the promise of God on his heart is as beautiful a sight as any plant in bloom.

But unlike our friends in the plant kingdom, we grow easily discouraged about God's promises if we don't see immediate proof of their fulfillment. We are so impatient, wanting God to fulfill in a matter of months what he has promised for years down the road.

When I first came to Visalia to pastor in a new congregation, my heart was alive with great vision for what God wanted to do in this fellowship. He had promised me that a fellowship could be built on the practical presence and headship of Jesus Christ, with intimacy and community available to every person. His power could live among a group of people willing to pay the price to abide in him and walk in his ways.

Two years into the promise if you would have met me most days, you would have found one discouraged young man. Nothing seemed to be going well. Most of the leadership that started with us had picked up and left. Though some of our gatherings were alive, most were quite a struggle. Community seemed an elusive goal that people would never accept in this culture.

I grew discouraged in God's promises, even doubting whether he had made them. If he had, was he playing some cruel trick, like the father who always promises to spend time with his children but never takes the time away from work to fulfill it? As Proverbs says, "Hope deferred makes the heart sick, but a longing fulfilled is a tree of life." Better never to have had promises than to have had them and never see them come to pass.

What do we say when promises don't come to pass? There are only three possibilities, and I've tasted them all:

First, we can be mistaken, believing our own desires to be God's promise. Present the promise in your heart to him, asking him to show you whether it was really him or not. If it was only your desire, let it go.

Second, we may have expected fulfillment too soon, and so give up too quickly. Our species seems to be an impatient lot. If too many days go by without some physical proof of God's promise, we grow discouraged. I relate well with Habakkuk, the Old Testament prophet of the late sixth century B.C. He offered God two complaints, both dealing with his impatience at God's moving. God's answer? "The revelation awaits an appointed time. . . . Though it lingers, wait for it; it will certainly come and will not delay."

I have to admit that for the most part I've always expected God's promises to be fulfilled in a time frame well ahead of his, and that is one sure way to destroy the very intent of a promise. We forget that God's promise is proof enough. If we can rejoice and be patient, that blossom will emerge as fully ripened fruit. His promises never fail. What I expected to happen in two years of church life needed another three or four years, because of the shaping that had to be done in us.

Third, promises go unfulfilled because we don't follow through on our obedience. Almost all of God's promises are conditional, assuming our continued pursuit of God and his ways. If the branch does not remain in the vine, the ripening fruit will wither even faster than it appeared.

Where there has been a problem with you and God's promises in the past, deal with it. God does not promise us to frustrate us or to be a source of confusion or despair. Can you think of a recent time when you've made a promise to someone? Especially think of the time when you expressly used the words "I promise..." What did you promise? More importantly, why specifically did you make your words a promise? Didn't you do it to set another person at ease? You wanted to quell any anxiety he or she might have and free him to act assured of your actions. Promises are intended to reassure.

Would God do any differently? You can't read Scripture without realizing that God is big on promises. We've already examined some of the more special ones that he has made to all of us: fulfilling us with joy, answering our prayers, and making us fruitful people. God's Word is full of others. Additionally, he makes promises to us individually, giving us insight into our personal lives. This is his way of borrowing joy from the future and letting us taste it in the present.

God accomplishes three things through his promises. First, he wants to stir hope within us. So much of our walk in him is predicated on hope—hope that God will actually do what he promises he will. Second, his promises set us at rest. He will accomplish what he has promised, so we need not try to fulfill it by our own strength. Finally, his promises free us to obey him each day, not pursue the fulfillment of our promises. Few of God's promises are arrived at directly. Remember, this is a kingdom where if you try to save your own life you're sure to lose it.

In these three things God's promises accomplish a deeper work: They are actually the means God uses to transform us. The hunger stirred by his promise, our need to learn trust, and our challenge to stay faithful all allow him to shape us. That is what is important to God.

> *Through these he has given us his very great and precious promises, so that through them you may participate in the divine nature and escape the corruption in the world caused by evil desires.*
>
> 2 PETER 1:4

Throughout Scripture God makes promises to people and fulfills them, and through that process he changes people to be more like him. The father of faith himself, Abraham, is perhaps the best example of this. God promised to make him the father of a great nation even though he had no children. For 25 years Abraham endured that promise, well past the time that he or his wife could ever have children naturally. Why did God delay? God's promise was to make Abraham the father of a great nation. That meant more than having a child; it meant that he had to be shaped as a man of faith. His promise provided the opportunity for that shaping.

In Romans 4 Paul pictures Abraham as a man who learned how to embrace God's promise, even though Abraham was not perfect. Genesis records his failures as well as triumphs, but through them he learned to trust God. That's why Paul made him an example of responding to God's promise with hope, not frustration.

". . . God, who gives life to the dead and calls things that are not as though they were." God called Abraham a father of a great nation before he was even a father. God sees the end from the beginning, and it is precisely this perspective that gives birth to his promises. Those promises share his perspective with us. We need to believe God's promises even when there is not a shred of material evidence to corroborate them.

"Abraham in hope believed and so became the father of many nations." Abraham's hope freed God's promise to be fulfilled. If he had given up he still might have had a baby, but he would not have been the example needed to stand as a father of an entire nation.

"Without weakening in his faith, he faced the fact that his body was as good as dead—since he was about a hundred years old—and that Sarah's womb was also dead." Faith never hides from facts. Abraham could look at the tangible evidence without weakening in his faith. Faith that has to hide from circumstances is not faith at all. But in spite of the lack of material evidence, Abraham had a promise from God. That alone was evidence enough to quell any fear.

"Yet he did not waver through unbelief regarding the promise of God, but was strengthened in his faith and gave glory to God." What circumstances surrounding you challenge God's promise? Don't let them convince you otherwise. Strengthen your faith by giving glory to God.

". . . being fully persuaded that God had power to do . . ." Look at the God Abraham served. God has the power to do anything. This is the one who created all things and even raises the dead to life again. His power wasn't limited by Sarah's dead womb. How big is your God? If he's not bigger than any circumstance you face, then you better spend some more time with him. Let him be magnified in your heart so that you know we serve a God who can do anything!

". . . what he had promised." Here is the clincher to Abraham's faith and of ours as well. God *can* do anything, but our faith can only be applied when we know what he *is* doing. He is able to do *anything*, but we can trust him to do *what he promises*. It wasn't Abraham's idea to be the father of a great nation. He might have already adjusted to the idea of being childless when God made him promises. That is why it is so important for us to hear God's voice in our lives. For faith does not rest on God's *ability*, but on his *activity*.

The young mother had been separated for a few months, her husband deserting her within a week after the birth of their third child. It was time that she look ahead and make some plans for the future. I was sure that's why she wanted to see me. As we began to talk she told me that she was not concerned, that God had promised her that her husband would return.

I probed her discernment carefully. I have too often seen people use God's name to cling to their own groundless hope—a made-up promise as an escape from facing reality. This situation sure looked like that, but something inside told me not to discount it. We talked openly about whether this was God or not, and though I couldn't tell her I heard God confirm it with me, I was convinced of her submission to Jesus. She was not trying to escape.

I encouraged her to stand strong in the promise, always open for God to show her differently if she was wrong. Nine months passed and nothing gave us hope of her husband's return. Then out of the blue he called one day. He had failed her, was deeply sorry, and wanted to come home. Over the next few months God did a marvelous work in bringing them back together—a promise fulfilled! Today they are in full-time ministry together.

Expect God's promises to come in springtime. When they do, hold on to them. If you're not sure, seek out another believer you trust for confirmation. Let God's promise set in your life, then prepare to watch both it and you grow through the days ahead as God brings that blossom through the process of becoming a mature fruit.

22

EARLY ENEMIES OF GROWTH

When anyone hears the message about the kingdom and does not understand it, the evil one comes and snatches away what was sown in his heart.

MATTHEW 13:19

Blame those pesky birds! As the seed bounced against the roadway, they were the ones to swoop down and grab the seeds. But in the parable of the sower, Jesus blames only the soil. It was too hard to let the seed into the ground.

I realize the sower was not planting vineyard seeds. That's not how they are propagated and they, unlike wheat or corn, do not need to be planted every year. But the applications of this parable are just as important in the vineyard.

Jesus told this parable to demonstrate the dangers to the kingdom of God taking root in our lives and bearing fruit. The first danger involves seed falling on the roadside. Because the seed cannot hide beneath the soil, birds (or the enemy) can snatch it away before it can even begin to grow. Yet Jesus doesn't fault the sower or the birds, but instead uses this picture to illustrate what happens in someone's heart that keeps seed from becoming fruitful.

The roadway represents people who hear the Word, but do not understand it. They've been touched by someone's word or had an experience with God's presence that led them to the

truth of the gospel. But if they do not grow in their understanding of God, that moment will quickly fade into memory
and the seed itself will be stolen by the evil one. What grants
God's power access to our lives is our understanding. Only by
changing the way we think and live can his life penetrate us
enough to let his life dwell in us.

Even though birds don't steal grape branches, it is interesting that the dangers which the vineyard faces in the spring
have the same catastrophic implications. For all practical
purposes there are only two dangers in spring that can
destroy the hope of harvest.

The first is an unseasonably late freeze. Once the vines
have budded, a hard freeze will destroy the buds and leave
the vines fruitless. New leaves will shoot, but there will be no
crop. Because the vine blooms extremely late, this very rarely
happens, but I did see its effects one year. The vines were as
brilliant green as ever and grew fiercely, but probing beneath
the leaves I couldn't find a single grape. The fruit had been
aborted.

The second danger, and this too is rare, comes from severe
hailstorms. Hail can rip the blossoms to shreds, with the same
results as a freeze. Leaves will regrow, grape bunches will not.
Would that it was as rare in the Father's vineyard! There are
not any direct spiritual corollaries to the frost and the hail, but
in Jesus' parable we do find their appropriate application:
People receive a touch of the gospel, but are cut off before the
process of fruitfulness can even begin.

How often I see people touched by the kingdom, even
responsive in an initial way to its truth. But it doesn't last. A
few months later will find them back in the same place they
were before. What happened? Was their touch genuine? Yes!
Did they really want it? Part of them did, but not enough to
seek to understand God's ways or the nature of his touch in
their lives. Without it the work of the gospel is destroyed.

This is not only a problem among new converts. Jesus'
parable of the sower is certainly not limited to people's first
response to the gospel. Jesus deals with the way we *continually*
respond to God. *Whenever* God touches our life in new ways

(which for a developing believer ought to be a frequent experience), we are presented with a choice: Are we going to let our understanding be shaped here, or are we going to quickly forget and walk away?

Meaningful experiences with God's presence are not sufficient in themselves to transform us. Only as we let God renew our minds with his truth can we escape the holds which the enemy has placed in our lives and find our full freedom in Christ. To walk with God we have to come to a place of thinking differently—to forsake our own wisdom and embrace God's instead.

I'm not talking here purely about academic interest. It is easy to study about God and have volumes of facts about him or Scripture memorized but still not have our way of thinking changed. Perhaps these are the people Paul admonished in 2 Timothy, ". . . always learning but never able to acknowledge the truth." Our understanding is not measured by what we know about God, but by how much we think like him.

And that is the challenge. Since he is so much higher than we are, and his thoughts so much greater than ours, we will have the unending joy of discovering how God thinks. Being in church leadership makes me a lightning rod for other people's ideas and opinions, especially when they are negative. The other day someone was expressing a concern to me about one of our worship leaders. "I don't think he is sensitive to God at all."

At moments like this I can't always resist responding, "And does God agree with you?"

By their confused silence and twisted glare I know I've sent the gears in their mind churning. What they really want to say is, "Of course; why else would I be telling you this?" But most of them have not prayed at all about such complaints, only assuming that God would surely agree with their assessment. How dangerous indeed! Whenever we think that our reactions so easily mirror God's greater wisdom and knowledge, we are in dire trouble indeed.

The more honest will respond, "I don't know." Now we have an opportunity to discuss their concerns as we seek God's mind together. His ways are so far above ours that we can only think like him if we're seeking him to make his Word clear to us.

The process of transformation is described as the renewing of our minds. God wants to free us from the twists and deceptions the enemy has inserted into our thought patterns, and through his wisdom create in us a whole new way of thinking. Instead of pursuing our own desires and appetites, we choose to live by every word that comes from God's mouth. Instead of giving in to anger and bitterness, we look for God to challenge it and excise it from our lives. Instead of assuming that God wants to bless the thoughts of the natural man, we realize that he wants to replace them with a heart of faith.

We grow in this understanding by having a heart for continual change as he transforms us into his image. That's why repentance is the key to life in God's kingdom, not only in coming into the door of God's kingdom but in living each day in it. I do not know what is best for my life, and so I need God to lead me each day by his Word and power. Increased knowledge will not result in increased understanding unless we're ready to respond to it and see our life change.

Why do we look in a mirror in the morning? Is it just for intellectual curiosity? Of course not. We look in the mirror to make adjustments. If my hair isn't combed, I comb it. If my shirt's not buttoned, I button it. If I'm not going to make any changes because of what I see in a mirror, then why look?

James in his epistle says that the same thing is true of the person who hears God's Word and doesn't do what it says. God's Word is the mirror. We must come to it to look for deficiencies in our lives, and then make necessary adjustments. If God's kingdom can't shape the way we live, it will quickly perish in our hearts.

Don't be embarrassed to admit your need for understanding to continue to grow, even if you've been a believer for a long time. It's amazing how much instruction our society gives about everything and yet how many believers feel that everyone should be able to figure out how to live in God's vineyard on their own. Only as you understand what he is doing in you can you respond to him each day with freedom and joy.

"Though it cost all you have, get understanding" (Proverbs 4:7). Here is how the blossoms set and begin to mature. The work that God started will go on to completion. If we're pursuing him every day we need not worry; the frost won't come too late, nor will the hail.

The gardener will see to that!

23

A PATTERN FOR NOURISHMENT

Beat your breasts for the pleasant fields, for the fruitful vines and for the land of my people, a land overgrown with thorns and briers.

ISAIAH 32:12,13

Obviously God as the provider is quite active in spring. He is the one who summons the vine to life again from the winter, and the one who creates new life in his followers. He calls the blossoms from the branches and by his grace makes us promises of good things that we could never earn from him.

But let us look now at God the gardener and see what he is doing as spring sweeps by. Not only will that perspective help us respond to him, but it will also show us how as his co-laborers we assist others in their springtime growth. God as provider demonstrates activity that we can never duplicate, but as gardener he is our model of ministry to others. So what does the farmer do in springtime other than training up the young vines, as we talked of earlier?

One day he might be on his tractor, plowing down the weeds that were incited by the spring rains, or spreading fertilizer beneath the vines. This time of year he'll almost always have a shovel with him, using it to scoop away small weeds from under the vine or to clip off a sucker.

Most of what the farmer does now looks far past spring-time, for now the vine does not have many needs. The rains water it, the soil nourishes it and the weeds are far too small to provide any real challenge to the vine. The farmer, however, is already looking ahead to summer, when the weeds will be much larger and can choke out the vine. The fertilizer, too, prepares the vine to endure the long haul of summer while the fruit ripens.

Now the farmer sets a pattern of nourishment that will sustain the vine through summer, when it will need it most. Here is where the foundation is laid even though the vine could do just as well without the little weeds pulled or the fertilizer spread. But the farmer knows that if these things are not taken care of now they will overwhelm the vine a few months later.

So in our lives, in the season of great joy and promise, God invites us to establish patterns of relationship with him that will endure the severest tests of faith. But too many of us cannot see the need. Everything is going so well just the way it is. Why do I need to let God deal with my fleshly desires, since he seems to be blessing me in spite of them? Why do I need daily time in the Word, since God seems to be speaking to me everywhere I turn?

It is precisely at times of great blessing, when God is so readily present, that the patterns for nourishment can be built in our own lives with the most effectiveness. God is easy to find—in our reading, our prayers and our touch with the body of Christ. There is no better time to set the patterns, or disciplines, for future relationship than now.

If we fail in springtime to set the course for our continued obedience and pursuit of God, when the promise delays and when the heat is turned up we will crumble. And instead of seeing our own failure to forge an enduring relationship with God, we will mistakenly blame him for deserting us in our time of need. But this God would never do!

All of us have to admit that it is easier to get serious with God when we encounter suffering than in times of bliss. God is so loving that he responds to this, but what will work better for us is to lay the foundations for that relationship in times of joy and blessing. Enjoy him during those times and use them to deepen your friendship with him. He will prepare you for the days to come. Isaiah warned us, "Seek the Lord while he may be found; call on him while he is near" (55:6).

When it looks like you hardly need to forge disciplines in your walk with God is the very time you must give it your attention. The enemy will try to convince you it is legalism, that you are trying to earn his presence by your works, but don't believe him. God is only training you for what he knows is coming. "Therefore let everyone who is godly pray to you while you may be found; surely when the mighty waters rise, they will not reach him" (Psalm 32:6).

Though the Word emphasizes this pattern of sowing and reaping, so many believers mistakenly think that their spiritual life will flourish regardless of the conditions in which they attempt to foster it. Somehow we assume that grace will cover for our spiritual lethargy, but it will not. Whenever we get just enough of God to survive the day, we've let the process break down. How we respond to God today has implications months down the road.

That's why people can miss some days of study and prayer and hardly notice any adverse impact on their relationship with the Lord. It hardly seems to matter, so they keep giving in to the excuses, not realizing that they are still reaping from what they sowed earlier. But eventually it catches up, and when they are left dry and empty, they can't figure out how it happened.

Nowhere is this more powerfully illustrated than in the vine. Not only does submission to the Lord's work of establishing discipline in our lives affect the harvest of next fall, but this emerging fruitfulness was established in that late spring and summer of the previous year. Grapes are a two-year crop. The bunches forming now were developed a year before while another crop was coming to fruitfulness. Then they were microscopic in size and hidden in the buds of next year's crop, but how the vine was cared for *last* year will determine the quality of *this* year.

What we do today affects what we'll be in Christ months and years from now. Grace does not change that. "Just as you used to offer the parts of your body in slavery to impurity and to ever-increasing wickedness, so now offer them in slavery to righteousness leading to holiness" (Romans 6:19). Wickedness makes wickedness easier to pursue. Righteousness makes holiness easier to embrace.

Spring is where these patterns are set. The roots are encouraged to go deep. The leaves spread their sails to catch the life-giving rays of the sun. The weeds are cut out while they are small, the insects are destroyed before they proliferate. It's time to give attention to your own spiritual patterns, drawing near to Jesus in those places we examined in the first section of this book. Don't wait for disaster to send you seeking in those areas for his presence; let them be shaped in times of joy.

The greatest danger we face when God blesses us is complacency. We don't need to participate; God will do it all. How wrong that is! If we allow ourselves to give in to complacency in springtime, look what will come of it:

> *You women who are so complacent, rise up and listen to me; you daughters who feel secure, hear what I have to say! In little more than a year you who feel secure will tremble; the grape harvest will fail, and the harvest of fruit will not come. Tremble, you complacent women; shudder, you daughters who feel secure! Strip off your clothes, put sackcloth around your waists. Beat your breasts for the pleasant fields, for the fruitful vines and for the land of my people, a land overgrown with thorns and briers.*
>
> ISAIAH 32:9-13

Whenever complacency grips our heart, we must call ourselves back to repentance. The farmer is doing all he can to ensure a future nourished by his presence. We need to do likewise.

Almost always long days lie between the promise and fulfillment, days where the real work of transformation transpires. At the times when God is moving powerfully in someone's life is the time we should be encouraging him to patterns of relationship that they will need for the future. Find four or five people who share your hunger and form a small discipleship group focused on building patterns of daily Bible study and prayer that are personally effective.

You cannot carry someone else to fruitfulness. You can only encourage him to build the patterns of nourishment into his life that will endure the heat of summer. Yet we have no clearer mandate than to make disciples of all nations. It's not enough to lead them to spring; we must also prepare them for summer, and be prepared ourselves.

24

OF FADING BLOSSOMS AND FUTURE FRUIT

One thing I do: Forgetting what is behind and
straining toward what is ahead....
PHILIPPIANS 3:13

Spring doesn't last forever. The fresh beauty of new life fades as the lengthening days and increased heat take their toll on the vineyard's beauty. Every year since the dawn of creation spring has passed into summertime.

The young, green leaves weather and darken, no longer tender and pristine. Their edges fray and split as the elements war against them. The blossom petals, small and pale as they are, have long since turned a dusty brown and fall unnoticed to the vineyard floor.

But I've never heard a farmer complain of the diminished beauty of his field. He is focused on the harvest, and summer is the next step to getting there. So even though the field looks a bit more ragged, he knows the real war has begun. Traversing the next three months will bring the tiny blossoms to their full fruitful splendor.

The greatest mistake the branch can make now is to cling to its fleeting beauty. It's a good thing they don't have brains like we do, or no doubt they would try to hold onto that beauty instead of letting it give way to the greater thing God wants to do. I can almost envision a branch trying to scoop up its fallen petals and paste them back on, fearful that its only claim to glory has been lost.

Isn't that what we do when we've come through a season of vision? We do all we can to hold onto those feelings even as God prepares to move us on. Fruit begins in spring, but it would never ripen there. In our own spiritual lives we cannot afford the luxury of trying to preserve the past, no matter how much we might have been blessed by it.

God moves on, just like the seasons of the vineyard. If we don't move with him we will not be fruitful. You can almost take a course on recent church history by visiting in the right order various church sanctuaries in your own hometown. In appropriate garb and liturgy you can taste of church life in the Middle Ages, in the Reformation, in the Anabaptist movements, or even in the Great Awakening. And you can find churches whose heyday might have been in the 40's and 50's still clinging to the songs and dress of those days.

Many represent a moment of God's renewal frozen in time. Often justifying it as an appreciation of God's work through history, it is usually an attempt to try to hold onto spiritual spring instead of risking the process of change. Why? Were those days any more holy than what God wants to do today? No! They are just more comfortable. But that is also their trap. Staying where we're comfortable doesn't always lead us to the changes God has for our lives.

I have nothing against celebrating the faith of those who have gone before us. There's much we should learn from God's hand moving in the past. Neither do I champion the notion that God is always in the latest innovation. What I am saying is that the process of fruitfulness passes through a variety of seasons, and that God's work in our lives does exactly the same. Whenever we preserve our traditions at the expense of following God's leading, those traditions and our lives are emptied of their power.

I know of nothing more tragic than empty, religious activity—people going through the motions but finding no joy and no power in them. That can happen when we try to force

God's work into our own molds. Jesus warned us against doing so:

> No one pours new wine into old wineskins. If he does, the new wine will burst the skins, the wine will run out and the wineskins will be ruined. No, new wine must be poured into new wineskins. And no one after drinking old wine wants the new, for he says, "The old is better."
>
> LUKE 5:37-39

The Pharisees were once again trying to trap Jesus by accusing his followers of not fasting. Jesus deals with their immediate question by saying that fasting isn't appropriate in times of joy, and since he, the bridegroom, was with them there was no need. But the day was coming when they would fast.

Then he told them that old wineskins are hard and rigid. When the wine in them begins to ferment, they are not flexible enough to handle the change inside and the pressure it brings against the wineskin. Instead of holding the wine, they burst. The wine spills out and the wineskin itself is destroyed.

Such a simple picture, yet everyone knew what he was talking about, because anyone who had ever put new wine in an old wineskin had lost both. His application, however, was new. Unless the Pharisees and the teachers of the law could find a new wineskin, they could not contain this new work of the gospel. Their old, rigid understanding of spirituality could not withstand the new wine of God's Spirit poured out in the gospel. To be part of God's new revelation they had to change, and their rigid commitment to their own security would not allow them to do that.

The same is true of us, in even such simple moments as God moving our spiritual progress ahead from spring into summer. If we choose to hold onto the past instead of following him, we will not find our lives either fruitful or fulfilled. At every moment we must risk the past to embrace the process of God's transformation.

That doesn't make history or tradition evil. The focus here is on our continued obedience to what God wants to do. It

shouldn't be either one or the other. The history of God's
work in our world or in our own lives can be a source of great
blessing if we're not trying to preserve it. Jesus contemplated
the possibility even as he spoke of teachers of the law who
have been instructed in the truth of the kingdom. "(He) is like
the owner of a house who brings out of his storeroom new
treasures as well as old" (Matthew 13:52).

If the two can be brought together, the result is most powerful indeed. But let us not move too hastily past Jesus' warning
in this parable. He concludes it by saying that we all have a
natural proclivity to hold to the past, refusing to taste the new
wine. "The old is better" sums up the flesh's drive for ease
and safety. Why change when we can just celebrate with
what's gone on before?

That attitude is your greatest enemy to moving on past
spring into summer. Risk the beauty of spring. Release the
blossoms as they begin to fade. They are only promises of
realities still to come, of fruit that will be a joy to you and an
even greater delight to the Master.

The summer will come anyway. There is no use resisting it.
You can pretend it is spring all you want, but that will not
change the reality. It is far better to embrace the summer with
God, than to try to hold God to a past that he doesn't dwell in.
Even if you like the spring, don't fear leaving it. It will come
around again. But understand that springtime is not idealized
Christianity. It is a wonderful time, indeed, but so is each
season of God's working in us. Because the greatest joy is not
in whether we're embracing promises or enduring hardships,
but in enjoying his friendship.

That friendship doesn't diminish regardless of the season.
Find him where you are; don't try to drag him back into a past
that wasn't half as good as you remember it to be. Your best
days are not behind you, at least not in God's kingdom.
Springtime is not just a few fun-filled days until we get down
to the cumbersome task of being a Christian. Each day holds
its own beauty; each season its own opportunities.

Summer

THE FRUIT MATURES

A sluggard does not plow in season, so at harvest time he looks but finds nothing.
PROVERBS 20:4

Though fiery at its apex, summer sneaks up on you hoping you won't notice. The other seasons are marked by a specific notice of their arrival: The outbreak of fresh green leaves from the swollen bud signals the spring; the turning of a leaf to crimson, the fall; and the first dusting of frost, the dawn of winter. For farmers, these signs are more accurate than dates marked on calendars.

Summer, however, has no blatant sign to mark its arrival. The days of spring quietly stretch out, getting longer and hotter. By the time June 21 arrives, it seems as if summer should be half over. In the San Joaquin Valley we will already have had nearly two dozen days over 100 degrees, some pushing as high as 108.

Growth has seemingly slowed as summer gets underway. Spring was far more spectacular, almost daily changing the landscape of the vineyard. Fresh canes exploded from the vine stretching to the heavens, until their own weight caused them to curl earthward again. Now this expansive growth slows as the focus moves from the leaves to what's beneath them.

The grapes have virtually sat idle since they were formed in early spring. They have grown very little and are about the size of BB's and almost as hard. Through spring the leaves were deployed—solar collectors for the energy needed to bring the grapes to maturity. Now, in their turn, the grapes begin to grow much more rapidly, softening as they are pumped full of the sweetened sugar produced in the leaves.

This process, however, is difficult to measure daily. The labor of the farmer has settled into the routines of irrigation and cultivation. There's not much he can do now to increase the crop, but his neglect of those duties can bring it to a swift end or severely damage its quality. These are days of hard work, far less beautiful than the blooming vines of spring and far less glorious than the joys of harvest. These are the days of persevering—the time gap between promise and harvest.

As is so often true in this age, the very thing that God intends to mature us can also be the very thing that destroys us. The same life-giving sun that beckons the grapes to ripen also creates a hostile climate which the vines must overcome. Too many days of high temperatures can put stress on the vine that will reduce the size and sweetness of its grapes. The sun also dries out the land, robbing it of the moisture the vine needs. The lengthened days and warmed temperatures allow the insects to multiply rapidly, an ever-present threat to the vines. The weeds, too, benefit from the sun as they continue to mount their assault on the vine's nutrient supply.

In our spiritual lives, it is during the time between spring and harvest that so many believers lose hold on their hope in God, and see the glory of God's promise fade in the hostile climate of this age. Because the fulfillment of the promise is not yet in hand, they give up, thinking that a promise delayed is a promise denied.

The farmer doesn't see summer as a delay—only a necessary part of the process to bring the promise of spring to the abundance of harvest. His eye is firmly fixed on the formation of that fruit. Summer is not the end. It will not last forever—just long enough for the fruit to ripen. Even though it is difficult, it can't be skipped. So he perseveres, not with resigned despair, but in hopeful anticipation.

Ever vigilant, the farmer cares for the vine through the summer, for danger abounds at every turn. He waters the vine when the soil dries up, tears out the weeds wherever they emerge, and destroys the pests which war against the vine.

Our spiritual summers demand the same vigilance of us. We cannot jump from spring to fall. We must endure the hot days of summer, ensuring by our perseverance that it matures us instead of destroying us. We must meet the challenges of summer head-on, persevering through its troubles so that the harvest is assured.

Our flesh will resist, complaining at what we will perceive as God's inactivity. But this is the enemy talking, wanting us to give up, discarding God's promise in anger that it is not yet sweet and edible. He can even convince us that it is all God's fault. He makes you wonder whether God tricked us with a promise he didn't want to fulfill, or whether he is faithful even through difficult days.

The men and women of God who are lauded in the Scriptures are those whose faith has traversed this chasm between promise and harvest. They have endured the onslaughts of summer, drinking deeply of God's goodness and staying the course while the fruit ripens. If we're going to be fruitful in God's kingdom we can do no less.

Let us not become weary in doing good, for at the proper time we will reap a harvest if we do not give up.

GALATIANS 6:9

25

THE LONG HOT DAYS OF SUMMER

Day and night your hand was
heavy upon me; my strength was sapped
as in the heat of summer.

PSALM 32:4

I have a new grapevine growing this year in my yard, and it is a good four years behind the other vines that grow near it. Just as the others are coming into full production, this one is starting over. There's not one grape bunch on it—just one small but stately cane growing up the pole to the arbor above.

This new vine is there because a vine died last summer for lack of water. I only have four vines, and they are watered by an emitter irrigation system which delivers water to each vine separately. Somehow the emitter beneath this vine had become plugged. I didn't notice it until the vine was withered so much that no amount of watering revived it.

The San Joaquin Valley is an irrigated desert. It is a rare drop of rain that falls here between mid-May and November. My wife, Sara, who was raised in the East still finds it almost unbelievable that we have to water everything that grows. And I'm just as shocked by the fact that in her home state few people have ever thought of watering their lawns, because the rains suffice. Without extensive irrigation systems in Israel around the time of Jesus, the orientation toward growing things was much more like Sara's experience than mine. They depended upon recurring rainstorms to water their crops. For plants to survive they had to have roots deep enough to ride out the sunny weather until another storm arrived.

But even with irrigation, vines are watered to drive the roots deep. My father did it every three or four weeks, depending on the severity of the heat. And when he irrigated, he didn't put a sprinkling of water on the surface, but deep-watered by flooding his field. This forces the roots to go deep instead of loitering near the surface. This not only keeps them well-nourished until the next irrigation, but deep roots also help anchor the vine firmly and give its roots greater breadth for drawing needed nutrients from the soil.

In a farmer's way of thinking, if my vine dies for lack of water, it's my fault. I was responsible to ensure that it had enough. Spiritually, however, God always provides enough water. The responsibility for how deep our roots plunge into it always depends on us. We are supposed to develop roots deep enough to outlast the heat of summer.

That's what Jesus was pointing to in the second type of soil in the parable of the sower. The seed fell on the rocks where there wasn't much soil. The plant grew quickly, but because it couldn't root deeply, as soon as the sun bore down on it the plant withered.

Again we'll take some liberty from our illustration of being branches on the vine. Branches don't have roots; only the vine does. Certainly Jesus' roots are deep enough to weather any crisis. Let's look at this process of deep-rooting, however, as an illustration of how the branch is joined to the vine. We could illustrate the same point by showing how partially broken branches will be exposed by the stress of summer. The demand for water and nutrients in the branch, combined with the weight of growing foliage and fruit, will cause an injured branch to break away from the vine. If, however, for this chapter we can think of ourselves as vines rooting into the soil, we will see more clearly what we need to be doing in our spiritual summer, particularly in the early days.

In spring, we discussed the importance of establishing patterns of nourishing ourselves daily in the presence of God. Now we see why these patterns are so important, and why they need to run deep. In the parable of the sower, notice how quickly those seeds grew that did not have much soil. Since they couldn't (or in our case, wouldn't) give attention to their roots, all their energy went to the outward growth. Such plants do grow quickly and look impressive.

Believers who spend little energy establishing their roots will demonstrate quick external growth. After coming to Christ they busy themselves with Christian activities and services. Others, though impressed with their zeal and energy, are worn out by their example. Many stand condemned by it, since their own growth does not seem as rapid. But the real test is yet to come.

Eventually the constant rains of spring give way to summer's heat. Now we'll see how deeply the roots have plunged into the soil. In Jesus' parable, they had not grown at all. As soon as the sun came out, the plants withered. The spring roots had not deepened to become summer roots. Jesus interpreted the parable: "Since he has no root, he lasts only a short time. When trouble or persecution comes because of the word, he quickly falls away."

No believer can remain in the safe cocoon of spring. The sun represents the trouble and persecution that every believer faces in this age. All may go well for awhile, but eventually suffering will come. The Word growing in our hearts will bring trouble and conflict.

When these come don't think them to be an indication that your spiritual life has suddenly taken a downturn. They are part of growing, and we are to prepare for them by having our root structure deep enough to withstand any trouble or disappointment, any onslaught of doubt or fear.

These roots symbolize the depth of our friendship with Jesus built before the sun gets hot. Scripture often exhorts us to seek God while he is near and easy to find. If we don't do this, times of trouble will overshadow God's presence and we won't be able to see him. That's why we're building patterns in spiritual spring that we don't quite need yet. Summer is coming.

Unfortunately, the busyness of our lives and our nature is more set on just getting by. We do it financially when we spend every bit of income we make, not ever saving up for the unexpected crisis to come. We do it with our time, filling up almost every waking moment with some kind of responsibility, so that like the priests who passed the wounded man on the road in the parable of the Good Samaritan, we don't have time to stop and help.

We also do it in our spiritual life when we have just enough prayer and worship, just enough Bible reading, just enough contact with other believers to get by. What happens when the heat is on? How can we make it if we've done just enough to get by in the good times?

Jesus invites us to a friendship with him that runs so deep, that nothing can separate us from his love. But how many of us have watched other believers cruise along wonderfully well in their spirituality until they meet some difficult circumstances or even very simple disappointments? How often have we done it ourselves?

Immediately our faith was challenged: "How could God let this happen?" Our relationships with other believers didn't prove strong enough: "I just couldn't tell anyone, I'd be too embarrassed." Our knowledge of God proved insufficient: "I just didn't know what to do." Most of all, our touch with Jesus was too easily severed: "I just couldn't find him no matter what I did." Roots that go deep are not affected by the temporal circumstances of what transpires above the ground. They can weather heat and pressure, drawing from God's life with the same joy as if it were raining.

The patterns of relationship, or spiritual disciplines, are how we sink our roots deeply into the reservoir of God's grace and faithfulness. We've discussed them before, but now we can see the depth that we need from them. They need to be so deeply ingrained in our life that we trust more what God is doing in us than the irrational conclusions which our flesh will draw about whatever difficult times we face.

How do we get our roots to go deeper? It really isn't so difficult a process. For a plant it happens quite naturally: The sun dries out the soil from the top down. As the abundance of surface water vanishes, the roots keep looking for it, no matter where they find it. Obviously that means they grow deeper, where the soil has not yet dried out.

The same is true for us. During some seasons, Jesus' presence seems to be everywhere. Every church service ministers directly to our needs. Every time we read the Bible we see so much in it that encourages us. Then one day it doesn't come so easily. Here is the time for us to seek a bit deeper. Unfortunately, however, many believers don't. They think something has gone wrong and grow discouraged.

But God has not gone anywhere. Circumstances may be drying up the surface water, but his life is still there for us to embrace. We only need to keep coming to him. If worship at church isn't as good as it used to be, it's easier to blame the worship leader, or other believers who aren't as ready to worship, than it is for us to seek him more fervently. We never see it as God inviting us deeper, past the goose bumps and the heart flutters, to the treasure of his presence.

When Bible reading or prayer time seems difficult and lifeless, don't give up and quit, intimidated that it is too difficult. Instead, read the Word more fervently. Look up words you don't understand. Cross-reference verses to see what else Scripture says on the same subject. Even reread the chapter, making your mind meditate on what you're reading instead of letting it slip to events and challenges coming up later in the day. If your fellowship with God has grown stale, press through. Invite another believer to an extended time of sharing and prayer, and begin to encourage each other with God's words instead of just running down the job and the weather.

In all our seeking, remember who the gardener is. He promised Isaiah that he would always provide enough water for his vines: "I, the Lord, watch over it; I water it continually" (Isaiah 27:3). He will ensure that we get enough of his life to thrive. For that we can trust him, even when it isn't all close enough to the surface to get at easily. It is nonetheless close by and that should encourage us to keep pressing toward him.

Roots that are fully developed provide the same continual refreshing as if we were planted near a spring. They don't learn to get by on less of God; instead, they find God at a deeper level and with a greater consistency. Scripture continues to compare our growth to plants that are not dependent upon capricious rainstorms, but abide by an ever-flowing stream. Though Jeremiah was not talking about grapevines here, his vision is no less applicable for a branch that deeply draws from the true vine: "It does not fear when heat comes; its leaves are always green. It has no worries in a year of drought and never fails to bear fruit." That's the heritage of deep-watered roots: We never lack, no matter how desperate the circumstances.

FRUIT IN A HOSTILE CLIMATE

Consider it pure joy, my brothers, whenever you face trials of many kinds, because you know that the testing of your faith develops perseverance. Perseverance must finish its work so that you may be mature and complete, not lacking anything.

JAMES 1:2-4

The clock moves past noon and the sun arches high over the vineyard, its unrelenting rays bearing down on the growing vines. Ripples of heat soar skyward making the distant vines look as if they are dancing. But they are not. Summer is not the season for dancing, at least on the outside.

The heat of summer in the San Joaquin Valley is oppressive, regularly pushing above the 100 degree mark. At the height of summer we often endure day after day of temperatures above 105 degrees, and sometimes watch the mercury stretch past 110. It gets so hot you can't even walk barefoot on the dirt without your feet being seared by the heat.

Not only is summer *hot* here, it is also far too *long*. Hot weather usually makes its debut as early as April and holds off its final curtain call until late October. During our hottest days, we don't even get relief in the evening. The temperature refuses to drop much below 90 degrees even in the few minutes

189

before sunrise. The heat hangs as thick as a theater curtain, and dead still, without a whisper of wind to freshen the stale, musty air.

Only fans and air conditioners, combined with our low humidity, make the heat bearable. But that's for humans; the vines receive no such luxury. They endure the full force of summer's fury. Though they need the sun to fuel the process of photosynthesis, which turns the nutrients into sugars, which in turn ripen the fruit, the heat it brings also stresses the vine appreciably. For grapes to ripen they need a certain number of sunlight hours above 77 degrees. So consistent is this need that scientists say you could count the hours to know exactly when to pick the grapes.

But the optimum growing temperature for the vineyard is in the 80's and low 90's. Above that the heat takes its toll on the vine. It's a mixed blessing, since the number of sunlight days we have over the summer make this a prime place to raise grapes. Our arid climate rarely offers us a cloudy day throughout the summer. But the heat that accompanies those sun-filled days also saps the vine of its strength and can diminish the quality of the fruit if it is too excessive.

This is summer in the vineyard, and it models one of the great paradoxes of our faith. Fruitfulness rises out of a hostile climate. The heat of trouble and persecution that bears down on us is precisely the environment necessary to mature the fruit.

It is a message so often missed in the New Testament, but only because it is unpopular, not because it is underemphasized in the text. Who wants to dwell on suffering when we can instead talk of prosperity, blessing, and the abundant life? But every major voice in the New Testament underscores the reality of our faith flourishing in a hostile age.

Yet none of the writers saw this as a cause for mourning. Quite the contrary: they were stirred to rejoice in the toughest of trials. Jesus' teaching on the vineyard accompanies the most severe trial his young followers had ever faced. In the next few hours Jesus would be betrayed and crucified. He warned them he was leaving them and fear ran rampant in the room. Over and over he appealed to them, "Do not let your heart be troubled."

He concluded his words with this: "I have told you these things, so that in me you may have peace. In this world you will have trouble. But take heart! I have overcome the world." He didn't hide the fact that his disciples must endure painful circumstances in this world. But they need not despair; he had overcome the world.

James picks up that same message: "Consider it pure joy, my brothers, whenever you face trials of many kinds." Why? Is it a good discipline? Should we put on a fake smile in the midst of pain, pretending that we're happy to suffer? No! It is a cause for rejoicing because *faith under test produces perseverance,* and perseverance is what takes promise to completion.

We don't rejoice in trouble for its own sake, but because we realize that it is only through the purifying of our faith during trouble that we come to fruitfulness. Don't resist such times, James encourages us. Though the trial itself won't produce the fruit, *our faith in the midst of it will.* If we are complaining at God, angry about the stresses in our lives and actively looking for some way to change our circumstances, perseverance will not be produced. Instead we'll find ourselves despising the very thing that can help us.

In other words, suffering believers have two choices: Either respond in faith and let it become part of the maturing process, or else respond with anger or resignation and see it accomplish nothing at all. Or even worse, our trials can produce sin. I've seen it often, both in myself and in others. Once we allow anger to fester in our heart toward God because he allowed us to face trials, it becomes extremely difficult to resist other temptations which the enemy launches against our lives. "If God is not helping me, I might as well go ahead and please myself anyway." How quickly the enemy can come in like a flood and destroy the promise that God has put on our hearts!

I have noticed an intriguing fact in many of the people I have counseled through crisis. Often they fight more despair and doubt over the fact that they *even* have trials than the trial itself could possibly have produced. Before we can handle the crisis God's way, we have to first reestablish their trust in him. Has it been destroyed just by the fact that all is not well? That's the enemy. He wants to take the stresses of this age to turn us against God.

To combat him, keep in mind that God is never the source of your trials. With all that is said of trouble and suffering in the Word, nothing indicates that God creates times of discomfort and pain to see how well his children are doing. The trials of this age are not like tests that teachers give us in school. God does not need to measure our faith, as if he does not know its depths. He does not orchestrate our crises any more than we would for our own children. Life in a fallen age provides plenty of inevitable opportunity for trouble and challenge.

There is exception to this, of course. God *does* judge rebellious sons and daughters. He will willingly bring external disaster to extend mercy to a wayward heart, and he had demonstrated that fact over and over again in Scripture. But that's not the issue for those firmly planted in the vine, following him with undivided hearts.

For these people, God in his magnificent grace takes even our worst circumstance and makes it part of the maturing process. He draws the good out of it in shaping us to be more like him. Throughout Scripture he promised us that we would never meet a test greater than we could endure, and that he will provide a way for us to escape the evil in it and to overcome it with his grace.

You can trust that promise no matter what difficulty you face. Don't give in to the overwhelming fear of the enemy who says you won't be able to make it. I've seen God demonstrate his faithfulness time and again even in the most devastating circumstances, for those who respond in the midst of them with faith.

That's why James told us to rejoice and Paul seconded his counsel in Romans 5:

> *(We) also rejoice in our sufferings, because we know that suffering produces perseverance; perseverance, character;*

and character, hope. And hope does not disappoint us, be-
cause God has poured out his love into our hearts by the
Holy Spirit, whom he has given us.

Any suffering can produce God's character in us if we allow God to work through it.

During the first year of my pastoral ministry I was coming into one of my own spiritual summers. I had just come through the excitement of joining a church staff and was seeing God allow my ministry to blossom in that fellowship. These were exciting, zealous days, and I had no idea how quickly summer would set in.

This time it came in the form of a kitchen accident. A pan of grease had caught fire in our kitchen, and in my ignorant attempts to deal with it I spilled the grease on my hand and ended up with third-degree burns to show for it. I remember the agonizing ride to the hospital, incredible pain throbbing not only in my hand but also my heart. Why did God let this happen? Why hadn't he healed me when I asked? This was going to ruin everything.

The days of recovery that followed were excruciating. The first day I nearly passed out in a doctor's office while he soaked my burns in peroxide. In the early days my anger toward God festered, but I stayed the course. I kept coming to him, even though I still complained to him that he didn't seem to care about my pain.

That's all perseverance means: to persist in the face of difficulty. Most of us don't, you know. When something bad happens we let our discouragement or confusion take control and we do things we would not do otherwise. But the godly respond with perseverance. Keep coming to God in spite of your hurts, doubts, or anger. He can handle it. "Remain in me" is the motto of the vineyard, and at no time is that counsel more important than during the stresses of summer.

Somewhere in the days of recovery God began to get through to me. He had not done this to me. The enemy wanted to use it to separate me from God. God wanted to draw me closer to him. Gratefully as I persisted through that long and painful healing I drew to God in greater depth than I had ever known before. I found a trust in God I had always wrestled with previously. I have never again since that injury blamed God for any pain in my life, something I had done with great skill and consistency since I was a child—from dentist visits to bouts with the flu.

All I had to do was keep coming to him, continuing in those same patterns of nourishment that had been established in more blissful days. When the heat is on don't try to bail out by making self-motivated changes in your life. Endurance is what is needed, not escape. If we'll just remain in the vine, the difficult circumstances we face will produce his fruit in us.

Character. God changed something in me through that experience that has left an imprint of his image on my life— fruit! Did God need to burn me to teach me that lesson? Of course not! He could and would have taught me the same thing in any number of other ways. Am I grateful I was burned? No, I can't say that either. But I *can* say that God took something very horrible and made it a great blessing in my life. He freed me, and I'm still enjoying its benefits spiritually long after the scars of the burn have healed.

How does character produce hope? When I see God so dramatically change my life in the midst of such an ugly circumstance I never have to fear anything else. If God could use that, he can use anything to bring me closer to him. That's hope—God is bigger than anything I'll ever face, and he is able to lead me through it to his glory.

27

ENEMIES OF MATURITY

*That Satan might not outwit us. For we
are not unaware of his schemes.*
2 CORINTHIANS 2:11

Every year they catch me by surprise. It begins with an air assault, and if I'm not in the back yard every day where my vines grow I don't even see them. Black moths flutter in over the fence and steal into the grapevines. There they lay hundreds of eggs and quickly die.

Days later the army hatches. Small yellow caterpillars with brilliant purple and black stripes fan out across the leaves, devouring them as they move. They leave behind only the veins of the leaves, eerie skeletons of life destroyed. Though they are hardly the size of a pinhead when they hatch, their sheer numbers can quickly overwhelm a cane. In a few days they can reduce a beautifully arching cane of greenery into a vegetative boneyard. If I am not careful the war can be half over before I ever knew it began.

Skeletonizers. Their name stirs up gruesome images. These are but one of the enemies that prey on a vineyard as the fruit matures. In fact the enemies of summer are numerous indeed and attack at every level of the vine's growth and development.

And isn't that just like our enemy. At the very time we are the most stressed, as vines are in the heat of summer, Satan rushes in like a flood. He rarely launches one offensive, but attacks on many fronts at the same time. Often when I am helping someone through a crisis, he or she will run through a list of all that's going wrong at the moment. "Believe me, Wayne, I could handle any one of these things alone, but together they're just too much for me to handle."

It sounds like spiritual summer to me, when the enemy rises up to destroy God's work. Regretfully, many believers, expecting the joys of spring to last through harvest, are left unprepared for the onslaught of conflict that summer brings. Discouraged by the difficulties they give up, cast off their fruit, and hope for better days ahead. But then when harvest comes and they have no fruit, they wonder why God doesn't love them enough to use them. To be fruitful we have to recognize how the enemy comes to destroy our fruitfulness, and then rebuff his every attempt.

During summer a vine is attacked at three different levels. First there are enemies that attack the roots, the lifeline of the vine. That's where unchecked weeds take their toll, as do nematodes, worms that live as parasites on the roots. Our friendship with Jesus is always in the enemy's sights as he looks for any way he can dislodge our affection and attention from our Lord. In the parable of the sower some seeds fell on soil that was covered with thorns. When the thorns, or weeds, grew up they choked out the new plants. "The one who received the seed that fell among the thorns is the man who hears the word, but the worries of this life and the deceitfulness of wealth choke it, making it unfruitful" (Matthew 13:22).

The enemy uses two weapons against our friendship with Jesus. The first is our anxieties. That may well be why Jesus told us not to have any. "Do not worry!" he commanded his followers. God will take care of you if you seek him above everything else. He wanted to keep our friendship safe from the destruction that worry causes. But I don't often see believers take effective countermeasures against anxiety and stress. Many people even seem to wear these as merit badges of how difficult their life is. What a deception!

Anxiety is the number one weapon of our enemy to destroy relationships. It first takes its toll in our friendship with Jesus, distracting our attention from him and even causing us to turn on him. How easily anxiety can make us blame God for not fixing the very thing we worry about! Almost all the seeds of our doubt and unbelief precede from our worries, as do envy and bitterness. If we don't find our way into a real trust in God's love, we will be threatened by other believers who don't seem to have the same struggles we do.

Nothing good comes from our worries. Identify them, then deal with them by bringing them to Jesus and asking him to teach you how to trust him more completely in those areas of struggle.

Satan's second weapon is the deceitfulness of wealth, whether we have money or not. If we lack it but seek it as the solution to our problems, greed will result. If we already have it, and most of us in the West do by worldwide standards, we risk becoming complacent and distracted. Both destroy our friendship with Jesus.

Of these two weapons of the enemy, complacency is probably the greater danger because of its subtlety. Though it is the opposite of anxiety, it produces the same result. Wealth can make us so comfortable, so happy, so convinced of its promise of security that its very existence threatens our need for God. Instead of seeking him desperately, we hold onto a safe piece of Christianity while we lose ourselves in the excessive luxuries and distractions that wealth offers. Don't get me wrong—God is not against legitimate enjoyments. He is only against us becoming so committed to our own amusement that we don't have the time or energy to pursue his ways.

When that happens our trust in God is destroyed, and our friendship with him is subverted by lies. We end up trusting more in our comfort than in him, and we may only come to see this deception when our wealth fails us. How quickly wealth can be swallowed up! How insufficient it will show itself against our real hungers and needs!

Like weeds, anxiety and wealth's deception need to be pulled out and cast aside wherever we find them. And we should be looking for them at every turn. Remember too that, like weeds, these are far more easily dealt with when they are small and hardly appear a threat, than when they have knotted themselves into a jungle.

The assaults don't stop there, however. The branch's leaves are also attacked. Skeletonizers are only one of a host of insects and mites that prey on the leaves. They either eat the leaves directly, or else suck the juices out of them. In so doing they destroy the vine's ability to process the nutrients into sugars that ripen the fruit.

There is no direct scriptural analogy for what the leaves might represent, but that which takes God's life and makes it fruitful in us is our obedience to him. It doesn't earn God's work in us, but our cooperation with him releases his continued activity on our behalf. Jesus linked obedience to fruitfulness. Those who do not discover the joy and freedom of obedience will never bear fruit.

The enemy will do all he can to impede that obedience with temptation and distraction. He will incite our selfish ambition, pride, and trust in our own wisdom. This list goes on, all of these siphoning off God's work in us so that we will not be fruitful. One of those, however, is particularly noteworthy. Jeremiah warned his hearers: "Many shepherds will ruin my vineyard and trample down my field; they will turn my pleasant field into a desolate wasteland" (Jeremiah 12:10).

Nothing can destroy fruitfulness faster than ungodly leadership—men and women who use positions of authority to manipulate and exploit people instead of serving their growth in Christ. Instead of leading them to greater dependence upon Jesus, insecure leaders cultivate dependence on themselves through a binding legalism that flies in the face of personal obedience to Christ.

We can't ignore this danger under the guise of preserving Christian unity. Bad leadership needs to be recognized and resisted. Don't allow anyone to curtail your own obedience to God in the name of loyalty to a man or his institution. Now that is not an excuse to go out on your own in anarchy, for that danger is greater than the one you are escaping. Rather find godly men and women whose heart is for *your* fruitfulness, not their own. There you'll find leaders after God's heart.

Finally, the enemy attacks the fruit itself. Fruit flies, bunch rot caused by worms eating the grapes, large flocks of birds, and mildew all assault the fruit directly. As the fruit ripens, the enemy launches a full frontal assault to destroy it. Just as we're learning love, patience, and kindness, he orchestrates circumstances to convince us that if we live this way, others will only take advantage of us. It's not worth it, he whispers. Through anger and bitterness he eats out our love, even using the way people treated us years before to rob us of the freedom to respond like God.

He also directly challenges the promises that God has put in our hearts: He is delaying or he didn't really mean it after all. But God does not delay; every promise he has made he is actively working to fulfill even as you read this page. Too many people misunderstand that fact. After weeks of personal ministry they grow weary of the difficult process by which God is transforming them. "When is God going to heal me?" they ask.

He is not *waiting* to heal them; he *is* healing them. That is the process. If you can only see it when it is finally done, you will have a miserable time in God's vineyard. From the day he promises to do so, God is at work to fulfill. Don't let the enemy trick you into thinking otherwise, or you will grow frustrated with God and cast off the ripening fruit before it matures.

There is one other source of attack on our fruitfulness that is difficult to grasp. I have never seen a farmer do this to his vineyard, but God himself will when the occasion calls for it:

> *Before the harvest, when the blossom is gone and the flower becomes a ripening grape, he will cut off the shoots with pruning knives, and cut down and take away the spreading branches.*
>
> ISAIAH 18:5

> *"Many times I struck your gardens and vineyards, I struck them with blight and mildew . . . yet you have not returned to me," declares the Lord.*
>
> AMOS 4:9

No farmer I know has ever pruned in summer, because it does exactly what God did here: It destroys the fruit. Neither have I seen any farmer bringing in fungus or insects to destroy his crop. What's at stake here? Why would God do such a thing to his own vineyard?

These instances do not represent the way God normally works in his vineyard. He is more committed to our fruitfulness than we are. Both of these occurred during Israel's rebellion. They were actively walking after other gods, but their God loved them so much that he would even do the most painful thing imaginable. He would cut off the fruit of his desire, allowing blight and mildew to destroy it, in hopes that his people would recognize their rebellion and return to him.

The prophet Joel encouraged God's people to recognize their own part in their destruction, and repent. Israel's fruit had been devoured by locusts and other destroying pests. He called them back to God, who graciously forgives and sets right again:

> *Despair, you farmers, wail, you vine growers because the harvest of the field is destroyed. The vine is dried up and the fig tree is withered; the pomegranate, the palm and the apple tree—all the trees of the field—are dried up. Surely the joy of mankind is withered away. Put on sackcloth . . . Come, spend the night in sackcloth. . . . Declare a holy fast . . . and cry out to the Lord.*
>
> JOEL 1:11-14

There are times when I have felt that same hand of destruction leveled at my life. My persistent stubbornness in the face of God's direction to me provided an opening for the enemy. I could almost see the ripening fruit wither on my branches. God was calling attention to my rebellion, inviting me back to humble submission. He loves us enough to rescue us even from ourselves.

The certain cure for almost any point of destruction in our lives is repentance. Whether it is God's hand judging our rebellion, or the enemy's hand thwarting our fruitfulness, the same remedy works for both. If we will humble ourselves before him, God will thwart the enemy's attempts and forgive us any complicity in allowing the enemy to gain footholds in our lives.

Unlike a real vineyard, which cannot defend itself, we ourselves play a key role in resisting the enemy's hand by recognizing his attempts and refusing to fall victim to his lies. Whenever he tries to destroy our relationship with God, or distract us from simple obedience to him, or attack the very promises that God is bringing to pass in us, we need not let him succeed.

Instead, we need to keep on remaining in the vine. In doing so we will have nothing to fear from the enemy because God as the caretaker is our ally in this war: "I will prevent pests from devouring your crops, and the vines in your fields will not cast their fruit" (Malachi 3:11).

He has his army in this war, too. There are a host of creatures in the vineyard that battle against the insects who destroy the vineyard. Small wasps, lacewings, praying mantises, ladybugs, and spiders eat the insects that prey on the vines. Like them, God's angels encamp around his followers and do battle against the forces of darkness.

We are not alone in this war, and its outcome is not in doubt for those who press through the conflict faithful to God's work in their life. He assures the victory, for he is a most vigilant farmer!

28

THE FARMER'S DILIGENCE

I went past the field of the sluggard,
past the vineyard of the man who lacks
judgment; thorns had come up everywhere,
the ground was covered with weeds, and
the stone wall was in ruins.

PROVERBS 24:30,31

Summer in the vineyard is an all-out war. It may not look that way to the casual observer who drives by on a summer day, for the vines may look content sitting out in the afternoon sun, but as we've seen, looks can be deceiving. Fruitfulness is a process laced with conflict.

That has been true since hours after Adam and Eve's fall in the Garden of Eden. God put them out of the Garden, and gave them a prescription for survival:

> *Cursed is the ground because of you; through painful toil*
> *you will eat of it all the days of your life. It will produce*
> *thorns and thistles for you, and you will eat the plants of the*
> *field. By the sweat of your brow you will eat your food.*
>
> GENESIS 3:17-19

For the farmer bringing a crop to fruitfulness is a never-ending struggle against destructive forces. Farming is not like writing a book; you don't spend a few years of diligent effort, achieve a finished project, and look back on it for years to come. Farming is doing the same tasks year in and year out, repeated again and again to bring the vineyard to succeeding years of fruitfulness.

One moment after the farmer plows the weeds down in a row of vines, new ones begin to grow. They too will have to be cut. As soon as a pest is expunged from the field, its cousins are already infiltrating. A farmer clears a field and plants his crops on it. At that very moment the war is launched. The wilderness will forever seek to reclaim the land taken from it.

A.W. Tozer in *The Root of the Righteous* expressed it this way:

> *Every farmer knows the hunger of the wilderness. . . .*
> *No matter how well-prepared the soil, how well-kept*
> *the fences, how carefully painted the buildings, let the*
> *owner neglect for a while his prized and valued acres*
> *and they will revert again to the wild and be swal-*
> *lowed up by the jungle of the wasteland. The bias of*
> *nature is toward the wilderness, never toward the*
> *fruitful field.*

He goes on to warn that "what is true of the field is also true of the soul." Maybe God had a deeper meaning in Adam's prescription than we originally thought. To be fruitful in God's kingdom we also have to be ever-diligent against the forces that seek to drive us back to the wild. Neglect in the kingdom of God is not a mere delay in our spiritual growth; it is an act of destruction.

There is no such thing as standing still in the life of God; either you are growing or you are dying. Those who think they can merely hold their own are only fooling themselves. Nothing in creation stagnates without dying.

One of the ways that farmers check the health of their vineyard is to look at the new leaves emerging at the end of each cane. That growth doesn't stop at the end of spring; it continues to the last days of harvest. If the growth stops or looks weak, the farmer knows something is wrong. Either the field is too dry, or needs fertilizer, or is being weakened by pests.

I do the same with people I care for. Often I ask them what God is doing in them right now. Is he drawing them deeper in prayer? Exposing a selfish attitude they hadn't seen before? Stirring their heart with new vision in ministry? Showing them something fresh about God's nature? If they can't respond with some measure of certainty, I grow concerned. Jesus said that the Father is always working. If we're letting him work in us, we will always have a new edge of growth and discovery. Lacking that, I'm suspicious of neglect.

When we neglect our spiritual life and cave in to the demands of the world we live in, God's work begins to wither and his work falls to ruin.

> *I went past the field of the sluggard, past the vineyard of the man who lacks judgment; thorns had come up everywhere, the ground was covered with weeds, and the stone wall was in ruins. I applied my heart to what I observed and learned a lesson from what I saw: A little sleep, a little slumber, a little folding of the hands to rest—and poverty will come on you like a bandit and scarcity like an armed man.*
>
> PROVERBS 24:30-34

In this vineyard the lesson of diligence is for branches as well as workers. God is certainly diligent on our behalf, but without sharing that same diligence for our own spiritual life, we will be destroyed.

Diligence is doing *what* needs to be done, *when* it needs to be done. It is not a matter of convenience. My father got up at 5:30 in the morning to sulfur his grapevines before the winds came up. I'm sure he would much rather have done it at 10:00, but it can't be done then, at least not effectively.

Many times I've seen him leave a party he was hosting at his own home, put on his work clothes, and go out to check his irrigation. When it's time to irrigate, you can't wait just because it is the Fourth of July or the date of the family reunion. When the water is running, it has to be checked whether you feel like it or not.

If we try to fit the life of Jesus conveniently into our lives we will always be disappointed with the results. I've dealt with many people seeking freedom from a major area of bondage in their lives. As we begin I encourage them to daily prayer and Bible study and participation with the body of Christ at least twice a week for a three-month time or until we break through that area of bondage. You wouldn't believe the excuses I get. "We really needed a camping trip." "My car broke down." "I was just too tired to make it."

The excuses themselves are fine; I don't have a problem with people camping over a weekend or having to work late when the need arises. But over a period of *three months* some interesting things happen. First of all, they make it to fellowship on an average of about twice a month, and rarely find time for personal study and prayer.

Second, they are greatly frustrated that the healing they seek seems to be eluding them. They are usually angry, mostly at God because they don't think he's doing anything. What always amazes me is that until I point it out they rarely see the connection between their convenience approach to their spiritual life and the fact that God is not working as fast as they think he should.

Spiritual life is real. It needs to be tended to *when* it needs to be tended to. For people that work eight-to-five jobs and compartmentalize their lives into work, recreation, and family this may be difficult to grasp. But having grown up on a farm, I understand it very well.

We cannot set a regiment for our lives that will work through every season. Instead, we have to know by following the Spirit's leading what is needed *today*. That may not always fit smoothly into my schedule. Perhaps (heaven forbid!) there might even be some cost in it and some difficult choices. We might have to say no to something good to embrace something far better.

Watching my father tend his vineyard taught me this valuable lesson. Some weeks of the year he had to put in 12- and 14-hour days to get the work done that needed doing. At other times the vineyard's demands would be light and he wouldn't need to work at all. This is when we took our vacations and he was able to catch up on other projects around the house.

To know what needs to be done, *diligence demands vigilance.* I'll have to admit I'm not very good at peeking into my grapevines. That's why one of mine died last year for lack of water. I should have noticed in time to revive it. That's also why insects can overtake mine so quickly.

A farmer, however, is ever-vigilant—always looking at the vines, noting their needs, and doing whatever the situation calls for to train up a vine, combat one of its enemies, or simply keep it watered. To be fruitful in God's kingdom requires the same vigilance. Daily we present our lives before God looking for areas of the enemy's attack, lack of nutrition, or creeping attitudes that are drawing us away from the Lord. Having seen any of these, we deal with them by whatever measures are necessary to bring resolve and keep us on the road to fruitfulness.

But be careful here that you don't get trapped into an exercise of personal introspection. We don't have to spend endless hours contemplating all that might be wrong with our spiritual life. God is our caretaker; all we need do is listen to him. He will show us where our attention needs to be drawn and what we need to do to continue the process of fruitfulness.

We can be that real about our spiritual life. It's not an ethereal concept. My life in Christ is as real as a grape branch. How is it doing? Is it growing? Is it being attacked? Is this time for rest, or should I be pressing into new areas of knowing God or new avenues of obedience?

That vantage point is where diligence flows from. Don't mistake it for busyness, thinking that an abundance of religious activity will stir fruitfulness. It will not. Don't mistake it for legalism, either, assuming you can earn fruitfulness by your performance. Diligence is only doing what the Spirit wants you to do every day, without excuse or delay because it might be inconvenient.

Much of the farmer's work along these lines is not spectacular. It won't draw the acclaim of crowds or win achievement awards. It's mundane work—shoveling weeds, tying up canes, or repairing broken wires. It's the kinds of things that need to

be done over and over again to bring the vineyard to fruitfulness.

The same is true of our spirituality. Don't seek the spirituality that is seen by others, for it is not the spirituality that
will bring you into freedom and fruitfulness. Instead, find a
daily diligence to Jesus' work in your life. If you don't, you
will not be fruitful and you'll wonder why. That's the way of
the sluggard, according to Proverbs: "A sluggard does not
plow in season, so at harvest time he looks but finds nothing"
(20:4).

A sluggard is not someone who doesn't want to find fruit at
harvesttime. He most certainly does, but every day he finds
enough excuses to put off the work that needs to be done until
it is finally too late. What a contrast from the one who is
diligent every day, nurturing God's work in his heart: "The
sluggard craves and gets nothing, but the desires of the diligent are fully satisfied" (Proverbs 13:4).

Maybe you have known great periods of joy and promise in
your life, but have never seen them come to full fruition. This
could be the reason. Learn from the farmer the importance of
daily diligence. Those who fit Jesus in only where it's conve-
nient, or who can be easily distracted by the demands of this
world and the expectations of friends and family, will always
sacrifice their spiritual growth.

God never intended that your spiritual life be your *first*
priority; he wants it to be your *only* priority. When you give it
that place you'll find direction and strength aplenty for fitting
in the things he wants of you at home, on the job, and even in
your recreation.

At whatever cost, do that. Cultivate his life in you with the
same reality and diligence that a farmer exercises in his field.
In doing so you will find spiritual reality become even more
real to you than the mundane world around you.

HAVING DONE ALL, STAND!

...after you have done everything...stand.
EPHESIANS 6:13,14

The summer comes slowly to an end. We're only two weeks away from the harvest now. The vineyard is in its final stages of production. The fruit is ripening, making measurable gains in sugar content every day.

Here in the most critical days before the harvest, where would you imagine the farmer to be? Vigilantly prowling his fields? Battling the unending armies of insects or weeds? Fretting what unseen trouble may yet be lurking out there to destroy his harvest? Hardly.

I'll tell you where my family was in the beginning weeks of August: We were high up in the Sierra Nevadas, camping.

Unbelievable, isn't it? But there really wasn't anything for Dad to do in those last few weeks. The groundwork had already been laid. Whatever he hadn't done before this moment wasn't going to make a difference anyway. The field was watered and the vines were sulfured to keep out the mildew. It was too late to spray for insects, since the insecticide would only hurt the fruit. No weed can grow tall enough in two weeks to challenge the vine. At this time the fruit is going to ripen no matter what you do. So we went camping.

One of the things a good farmer has a firm grasp of is where his work ends and God's begins. A farmer can only do so much. He can water, cultivate, fertilize, and prune, but he cannot make anything grow—not one bunch of grapes, not even a leaf. Only God can do that.

I'm switching crops again, but Jesus told a parable about wheat that illustrates this point perfectly:

> *This is what the kingdom of God is like. A man scatters seed on the ground. Night and day, whether he sleeps or gets up, the seed sprouts and grows, though he does not know how. All by itself the soil produces grain—first the stalk, then the head, then the full kernel in the head. As soon as the grain is ripe, he puts the sickle to it, because the harvest has come.*
>
> MARK 4:26-29

Only God can make things grow. That's true of plants around us, and also true of the fruit in your life. This is not Jesus' guide to farming; he was talking about the growth of the kingdom. We can sow and we can reap, but we cannot make one thing grow. To know the peace of God even in the most difficult of circumstances we have to know where our responsibilities begin and end.

It's a lesson that God needed to teach. Jonah didn't want to go to Nineveh because he suspected that those wicked people who were Israel's vicious enemies would repent at his message. Instead of destroying them as promised, God would forgive their sins and extend his grace to them. Jonah didn't want that to happen, and that's why he ran away on a westbound freighter.

Though God eventually brought him to Nineveh willing to obey, Jonah still despised the people he preached to. They did repent, and Jonah was angry. He sat outside of town and sulked, begging God to kill him because he did not want to be a source of salvation for his enemies. What an attitude! Jonah had confused God's responsibilities with his own.

To teach him a lesson, God let a vine grow up over Jonah in a single day. Jonah was thrilled with the shade it provided. But the next day a worm ate the vine, and Jonah sat without relief under the blistering sun. "Do you have a right to be angry about the vine?" God asked him.

"I do," Jonah replied. "I'm angry enough to die."

Jonah missed the point, but God didn't let him get away with it. He told Jonah that because he had not made the vine grow, he had no right to be angry when it was gone. And if he cared so much for a vine, why wouldn't he be concerned about a great city full of people that God loved?

We don't make things grow, and we're not responsible for results; God is. Discover that fact and you'll have found the secret to the Lord's peace. All we need to do is obey Jesus, and God will see to it that his purposes are accomplished.

That understanding is the source of patience, and the best farmers are patient farmers. A farmer who works the land near my home is not so patient. He is always working his ground with one implement or another. Going over the field dozens of times when a few trips would suffice, he adds greatly to his cost of operation. Last year he planted his cotton too early, and a late spring rain forced him to plant the whole field all over again. He's young; he'll learn.

My father is the most patient man I know. Whether being a farmer produced this in him, or whether he chose farming because it fit his temperament, I don't know. But my father has a keen sense of what is his responsibility and what is God's. And he flatly refuses to take over God's.

When the rains came and destroyed his crop one harvest, his faith in God never flinched. I would have lain awake at night fretting, pacing the patio rebuking the storm, screaming at God in case he had forgotten me under the cloud cover. But I never saw my dad do any such thing. I'm sure he didn't enjoy seeing a year's worth of labor wiped out in a few hours, but he didn't get angry or shake his fist at God. Instead he threw up his hands, cocked his head with a smile that revealed the inner peace that guides his life, and said, "What else can I do?"

What else can I do? We could all learn to use those words more—not in frustration or anguish, looking for desperate alternatives, but in the simple recognition that I have done what I've been asked to do, and the rest is in God's hands. We can sow and reap, but only God gives the increase. You learn that in a vineyard. City life reinforces the ridiculous notion that if things aren't going our way it's because we aren't trying hard enough.

Do you know how many believers live in the bondage of that kind of thinking in their spiritual life? Every time something goes wrong they blame themselves. So they redouble their effort, thinking that if they can just do more, maybe things will turn out their way. But it's just not true. Some things we can do, some we can't.

When you work with growing things you have to be patient. You have to do your part and let God do his, and try not to get the two confused. We can't expect God to plant or weed, since he wants us to do that. But he will make the branch to grow and the fruit to ripen. Trust him.

Whenever I read Ephesians 6, I think of those August vacations. "After you have done everything . . . stand!" When you've done everything you know to do, even if circumstances aren't coming out the way you thought they would, just wait. God will go beyond your abilities to accomplish his purposes.

He wants us to trust that fact and not confuse diligence with prevailing by our own efforts. Our efforts are only directed at abiding in the vine as a daily reality. If we do that, and simply do whatever God shows us to do, he will be free to accomplish everything he has chosen to do with our life. When we try to possess for ourselves the promise of God, we will be forever frustrated in his kingdom. Only God can make things grow.

We can trust his plans. When we've been obedient, we need only to be patient. James saw the attribute of patience displayed in farmers and encouraged us to follow their example in regard to the Lord's coming:

> Be patient, then, brothers, until the Lord's coming. See how
> the farmer waits for the land to yield its valuable crop and

*how patient he is for the autumn and spring rains. You too,
be patient and stand firm, because the Lord's coming is
near.*

JAMES 5:7,8

If we need to wait patiently for his final coming, how much
more now in the situations and circumstances we face. I see
too many people at the very threshold of the promises God
has made to them who just can't wait until the final work is
done. They grab for a more immediate substitute only to
discover later that it falls far short of God's promise.

Sometimes the best thing to do is just to stand firm. It
might help to throw up your hands and smile peacefully,
"What else can I do?" Especially as the fruit ripens, we need
to learn that lesson well. Any reliance on our own efforts
instead of God's power will only spoil the harvest.

SOFTER AND SWEETER

*Take my yoke upon you and learn from me, for
I am gentle and humble in heart, and you will
find rest for your souls.*
MATTHEW 11:29

In the last few weeks before harvest the grapes ripen rapidly. Two dramatic changes take place in these final weeks to finally make them the succulent grapes the farmer desires.

By early August the grapes have grown almost to full size. But if you pick one and bite into it then, you'll be greatly disappointed. The grapes are still hard, and tart enough to pucker your lips. It is during these final weeks before harvest that the grapes fill up with sugar, making them soft and sweet.

The leaves are in full production at this time, pumping the grape bunches full of sugar. Almost daily you can taste the changing sweetness as the sugar content soars. This influx of sugar also softens the pulp inside the grape. As you bite through the firm outer skin, you'll find that pulp has softened inside so it almost explodes in your mouth.

When the grapes turn soft and sweet, harvest is at hand. Today with special instruments farmers can measure the exact sugar content and know for sure when the grapes are fully ripe. Farmers of old, however, trusted their eyes and taste buds to tell them the same thing.

Softer and sweeter. The same things that signal the maturity of a grape also signal the maturity of a believer. As God brings his promises to completion in our lives, one of the signs that he is about through is the softness and sweetness that floods our demeanor. Earlier, in the midst of promise and warfare, we might find ourselves a bit harder, full of arrogance—fighting and striving in our own efforts to accomplish God's work. But the perseverance of summer yields its best fruit when in the final days before fulfillment God changes our heart, softening it with humility and gentleness and sweetening it with lovingkindness.

It is the final test I look for as people are being shaped and prepared for ministry in God's promise. It is the surest sign of harvest I know. Others may think themselves ready, pushing and manipulating their way into God's promise, but as long as they trust in their ability to make a place for their lives, you know they are not done yet. God still needs to bring the brokenness, humility, and dependency upon him that softens the edges of our lives.

When that happens people always have a greater compassion for other believers struggling around them, not less. They abandon anger, legalism, and manipulation as tools to accomplish the work of the kingdom. Though they are confident in God's work through them, they have a bedrock understanding that it comes only by his grace, and they know that it is God alone who will fulfill God's promises.

What oozes from their life now is the sweetness of God's character. That's the fruit he has been producing all along. The promise that may have signaled either a ministry he wanted us to discover or a blessing he wanted us to receive was only given to us in order to accomplish the greater work of shaping our lives to be like Christ. The fruits of the Spirit—love, joy, peace, patience, kindness, goodness, faithfulness, gentleness, and self-control—were all demonstrated again and again in the life of Jesus. These signal a person who is softened and sweetened by God's presence.

But in all honesty they are not the attributes most desired or engendered by the world system. Look again at the fruits of the Spirit. Imagine a person who exhibited those traits in everything he did. How would the world regard such a person? As a softie, wouldn't they? And it wouldn't be a compliment.

Anyone who has ever been on a school playground knows that those who are good and kind are either laughed at, called names, or exploited by others. The world system is clear: If you want to make it in this world, you have to be tough. You have to know what you want and grab for it, because no one is going to give it to you. Don't show any sign of weakness (meaning, kindness or goodness), because someone is waiting to take advantage of you the moment you do. Those are the rules. Everyone who succeeds learns them early and follows them adamantly.

Everyone except Jesus. His life demonstrated an inner peace that others could not destroy. He was kind to the outcast and never took advantage of anyone, not even his own disciples. In every conflict he faced, through every lie directed against him by those who sought to destroy him, he only demonstrated the gifts of the Spirit.

Did they call him a softie? Not that we know of. In fact, many people were scared by his authority, even though he held no political power nor ever enforced his will on anyone. He went about doing good, but this only threatened those who would not allow God access to their lives. "We've never seen anyone like this!" the people gasped, even as they looked for ways to kill him.

Softness is not weakness; in God's kingdom it is the measure of strength. The disciples didn't understand this fact even after walking with Jesus a few years. James and John wanted to call down fire from heaven when people in a Samaritan village wouldn't extend hospitality to him. They were ready to usher in his promise the world's way. "We'll show them who's boss."

I can see Jesus perhaps even smile as he shook his head. Still kids, he thought. Just like a farmer who bites into an early August grape—"No! They're not quite ready yet." Is that what he meant when he said his time had not yet come? Was he waiting for these first bunches to sweeten up enough not to destroy the kingdom he had brought?

But they eventually learned the lesson. That same John was the one who repeated over and over again those most simple and most powerful words of Jesus: "Love one another." Jesus finally got through to him.

All too often I've seen people loaded with knowledge and zeal but still captives of the world's system. Their lives are always harsh and their words judgmental—and in their wake are offended people, not by the gospel but by the way they've been treated. Eager to serve God, or perhaps themselves in his name, they push their way in, striving for success, acclaim, and affirmation from their peers.

They want to be somebody. But as long as they want to be somebody their ministry will be polluted. Even in places where God has genuinely called them they are defensive and easily threatened, and they compensate for that by aggression and manipulation. Where they don't succeed, they are frustrated and bitter at those they think are impeding their ministries.

That's how I can tell when people are ripe for ministry. Those whom God has prepared have been softened and sweetened, and reflect the same humility and gentleness that Jesus did. They are not advancing their own agenda, angry when they don't get what they think God has for them. They don't threaten to leave and go somewhere else "where their gifts will be appreciated."

Why? Because through the stresses of summer they have learned to trust God. They know that he opens doors and shuts them, and when he does, no man stands in his way. Learning that lesson is the last stage of maturity before we can participate in God's harvest. If we don't learn it our misplaced passion can easily crush the very people we're called to touch with his life. Jesus was gentle and humble in heart and told us to take the same yoke on ourselves. The early church was often exhorted to humility and gentleness. They knew how delicately people need to be treated when they are treated in God's name.

The end product of summer, for those who traverse it with perseverance and faith, is a gentle and humble spirit. There is no more accurate sign of maturity than those who treat others, all others, with kindness and gentleness. When that settles on your heart, you know that summer is over. Let the harvest begin!

Fall

THE JOY OF HARVEST

Those who harvest it will eat it and praise the Lord, and those who gather the grapes will drink it in the courts of my sanctuary.
ISAIAH 62:9

To the grape farmer there is no scene more awe-inspiring than swollen grape bunches cascading out of the leaves like a billowing fountain. All his effort over the last year has aimed toward this one moment.

But as beautiful as that is, it is not as idyllic as it may sound. The vine is actually not as beautiful as it was in the spring. The vine sags under the weight of the fruit like a tired, swaybacked horse. The leaves are ragged and frayed, dulled by a heavy cloak of dust. Some have yellowed and others have wilted completely. Many have pieces ripped away, remnants of summer's warfare.

Though scarred and bruised, the vines emerge laden with fruit. Their beauty lies not in their impeccable outward beauty or order, for that's only for plants that flower in safe greenhouses or backyard gardens. The farmer cherishes the vines because they have completed their work and are full of the ripened fruit he desires.

The war is over and the vines have won. Harvest is at hand. The farmer doesn't care so much how the vine looks, but what kind of fruit hangs from its branches. The grape bunches testify to its success. Indeed, its purpose was never to look good—only to produce fruit.

The vineyard uses the entire growing season to develop and ripen its fruit. As the approaching fall brings cooler temperatures and shorter days, the grapes bulge with sweetness. The farmer waits until the sugar content is high enough to suit his purpose, then sets the knife in the field to garner the fruit.

There are days of great joy. Farmers have no way to measure their success weekly or even monthly. Their labor is directed toward one small span of time when the harvest is gathered. Depending on the farmer, he may gather the grape bunches directly for use as table grapes, or process them into wine, or (as in my father's case) lay them on the ground in the sun to dry as raisins. Scripture makes reference to all three uses.

As much as I hated farmwork as a child, some of my sweetest memories include the last ride on the tractor into the barn. The trailers were stacked as high as possible, trying to make that trip the last instead of having to come back again. The sun-ripened raisins formed a mountain as they sloped down to the edges of the box.

The crop was in. We had beaten the winter storms for another year, and now the crop was safe. The hot, dusty work was over. I remember on more than one occasion surveying the awesome sight of row upon row of boxes stretched out across the top of the hill where the outbuildings on my father's farm stood. A year's worth of labor and all of my father's income for an entire year sat beneath the haystack plastic covering the boxes.

The last act of harvest was always a celebration. Shouts of joy, song, and laughter filled the air on that final ride home. Afterward we would clean up and go out to eat—a feast to celebrate the harvest and the gracious God who made it possible.

I suspect that the final harvest in the kingdom of God will be like that. Paul speaks in 2 Timothy 4 of his departure to the Father and the joy that awaits him in God's presence for his ministry faithfully executed. Revelation tells of a marriage banquet where we sit down with the King and feast in his presence. What a great day that will be for all who have been faithful!

But like the vine, we have not been shaped for only one harvest. There are many seasons in our spiritual growth when the fruits of our labors are rewarded and we get to see the result of the Father's dealing with our lives. Those too are days full of celebration. And they are often days of understanding as to why God didn't always intervene in our circumstances the way we thought he might. He was producing something far better than our own temporal conveniences would ever allow.

But let us not forget who shares the greatest joy—the gardener himself. What a delight must come to his heart when he sees that the necessary difficulties and pain have produced in his children the peaceable fruits of righteousness! Remember, it is *his* work, not ours. He is ultimately the victor and we are his prize.

This is worship in its highest form, for God knows no greater joy than to receive the fruitfulness of his sons and daughters. Let's look at this mystery of harvest and pledge ourselves to stay with the growing until we have fruit to present before him—not for our own benefit, but for his eternal pleasure.

31

OUT OF
WATER—
WINE!

*Celebrate the Feast of Harvest with the
firstfruits of the crops you sow in your
field. Celebrate the Feast of Ingathering
at the end of the year, when you gather
in your crops from the field.*

EXODUS 23:16

The wedding was over. The feast to celebrate it was in full
swing. The joyful sounds of animated conversation and dancing filled the room. So far everything was going well—but it
did not look like it was going to continue. Disaster lurked in
the wings and was about to come to center stage. The groom
had not ordered enough wine for his guests, and it had run
out before they had.

This was the context of Jesus' first miracle: A party was
about to die. Yet even though this was an embarrassing social
blunder, as far as needs go I wouldn't rate it very high on a
significance scale. Surely the need here was not as great as
Mary's brother dying, or of being caught in a raging midnight
storm on the sea of Galilee.

I wonder if Jesus felt the same way. Is that why he resisted
his mother's well-intentioned attempts to involve him? Maybe

the wedding was from her side of the family and far more significant to her than it looked on the surface. Yet Jesus acceded to her desperate appeal.

He told the stewards to fill the washing pots to the brim and take some to the master of the banquet. They did so, and found out that somewhere between the time they had filled the pots and when it was tasted by the master of the banquet it had been changed into wine, better wine than had been used earlier.

Those that knew how the wine came to be there were awestruck by the miracle. But most at the party hadn't paid enough attention to recognize it. Yet the man who recorded the event had, and he told us that on the basis of this miracle the disciples first put their faith in Jesus.

Out of water he made wine! That he did it should not be significant. As C.S. Lewis pointed out in an essay on miracles in *God in the Dock*, this was something he had done before— many times before:

> God creates the vine and teaches it to draw up water
> by its roots, and, with the aid of the sun, to turn that
> water into a juice which will ferment and take on
> certain qualities. Thus every year, from Noah's time
> till ours, God turns water into wine. That, men fail to
> see.

What was significant this time is that Jesus did in a moment what he normally does over an entire growing season. Out of water, soil, and sun he produces a harvest, the final product tasting far better and offering far more nourishment than any of its individual parts could do alone. To do it he uses a grapevine. Can anyone else mix water, dirt, and sunlight and produce anything to compare?

This is the Lord of the Harvest, who made himself known at a wedding feast. Lewis goes on to draw a powerful point: If such miracles only convince us that Christ is God, they have only done half their work. Miracles are "a retelling in small letters of the very same story which is written across the whole world in letters too large for some to see." Thus this

miracle only has its full impact "if whenever we see a vineyard or drink a glass of wine we remember that here works He
who sat at the wedding party in Cana."

Year in and year out nothing speaks more clearly of God's
involvement in our world than his bringing crops to harvest.
As the green grapes fill with sugar they yellow slightly. To the
keen eye of the farmer that change signals the approaching
harvest. A quick taste will confirm it. Soon the other bunches
on the vine will follow. God has brought another crop to
harvest.

Not surprisingly, harvest and joy are closely connected
throughout Scripture. In an agrarian society that predated
cold storage and prepackaged food, the harvest was a lifeline.
The previous year's food would be running low, paced to last
through the year. That may not be easy for us to grasp with
adequate fervor when our supermarkets are loaded with food
every day of the year. How can we recognize the vulnerability
of their harvest when we can replace the freeze-devastated
citrus crop of California by shipping in oranges from Florida,
or vice versa.

For a society without those luxuries, the harvest was a
genuine time of celebration and thanksgiving. In fact God
ordained two feasts to bracket the harvest. The Feast of Harvest came at the beginning as precious firstfruits were offered
to God in thankfulness for another crop. The Feast of Ingathering marked the successful completion of the harvest
itself.

Both were to be celebrated before God. He, not nature, had
provided bountiful for the year to come. The expression of his
faithfulness as shown in that crop was cause for true rejoicing. Even for heathen nations, the apostle Paul identified
God's testimony of kindness in the harvest: "He has shown
kindness by giving you rain from heaven and crops in their
seasons; he provides you with plenty of food and fills your
hearts with joy" (Acts 14:17).

To those who see his hand in the harvest, he wants our
hearts to be filled with joy, and even more so in the spiritual
harvest than in his physical provision for our lives. Out of our
broken lives God brings forth fruit of his kingdom. It is *his*

doing and should be marked with joy in our own lives. Maybe that's why God chose a vineyard to represent our spiritual growth. Even the fruit of the vineyard speaks of joy.

Grapes and raisins were desired treats in days prior to chocolate cake and ice cream. They not only provided nourishment but offered a sweet contrast to the harsher grains and meat that made up most of the people's diet. Remember how awed the Israelites were when the spies brought back grape bunches from Canaan that had to be carried on poles because they were so large?

But even more than these, wine is the most-used scriptural symbol for joy. When Solomon expressed his delight in the Lord he exalted it above wine, evidently the standard by which other things desirable were measured: "We rejoice and delight in you; we will praise your love more than wine" (Song of Songs 1:4).

When God gave instructions to the Israelites about using their tithe, wine and celebration were a big part of it: "Use the silver to buy whatever you like: cattle, sheep, wine or other fermented drink, or anything you wish. Then you and your household shall eat there in the presence of the Lord your God and rejoice" (Deuteronomy 14:26).

I realize that these uses of wine are confusing for many of us today. The church I grew up in found it inconceivable that Jesus would go to a wedding to change water into wine. (Most of them would have gone to a wedding party to turn wine back into water!) We even defined wine as unfermented grape juice. I grew up thinking the Greek word for wine was "Welch's."

To this day I am still a teetotaler, despising any kind of strong drink because of the destruction it foists on our society. I have counseled too many people who were the victims of alcoholic parents, too many who battle its temptation. One of my best friends I grew up with since kindergarten was killed by a drunk driver in his first year of college.

Scripture is not oblivious to this dark side of wine. Though it was a drink to be shared with joy at celebrations, drunkenness is resoundingly condemned throughout Scripture.

Proverbs tells us that wine destroys those who give themselves over to its power. They will end in poverty and shame. Wine is even used as a symbol of the last great evil civilization that will fill our world: "Fallen! Fallen is Babylon the Great, which made all the nations drink the maddening wine of her adulteries" (Revelation 14:8).

The reason wine makes a powerful symbol of the joy and freedom that God wants to bring to his people is that, like all his other gifts (ministry, food, sex), they have potential for our enjoyment or our destruction. What makes the difference is whether we partake the way God has directed, or whether we spend them on our own pleasure, using them as substitutes for God himself.

That's what happens when people abuse alcohol. Instead of letting God address the hurt or loneliness, they try to bury it in a bottle. But the ruse only lasts a moment, and when the horrors begin so does another search for their God-substitute. Drunkenness turns people over to the power of alcohol, which only seeks their destruction.

Instead, we are exhorted to let God alone be our source of help through any pain or trial. Thus wine can be a symbol of either the enemy's work or of God's. Perhaps no Scripture brings that together as well as Ephesians 5:18: "Do not get drunk on wine, which leads to debauchery. Instead, be filled with the Spirit."

Scripture's use of wine as a symbol of joy does not mean that it contains real joy. Pursuing it there or any other place outside of God will only lead to an unfulfilling, compulsive search that will not end in our satisfaction, but only in persistent frustration and eventual destruction. Wine is only a symbol of the joy and celebration that come from his presence.

That's why Paul tells us not to be drunk with wine like the world, but filled with the Spirit. He is the source of our joy. Thus wine is also linked to the Holy Spirit as well as to joy. He is the new wine, and we are encouraged to drink freely and often from his fountain.

Celebration and joy are major themes at harvesttime. Even though it was purchased by the pain and toil of summer, this celebration is the ultimate reason for our suffering. There is even a hint of that fact at the last meal that Jesus shared with his disciples. What a confusing night for his men—he talked of his impending departure as they shared the Passover meal! As they ate, he talked of his body broken and his blood shed.

They were confused and afraid. What kind of ordeal was he describing? But when Jesus spoke of his dying he took the cup in his hand. A cup of wine! Previous to that moment there was nothing in the Passover making wine a symbol of blood. There was no need to, for the blood was smeared on the doorposts from the sacrifice. The unleavened bread and bitter herbs were to remind them of their slavery. But this was not the time for pained recollection, but a celebration with thanksgiving that God had passed over them and spared their lives to take them out of Egypt. That celebration was in the wine.

It was at this meal with his disciples that Jesus vested in the wine the symbol of his sacrifice. The very cup that symbolized celebration even in the midst of tragedy would carry that symbol into the New Covenant. Jesus didn't want us looking back at the cross with gruesome anguish; this was to be a cup of celebration. The blood had been shed and the work of redemption was complete—at great pain, but resulting in even-greater joy.

So he took the cup. "This cup is the new covenant in my blood, which is poured out for you." Pain and celebration brought together in the fruit of the vine. As we begin our own season of harvest, let us remember whose blood made it possible, and celebrate his love for us. For it is all of *his* hand, not our own. He alone can make wine out of water, and he alone can make fruitful vines out of fallen humanity.

FOR ALL
TO SEE

By their fruit you will recognize them.
Do people pick grapes from thornbushes,
or figs from thistles?
MATTHEW 7:16

As I've said all along, my father is an exceptional farmer. He cares for his vineyard with exacting standards in order to coax maximum fruitfulness from each vine. But it has not always been so.

For a period of about four or five years during my early teens, my father's vineyard didn't look as well-cared-for as it does today. Even the neighbors noticed. The weeds grew taller, the pests were more numerous, and the long-term maintenance needs of the vineyard were neglected.

You might call this my father's fanatic stage. There was a fresh revival going on in his spiritual life, and he was more excited about the things of God than I had ever seen him. He was always rushing off to a prayer meeting or conference or helping someone in need. Many Christians at that time were certain that Jesus' second coming would happen before we ever reached the 70's.

In that spiritual climate the vineyard just didn't seem all that appropriate. If irrigation or spraying had to wait an extra week, that was too bad. We were involved in the business of God's kingdom; let God take care of the vineyard.

My dad looks back at that time with a glimmer of laughter in his eyes. He sees now the folly of thinking that to serve God with all one's heart means we have to neglect our responsibilities in this age. At the time, however, the toll it took on the vineyard was very real. Without proper care the vineyard was not fully fruitful. Make whatever excuses you like, but the proof was in the fruit itself. These were not well-cared-for vines.

In every grape the history of the vine is told. If it was a good year with proper care, the fruit will burst with sweetness. If it was neglected, the fruit will be small and rather tart.

Fruit doesn't lie. As we saw earlier, it is the overflow of the vine's life. The greater the overflow, the sweeter the fruit. As a branch joined to Jesus himself, we are part of the healthiest of all vines. If we have kept ourselves firmly rooted in him through the stress of summer, his life will overflow in us. If not . . . well, this fruit doesn't lie either.

The proof of a branch's life is found in the harvest. Its diligence will reap an abundance of fruit, useful for the Master in extending his kingdom. His character having been developed in us, we will now be useful in demonstrating his love and grace to others. That's why, as we shall see in the next chapter, harvest is a time when ministry pours out of our lives to others.

But there is another side to the harvest, one that is not so joyful. For those who have not pursued friendship with Jesus wholeheartedly, but have neglected their spiritual nourishment, harvest exposes that reality. Now the inner life is seen for what it is. If we resisted the Master when he sought to prune us, or have cast off our fruit in the weariness of summer's wasting heat, we will have nothing to show for it. If we have only stayed close enough to Jesus to survive, our fruit (if it exists at all) will be pale and tasteless.

Worse yet, if we have only pretended to draw life from Christ, but have in fact resisted his work in us while we've served ourselves, our fruit will bear our own likeness and not God's. The fruit testifies to the source of the branch:

Their vine comes from the vine of Sodom and from the fields of Gomorrah. Their grapes are filled with poison, and their

clusters with bitterness. Their wine is the venom of ser-
pents, the deadly poison of cobras.
DEUTERONOMY 32:32,33

You can't fool the fruit. It fully expresses the life of the vine. That's why Scripture views the harvest in both positive and negative terms. It demonstrates the quality of our lives, whether good or bad. Thus harvest is used to talk of both the triumph of the righteous and the outpouring of God's wrath against the wicked—joy or judgment.

In fact, most of the references in Scripture to the winepress, an important tool in the Hebrew harvest, have to do with God's wrath. Where evil reigns, the harvest presses out the wickedness in judgment: "Swing sickle, for the harvest is ripe. Come, trample the grapes for the winepress is full and the vats overflow—so great is their wickedness!" (Joel 3:13).

In the last days of human history our world will undergo a final harvest. The events of the last days are formulated to bring each person to full ripeness. In the face of the cataclysmic events of Revelation, people's hearts will either be stirred to a greater pursuit of God or will plunge even deeper into darkness. Then the harvest will come. For the wicked it will be a terrible day indeed:

Still another angel, who had charge of the fire, came from the altar and called in a loud voice to him who had the sharp sickle, "Take your sharp sickle and gather the clusters of grapes from the earth's vine, because its grapes are ripe." The angel swung his sickle on the earth, gathered its grapes and threw them into the great winepress of God's wrath.
REVELATION 14:18,19

For those who remain in Christ, however, there will be no terror in that day. For then God will vindicate his goodness, gathering the righteous to himself and forever holding us in his presence. No longer will we have to struggle against the wickedness of the world or the resistance of our flesh. For us that day will be joyful.

So it is in the periodic harvests that God calls out of our lives; the fruit that has largely gone unseen and perhaps unnoticed now takes center stage. Now we can be seen for what we really are. That's why Jesus told us that the fruit borne at harvest reveals a lot about people. Though he warned us not to judge others, he did say that we had a responsibility not to be gullible to the counsel and ministry of those who don't really belong to him.

He didn't want us to judge each other's motives or to make assumptions because of their boasts or their failures. Look at the fruit instead, he said. That will tell for sure what they are on the inside:

> *Watch out for false prophets. They come to you in sheep's clothing, but inwardly they are ferocious wolves. By their fruit you will recognize them. Do people pick grapes from thornbushes...? Likewise every good tree bears good fruit, but a bad tree bears bad fruit. A good tree cannot bear bad fruit, and a bad tree cannot bear good fruit. Every tree that does not bear good fruit is cut down and thrown into the fire. Thus, by their fruit you will recognize them.*
>
> MATTHEW 7:15-20

Jesus' words leave little room for negotiation. There is no way a grape branch can produce thorns, or a bad tree good fruit. If a branch bears thorns, then it is attached to a thornbush. For too long our qualifications for Christian ministry have focused on expertise, gifting, anointing, or ability to say what we want to hear. Jesus tells us to look elsewhere: to people's true character. How are they when they think no one is looking?

Do they tell the truth when they are asked? Are they gentle, even with those who may dissent? Do they exemplify love and mercy? If so, trust them. Jesus didn't mean they had to be perfect, but that they *do* need to bear the character of Jesus in their attitude and demeanor. There is no more important qualification for ministry.

If they don't exemplify that character, Jesus warned us, get away from them. If they get angry when confronted, or lie to cover up their sinfulness, or treat others harshly and with arrogance, they are wolves in sheep's clothing. They are only around for what they can get from the sheep—power, money, or even a sense of personal success.

Trust the fruit, Jesus said. We would all do well to examine our own lives to see if our hearts are really drawing life from him. Fruit cannot be faked. Though a person may for a time be able to pretend some godly attribute for a brief season, in his weak and tired moments his real nature will slip out and be exposed. Only the fruit produced by God himself can withstand the heat of battle.

Fruit makes the invisible visible. It shatters all pretense and over time serves as a true marker of the depth of our friendship with Jesus. Has it been neglected or nurtured? The fruit will tell. Stay faithful to him and you will see this fact emerge. Rest assured that it is the only way it will appear. Don't expect grace to cover up your neglect by producing spiritual fruit. Grace can restore us to God's presence, and it can forgive our sins and offer us a fresh start, but grace will not produce fruit when we have not paid the cost to remain in the vine. It will not make up for the times when we have given in to the enemy's lies and aborted our own fruit to save our hide in times of stress.

God's harvest may surprise us. The people we thought were pursuing God because of their gifts, temporal success, or charming words may not turn out to be his followers at all.

> *Not everyone who says to me, "Lord, Lord," will enter the kingdom of heaven, but only he who does the will of my father who is in heaven. Many will say to me on that day, "Lord, Lord did we not prophesy in your name, and in your name drive out demons and perform many miracles?"*
>
> *Then I will tell them plainly, "I never knew you. Away from me, you evildoers!"*
> MATTHEW 7:21-23

In the final analysis the acts of power we participated in, or the numbers of people touched, or the acclaim we received from others will be meaningless. All that will matter is our friendship with Jesus.

33

THE HARVEST AS MINISTRY

Look at the fields!
They are ripe for harvest.
JOHN 4:35

You probably don't think much about it when you sink your teeth into a delicious bowl of fruit. As the sparkling sweetness explodes in your mouth it is too easy to forget that the fruit is also a seed. That is how plants multiply for future generations.

The earliest passages in Genesis tell us that God created fruit for this dual purpose—food to be eaten and seed to be sown. So it is with the fruit of our friendship with Jesus. As he shapes us into his image, that fruit is what God wants to use to draw others into the kingdom. Because their unregenerate hearts cannot behold the invisible God, they need to see him in us first.

How will they know his love if I don't love them? How will they understand his gentleness and forgiveness unless I demonstrate it? How will they know he is faithful unless I am faithful in my relationship to them?

The fruit of our lives has its greatest use in this age by demonstrating God's reality and nature to others. During days of harvest not only do we enjoy and celebrate what God has accomplished in us, but we also see God use us to touch the lives of others. Harvesttime is ministry time, the fruit of

239

our lives reaped, so that a further harvest of new branches will result.

Harvest is a twofold analogy in Scripture. Not only does it refer to the fruit of transformed character in our lives, but from a different vantage point it also refers to the unsaved as a ripened harvest, those who have been prepared to meet the Lord. These are not unrelated. The demonstration of God's nature in us is the means by which God propagates the gospel. We are workers called into that field to make him known.

This is not a burdensome task to be met through a complicated evangelism program. This is something that people who have been changed by God can't help but do. Our changed lives can't help but demonstrate to people the reality of God.

Whenever Jesus referred to this kind of harvest, it seemed to have no seasonal limitations. "Do you not say, 'Four months more and then the harvest'? I tell you, open your eyes and look at the fields! They are ripe for harvest." There are always people around us ready to respond to God. Jesus spoke from experience; he had just found one earlier that morning.

He was passing through Samaria, tired from the journey. It was almost noon, and instead of going into town with his followers to find lunch, he sat down by an out-of-the-way well. Was he lying in wait for the conversation to come, or did he just take advantage of the moment. I suspect the former. In either case, a Samaritan woman came to draw water.

Outside of town? In the heat of midday? Unusual. Everyone else had come earlier in the day, or were to come later. Those that needed water at that time could get it in town.

Unusual? Yes, but not unplanned. Here was a woman who had charted her course specifically so she would not be seen. Later on we find out why. Here was a woman who had been married five times, and each time had ended with rejection. In this society women didn't have the right to divorce. The man she lived with now was only exploiting her, extending her neither his pledge nor his name.

Imagine the stares she got from her community—those long, down-the-nose glances of people who would wince as if they had just smelled manure, and then would hurry away lest they would somehow be infected by her. She couldn't face it anymore, so she sneaked off to the farthest well at the hottest part of the day to be alone.

Even at a distance she would notice someone there, a stranger sitting by *her* well. I wonder if she thought about going back and trying again later. But she would look ridiculous, wouldn't she? She was halfway there with an empty pot on her head. She wasn't looking for relationship; she just wanted to be alone.

But it was not to be. She didn't speak to the stranger, whom she now recognized to be Jewish. She wanted to draw her water quickly and hurry away from the awkward moment before he said anything. But Jesus was ready for the ripened harvest. "Will you give me a drink?" he asked.

Her worse fear had come true. "At least he doesn't know me," or so she thought. She at least didn't see him wince when he spoke to her. In fact, she winced first. "You are a Jew and I am a Samaritan." If you don't know the real reason to despise me, shouldn't this be enough?

But Jesus kept on, ignoring her plea to be left alone. Let me note two important things that happened here. First, Jesus took the time to get to know a woman and her need. Where others saw a sinful woman, he saw someone thirsting for something she had never found. Without condoning her sin, he looked past it to the thirst that drove it, knowing it wouldn't be quenched now by number six. This was a woman who needed to drink from God's fountain.

Second, Jesus added some divine insight: "The fact is, you have had five husbands, and the man you now have is not your husband." He knew!

"He told me everything I ever did" is how she later reported the encounter to her friends. This man knew me and still extended to me what no one else had—an offer to be included, an offer of life. Jesus showed her God's love, and she came to believe in him.

When the disciples got back with lunch, they were amazed that he was talking with a woman, much less a Samaritan. Did they wince in disdain at her? No matter, she was off to tell her family, "Could this be the Christ?"

Eventually her family and friends came to faith as well—all because Jesus spent time with a woman who needed God's touch. No evangelistic rally downtown would have attracted her. She ran from crowds. This harvest needed a one-on-one encounter.

I don't begrudge evangelistic rallies at all, but let's not be tricked into thinking that these are the best or only way Jesus wants to touch the lost. No doubt these are the easiest, but God has other ways too. I am concerned with this superficial view that many people have of ministry which prevents them from getting to a real touch with people. Ministry is not standing before huge crowds holding them in spellbinding oratory. Those can be expressions of ministry, but this example gets far quicker to the heart.

Too many of our models lead people to covet not the personal touch with rejected and hurting people, but creating organizations and investing ministry in preplanned programs. I don't want to indicate that such methods are wrong, but I do want us to take an objective look at how effective they are. What too often happens is that people with the most heart for ministry end up administrating programs instead of ministering to people. Programmed action too easily replaces the power and love of God reaching out to touch others through changed lives.

We do not find the real ministry of the kingdom by finding a niche in a religious organization. We find it when we see God using us to touch other people. Of course there's a place for coordinated outreach, but I want to encourage those whose obedience doesn't fit such models. Don't be frustrated when others receive notoriety for their efforts that seems to escape you. Don't look for the applause of men—only God's approval. Our ministry is far better measured by our faithfulness to him than by finding the accolades of the religious sector of our society.

After his encounter with the woman at the well, the disciples tried to get Jesus to eat. But he replied, "I have food to eat that you know nothing about." There is something about being part of God's plan that is its own reward. "My food is to do the will of him who sent me and to finish his work."

If that doesn't describe a branch nourishing off the vine, I don't know what does. Our obedience to God and participating in his work is our nourishment. Expect many distractions to try to sway you from this sustenance. Perhaps Jesus would have preferred the walk into town with his friends over staying at the well for another moment of ministry, but he chose the Father's desire. In doing so he found fulfillment more real than the lunch they brought to him.

Then he told them about the harvest:

> Even now the reaper draws his wages, even now he harvests the crop for eternal life, so that the sower and the reaper may be glad together. Thus the saying "One sows and another reaps" is true. I sent you to reap what you have not worked for. Others have done the hard work, and you have reaped the benefits of their labor.
>
> JOHN 4:36-38

Jesus affirms that we are not only branches on the vine, but also workers in the vineyard. Some sow, some reap, but all rejoice together as new lives are brought to Jesus. Don't exalt one above the other. The Corinthians did, and it produced a wealth of discord among them. Those who reap often reap where others have already done the harder work of sowing and nurturing.

In a recent reading through Acts I noticed something I had never put a finger on before. Do you know what was the most major deterrent to the spread of the gospel? Not persecution. Not false teaching. Not the materialistic culture. Not the complacency of believers.

What continued to assert itself over and over again was *jealousy*. Paul and Barnabas would go to a synagogue to proclaim that the Messiah had come. They always found receptive hearers. Tell us more, they would plead, and invite them back next week. By the next week the place would be packed with people interested to hear what Paul and Barnabas would share. Those who had been around the synagogue for a long time found that offensive. Why should the crowds come now? Their jealousy caused them to reject what had stirred their hearts only a week before.

Jealousy is a powerful force. More than we would care to admit, it will cause us to reject both the truth and those who incite our jealousy. That's what John the Baptist's disciples tried to tap when they reminded him that Jesus' ministry had grown larger than his. In fact, some of his followers were now with Jesus. But John didn't bite: "A man can receive only what is given him from heaven."

To this Paul added, "What do you have that you did not receive? And if you did receive it, why do you boast as though you did not?" There is too much jealousy and too much boasting in the body of Christ today over things for which God has responsibility. Resist it. Find your own obedience to God and pursue it whether or not it ever earns you any acclaim.

Fruitfulness for the vine comes in its season. The harvest may be ripe, but the harvesters may not be. As ready as the field was, Jesus sent his disciples back to Jerusalem to wait for the power that would come only from the Holy Spirit. The more God shapes you in his likeness, the more your ministry opportunities will increase.

As God solidifies that work in you, let your life reach out to others. Practice hospitality, especially with the world. Don't limit your activities to the safely religious, but cultivate relationships with unbelievers so that they can taste God's character through you. Get involved in your community with nonbelievers at work, in your neighborhood, or through other activities and outreaches.

Through these relationships God will show himself to the people around you. Let God choose how that happens. A vine does not harvest itself; the gardener does. Our activity at harvest is not always intense; often we find God moving through us most powerfully when we're hardly even aware of it.

34

JUST WHOSE FRUIT IS IT ANYWAY?

*When the harvest time approached, he sent his
servants to the tenants to collect his fruit.*
MATTHEW 21:34

We examined the parable earlier when we dealt with our
dual role in the vineyard, but there's one word in it that I want
to highlight now. Jesus told a story in which God planted a
vineyard and entrusted its care to farmers. At harvesttime he
sent his servants to collect the fruit. You know the story: They
preferred killing his servants, and even the landowner's son,
to sharing *their* fruit.

Their fruit—that's how they thought of it. "It's ours. We
made it. We'll do with it what we want, and we don't want to
share it."

Never mind that God had built the vineyard, planted each
vine, and held title to it all. Jesus said it was his fruit—the
landlord's, that is. He only assigned *care of the vineyard*, not
ownership of its fruit. But the farmers failed to understand that
fact, so instead of giving the landlord his due, they took for
themselves possession of that which only God could produce.

It wasn't their fruit, but God's. Here is a lesson for both
branches and vineyard workers alike. The fruit borne on our
limbs or in our corner of the vineyard *never* belongs to us.

245

Nothing will destroy the joy and bounty of the harvest faster
(and turn God's blessing into our own source of destruction)
than to misunderstand this foundational truth of the vineyard.

Israel missed it. God blessed them with great fruitfulness,
but instead of offering it back to God in thanksgiving, they
used it for their own desires. Hosea confronted them with
their unfaithfulness:

> *Israel was a spreading vine; he brought forth fruit for him-*
> *self. As his fruit increased, he built more altars; as his land*
> *prospered, he adorned his sacred stones. Their heart is de-*
> *ceitful, and now they must bear their guilt. The Lord will*
> *demolish their altars and destroy their sacred stones.*
>
> HOSEA 10:1,2

Once God's fruit becomes ours, any number of things can
happen, none of them good. We either use God's blessing for
our own indulgence, or even, as in this case, to create our own
gods and systems of worship. The fruit belongs to *God.*

The story is told most clearly in the vine itself. The fruit
does not benefit the branch that bears it. The leaves nourish
the vine and make it stronger, but the vine cannot utilize the
fruit for its own needs. It cannot draw on its stored energy or
taste of its sweetness. Whatever goes into the fruit is the
abundance that the vine gives up. It belongs to the gardener,
to pick and use as he sees fit. It can either be food for the
hungry or seeds for new generations, but it cannot nourish
the vine.

But how we try to make it so! All too often when we have
been blessed by God with gifts, or ministry, or influence, or
changed lives, or even material goods, we have suddenly
turned to treasure those things more than God himself. It was
far easier to seek God when our circumstances were desperate, when our lives were broken and despised. The gifts of
God have always represented a greater threat to his people
than any hardship.

The Israelites rarely forgot God when they were under
attack or caught in famine. But in times of peace and tranquility they forgot God and turned to serve themselves either

directly or through idols of their own creation. Their failure must be our lesson: God's blessing is not for ourselves; we are blessed to be a blessing to others.

Fruit is borne to be given away. Hoarded fruit on the vine will only spoil and rot. If it's not picked and put to some other use, its blessing is lost. It is perhaps the saddest commentary on our generation that so much of our view of Christianity is tainted by our own self-interest. To get people to worship, we must promise them the peace and tranquility it will bring to their heart. But worship by definition is self-abandonment. It is adoration of God, my heart presented to him for his blessing and joy. Anything less than this perverts worship into an exercise for our own blessing.

The same is true of ministry. If we can't hint to people that their service to God won't be richly rewarded in some material way, many are not interested. "What's in it for me?" is the cry of the world, but we dare not answer it in the church of Jesus Christ. It will not lead any of us to the depth of fruitfulness that God desires of us.

In his kingdom *giving up* is the key to life. No one demonstrated this better than the true vine himself. In living among us, Philippians tells us, he emptied himself, not even regarding his equality with God as something he had to hold on to. He gave it up to become a servant among us.

Nothing marked his life better than his constant choices to give up his own temporal desires to obey his Father. He gave up fame and notoriety by refusing to use the power of God for his own advancement. He gave up his own safety by refusing to compromise truth in the face of religious leaders who wanted to contain him. He gave up his own personal comfort to bring God's kingdom throughout Israel. At the end of his life was the greatest giving up of all: He gave up his spirit to God.

In giving up he found the secret to being fruitful to God. All he did abandoned his own self-interest so that God the Father would be glorified: "I have brought you glory on earth by completing the work you gave me to do."

Do you remember the lesson of the blossoms in spring? For fruit to form the blossoms have to wither. If we cannot let go of

God's promise in trust that he will fulfill it, all we will have is dead blossoms. That lesson foreshadows what we must embrace wholeheartedly in the fall. Now the fulfillment of God's promise must be released yet again. It will do no good for him as long as we cling to God's blessing for our own personal gain.

We grow in the kingdom of God not by what we gain but by what we give away. Life doesn't come where we look to please ourselves, but where we deny our own self-interest to embrace something far larger and far more wonderful:

> *If anyone would come after me, he must deny himself and take up his cross and follow me. For whoever wants to save his life will lose it, but whoever loses his life for me will find it. What good will it be for a man if he gains the whole world, yet forfeits his soul? Or what can a man give in exchange for his soul?*
>
> MATTHEW 16:24-26

The character shaped in our lives must be at God's disposal to use as he sees fit to nourish others, or to multiply his vineyard. The promises he fulfills in us must lie at his disposal. Even falling in love with God's promise fulfilled can be an idol that separates us from him.

A branch in God's vineyard must be willing to risk anything at any moment in obedience to God. I see this struggle most whenever we talk about multiplying ministry in the fellowship in which I pastor. The church in our generation has never been so good at that. Oh, we can expand ministry just fine until it becomes a huge machine, unresponsive to the needs of people. But multiplying ministry through planting churches and dividing existing groups is always a challenge.

I am convinced by everything I've shared in this book that church life, in order to fulfill its New Testament pattern, must be community-based and not program-based. In other words, life in the church isn't measured by the power of our Sunday gathering or how well our programs work, but how effectively we release people to touch each other with the ministry of Jesus. That necessitates some form of small-group arrangement where people can be known, loved, discipled, served, and challenged to the fullness of life in Christ.

Any group that does that well, however, grows beyond its ability to continue doing it. Increased size means that relationships give way to procedures, and spontaneity to planning. The only remedy is to let the group multiply, forming new groups out of the one that has grown. But nothing challenges people more. Not only is change itself threatening, but tampering with relationships that have been key in God transforming people is sure to cause a stir.

I understand this, but we also need to understand that the only reason they had relationships made available to them in the first place was because another group before them paid the price to multiply. The transition is always difficult, but it must nevertheless be pursued. For that to happen, people have to be willing to release God's blessings with a spirit of generosity.

Letting God have the freedom to make those changes as he desires is what being a branch or a worker in his vineyard is all about. The fruit he has created in us was always intended to be a source of blessing for others. Cultivate that mentality, and when God gives the increase it will never be a source of frustration but a joyful adventure.

God sought to sow a spirit of generosity into the very fiber of his people. Even their physical crops were not to be harvested completely. Instead, the reapers were to leave some for the gleaners:

> *When you reap the harvest of your land, do not reap to the very edges of your field or gather the gleaning of your harvest. Do not go over your vineyard a second time or pick up the grapes that have fallen. Leave them for the poor and the alien. I am the Lord your God.*
> LEVITICUS 19:9,10

God wants his people to be a generous people, never hoarding for themselves his blessings, but realizing that since it all came from him anyway, it is all his to use for his glory. As you come to the days of harvest, keep that in mind. What God produces through our lives he intends for *his* glory, not our own.

WHAT HAPPENS WHEN THERE IS NO HARVEST?

Though . . . there are no grapes on the vines . . . and the yields produce no food . . . yet will I rejoice in the Lord.
HABAKKUK 3:17,18

Can one embrace the promises of God in spring, endure in them despite the perils of summer, and still come through the harvest with no fruit to show for it?

It happened to my father in at least two seasons that I can remember. After nurturing the crop to completion, Dad still came up empty. The crop matured well enough, but the problem came at harvest. Because he makes raisins of his grapes, he picks them and lays them on the ground to dry on paper trays. This is when the raisin crop is most vulnerable. Should it rain heavily during those few days, the entire crop will rot right on the ground.

I've seen it happen. There are few things more frustrating and no feeling more futile. All the labor of a year is wiped out by a freak storm from the subtropics. It's not at all common for rain to find the San Joaquin Valley in September, and that's why he laid them on the ground. But twice he paid for it rather severely.

There are other dangers that can net the same result at harvesttime. Insects or birds in large enough quantities can settle on a crop and devour it. I've not personally seen this happen, but one year experts were concerned that large flocks of starlings were gathering in our valley. We were told they could pick a field clean in a few minutes. Gratefully, the threat never materialized.

The enemies of fruitfulness don't just give up because fall has come. My father never thought his crop was safe until it was delivered to the packer. Then he could relax. Harvest was over.

Can this happen in the Father's vineyard? Can we faithfully pursue God with all our heart, only to have fruitfulness snatched away from us at the moment the promise emerges? I think not. But if I don't qualify that statement I'm afraid you'll misunderstand it, and with it God as well.

The reason I would say no is because Isaiah's words are so clear:

As the rain and the snow come down from heaven, and do not return to it without watering the earth and making it bud and flourish, so that it yields seed for the sower and bread for the eater, so is my word that goes out from my mouth: It will not return to me empty, but will accomplish what I desire and achieve the purpose for which I sent it.
ISAIAH 55:10,11

As long as we continue to remain in the vine by remaining in Christ's Word, it will bear fruit in our lives. What needs to be qualified is that it often may not be the fruit we anticipate. Many of us carry unrealistic expectations of what that fruitfulness may mean. We confuse being fruitful with being successful in the world's eyes, or living in comfortable bliss. We couldn't be more wrong.

Take Stephen, for instance, who was brutally murdered for his faith. He was the first nonapostle to emerge in the early church with a powerful and fiery ministry. Just as he was coming into his own, perhaps after his first and what proved to be his last sermon, he was stoned. Was Stephen a harvest aborted? It may look like that to some, but God allowed him to be stoned and used it for his greater glory.

His life bore fruit, and still does through the testimony of Scripture. All our fruitfulness will not be borne in ease or even in this life at all. The obstacles of this world and the assaults of the enemy will provide constant challenges, and though our circumstances may not always come out as we expect, we can always expect God to be glorified through us.

The enemies of the harvest are many. That is why we cannot confuse open doors with lack of opposition. Paul didn't. He spoke of staying on in Ephesus "because a great door for effective work has opened to me, and there are many who oppose me" (1 Corinthians 16:9). The litany of his struggles on behalf of the gospel was legendary:

Five times I received from the Jews the forty lashes minus one.
Three times I was beaten with rods,
once I was stoned,
three times I was shipwrecked,
I spent a night and a day in the open sea,
I have been constantly on the move.
I have been in danger from rivers,
in danger from bandits,
in danger from my own countrymen,
in danger from Gentiles;
in danger in the city,
in danger in the country,
in danger at sea;
and in danger from false brothers.
I have labored and toiled and have often gone without sleep;
I have known hunger and thirst and have often gone without food;
I have been cold and naked.

2 CORINTHIANS 11:24-27

Does this sound like a man loved of God? If not, then perhaps your perception of God's love is skewed. For Paul was loved of God as are you, but that must not translate to the false expectation that God's love will insulate us from all pain and discomfort in this age. Rather, his love will carry us through them to the fullness of his glory and to an even greater harvest.

Even as Paul sat in a prison cell in Rome, abandoned and lonely, his execution just around the corner, his heart was steadfast in the Lord's victory. He didn't doubt his own fruitfulness even though many of the churches in Asia had abandoned him.

> *I have fought the good fight, I have finished the race, I have kept the faith. Now there is in store for me the crown of righteousness, which the Lord, the righteous Judge, will award to me on that day.*
> 2 TIMOTHY 4:7,8

Don't look to your circumstances for the measure of your harvest. You simply cannot trust your perceptions of them. The only way harvest is aborted in the life of a believer is if we give in to the enemy's devices to abandon our faith in the midst of difficult times, or if we suffer God's judgment because of rebellion. God did this to Israel, and will with us if we abandon him.

> *"I will take away their harvest," declares the Lord. "There will be no grapes on the vine. There will be no figs on the tree, and their leaves will wither. What I have given them will be taken from them."*
> JEREMIAH 8:13

What does all this say about my father's failed harvest? Did God wipe it out because of rebellion? No! Whether the enemy thwarted Dad's harvest, or whether he was simply a victim of capricious weather, what was really at stake was his faith. Here's where I learned more about faith than in any other single experience.

Many times I had seen rain clouds threaten and had prayed earnestly that God would protect our crop. I remember times when the rain pummeled our neighbors' vineyard but stopped almost directly along our property line. How we rejoiced at God's hand that spared us!

But the first time God didn't stop the rains, I watched my dad carefully. I saw him one afternoon staring out at his field, the rain pelting down in sheets. An inch had already fallen on the drying grapes a few days before and had damaged them severely. This second storm would spell their end. He knew that. I saw the helplessness and disappointment in his eyes and I felt as bad for him in that moment as I've ever felt for anyone. Didn't God care? How could he let this happen?

"What are we going to do, Dad?" I asked, wondering how we would eat in the coming year.

Through his disappointment his response was clear: "The Lord is faithful." After a long pause, "We'll just have to see how the Lord will provide for us in the year ahead."

And provide he did. I didn't miss any meals that year, but more importantly, I learned a valuable lesson. Confidence placed in a completed crop or a hefty bank account is a vain hope. Hope is better placed in God, who has more options to fulfill his will than we could ever guess.

Crops can be lost, just like circumstances in our life can be troublesome, but those are just circumstances. They needn't destroy our own personal fruitfulness for the kingdom. Far from it. What I learned in this circumstance is that even the most difficult trials can enhance our faith and therefore our spiritual fruitfulness. That's why the prophet Habakkuk could exclaim:

> *Though the fig tree does not bud*
> *and there are no grapes on the vines,*
> *though the olive crop fails*
> *and the fields produce no food . . .*
> *yet will I rejoice in the Lord,*
> *I will be joyful in God my Savior.*
> *The sovereign Lord is my strength.*

HABAKKUK 3:17-19

What an eloquent testimony of faith! God is our strength, and he is powerful enough to bring us through any circumstance, all the while making us more fruitful for his kingdom.

36

THE GROWING IS NOT YET OVER

*Let us live up to what
we have already attained.*
PHILIPPIANS 3:16

In the euphoria of harvest it is easy to reap the fruit of our past diligence, and lose sight of its continuing necessity. We see God using us and overlook our need to remain in the vine.

Admittedly the branch doesn't do much to participate in the harvest. After the grapes have matured they just hang there for whatever purpose the farmer desires. There's nothing more the branch can do for them. Does this mean it is inactive at the harvest? Hardly!

Scientists tell us that in the final stages of ripening, all the nutrients of the vine are drawn into the grapes. When the grapes are ripe there is little reserve anywhere on the vine. It has all been used to ripen the grapes. After that, the branches don't stop growing.

They continue to produce nourishment, which is stored in the trunk and roots of the vine. These storehouses were virtually depleted at summer's end as all the energy was going into the fruit. Now they are replenished. This growth continues until the very last days of fall, when the leaves finally wither and fall to the ground.

The cycle of sowing and reaping continues. Strength gained now will reap benefits in months to come. Next year's crop is already being formed in the buds of the first-year canes. This crop is being finalized, and if the branch were to let down now, next year's crop would be impaired.

The nutrients stored now will not be needed in the coming winter because the vine will go dormant. But it will be there next spring, when the branch explodes with new life. Before those leaves will be strong enough to produce their own nutrition, they will live off what it stores now.

"Remain in me." There is no season that the branch can afford not to heed that admonition. As much as in summer, our diligence to walk with Jesus and obey his commands must remain our priority, even though in these days it may seem less urgent. As God uses us to extend his kingdom, it is easy to neglect our own spiritual nourishment as we get distracted from cultivating our friendship with Jesus.

But it must continue at all times. We cannot allow ourselves to think that just because we are giving out, we can get by without being nourished. How many of us have seen men and women mightily used of God, only to suddenly take a big fall? The vineyard teaches us that such falls are not sudden at all. They result from preceding days of not remaining in the vine and drawing its life.

Perhaps such believers allow themselves to give too much. Their voice is the only teaching they hear, and their feeding comes by what they plan to share with others. But when our own relationship with the vine is severed, no matter how great the harvest we're in the midst of, we have begun to wither. An inner emptiness even in harvest can tell us that we've lost connection with the vine.

At all costs, cling to your friendship with Jesus as more valuable than anything in this life. Cherish his presence and go there often to replenish your life in him. Allow it to deepen. Listen to his voice and let him show you what he is doing in you beyond the harvest itself.

The cycle continues. A vineyard does not bear fruit once and then die. The hungers and vision that stir within it are for crops still to come. This is a good reminder for us and an encouragement to always continue growing. Throughout our lives there will be many seasons of fruitfulness, but if we ever look for one of them to be complete, I'm afraid we'll be disappointed. If one season of fruitfulness doesn't fulfill all your dreams and visions, don't be surprised. God will bring you to another season, and still another beyond that—until the day when final harvest comes and his reapers bring history to its conclusion. This is the harvest for which we all yearn with passions that will never be fulfilled in this age. We were not created for the sinful, finiteness of this world. We were created for all eternity in purity with Christ forever. Don't expect all your dreams to be fulfilled here.

Even those in the great roll call of faith in Hebrews 11 didn't receive the fullness of what was promised them in this life. "These were all commended for their faith, yet none of them received what had been promised. God had planned something better for us so that only together with us would they be made perfect" (Hebrews 11:39,40). All of God's working in us does not have its fulfillment here. He is preparing us for a greater day.

Here we know in part and see in part, but then the perfect will come. Then we will come into the full fruitfulness for which God chose us from the beginning. Look forward to that day with great anticipation. Our lives here are not worth clinging to. We are but a vapor, here for a moment and then gone. If we could really see our lives that way, no amount of suffering could thwart us, no pain could overwhelm us. God is preparing us for all eternity in his presence. What we've valued most dear in this life of eternal consequence is being saved for us there.

The branch is now ready for the winter ahead. Its storehouses are fully replenished. The euphoria of harvest ends, but it opens the door to an even more wondrous season beyond. You can already feel the chill in the air. Winter is at hand.

Winter

DAYS OF REST AND PREPARATION

In repentance and rest is your salvation, in quietness and trust is your strength.
ISAIAH 30:15

After the harvest, the vines begin to fade. The leaves yellow, having finished their task. The nutrients not used in this year's grape production have been stored for next year. The vineyard is shutting down, preparing for the winter rest that will recharge it for another year of fruitfulness.

Winter is at the threshold. It finally steps through the door at the first freeze, which in this valley usually comes in the waning days of November. Then rest comes quickly as the leaves turn a dirty brown, wilted reminders of a rich heritage, and fall earthward.

Early winter does not showcase the glory of the vineyard. No longer manufacturing their fruit, they have withdrawn their life-giving sap in response to the cold. The nearly barren canes curl upward against the sky, dark scrawls against the gray cast. The few leaves that are left dangle precariously from the branches, waiting for the slightest zephyr to pluck them free and settle them gently to the earth below.

The vineyard lies in chaos. Debris fills the rows between the vines. The canes, no longer hidden by their leafy dress, twist and turn inside each other in vivid disarray. Dark bunches of rotted grapes missed in the harvest hang limply,

uncovered by winter's nakedness. The wounds of the growing season are obvious. Some canes have broken off, while
others were split open by the weight of the ripening grapes.
They have even pulled down the wires between the vines as it
slumps from grapestake to grapestake.

This chaos of early winter stands in marked contrast to how
the vines will look at its end. Only a few months from now
these vines will stand pruned and neatly tied to a restretched
wire. The debris below will be worked into the soil, compost
for next year's harvest. Winter is where the growth cycle
begins. I have waited to the end to describe it, for it is only in
the aftermath of fruitfulness that we can understand its value.
It may seem harsh for the vine, but it is not. The vine actually
goes into rest so that the farmer can restage it for the year to
come.

We have winters, too, in our growth cycles. But these are
not the times when our love for God grows cold and he seems
distant. That's not winter. Spiritual winter comes when the
external fruitfulness of our life begins to fade, and God rests
and prepares us for another crop.

Often our circumstances will signal the coming of winter,
just as in the vineyard. They seem to turn against us. We are
doing all the same things, but nothing is as fruitful as it had
been before. Why is everything drying up? Will I ever be
fruitful again?

We've all been through moments like that and instead of
recognizing the onset of a new season, we usually redouble
our efforts to try to keep winter from coming. We pretend
instead that it is still fall—and try all the harder to produce
fruit by our own efforts.

Far better that we give in to God's work, for he is not distant
at times like this. He draws even closer to do a deeper work in
our heart. He doesn't relish the pain we face, but it is as true of
vines as it was of his own Son: We do learn obedience by the
things we suffer. If you will let your heart come to rest in him,
you will find your fellowship with him at such times far
greater than before.

This is where we must learn to rest in him. He is doing a work now, and that mostly without our help—only our continued surrender to his pleasure. If we learn to rest in him in winter, it won't be long until spring sweeps across our spirits again and fruitfulness once again graces our branches.

37

HELP, MY GLORY IS FADING!

Forgetting what is behind and straining toward what is ahead, I press on toward the goal to win the prize for which God has called me heavenward in Christ Jesus.

PHILIPPIANS 3:13,14

It's not easy to watch God's glory fade, and even harder not to do anything about it.

We've already seen two previous instances when the branch has to let go of God's working in one season to embrace his leading into another. The blossoms of spring needed to wither and fall so that the fruit could form. In the fall the ripened bunches had to be surrendered to the farmer for use as he saw fit. Now the branch must yield again, but this time it is a far greater yielding. For now it is not just blossoms and fruit that need to be let go, but the glory of the branch itself must surrender to the creeping coolness of winter.

To be a good branch on Jesus' vine it seems that you really have to do only two things: one, remain in the vine, treasuring friendship with Jesus every day, and two, let go of everything else, even the success of the harvest. Never hold onto God's work from one season or another. Serious disciples learn the secret of letting go. God moves on and invites us to go with him.

The glory of the vine cannot be found in its blooms, its fruit, or even its leaves and canes. Its glory exists only in the relationship it holds with the vine. That never changes. From season to season the one constant source of fulfillment is our friendship with Jesus.

One of the benefits of shifting seasons for us branches is the testing of our hearts. It is easier for us to fall in love with the trappings of Christianity than to keep our love for Jesus aflame. Almost without noticing, we substitute those trappings for the relationship itself, finding ourselves passionate for forms of worship or ministry more than we are for him. It is a subtle trap, and any disciple who doesn't admit to falling its victim is not telling it straight or not thinking it straight.

As a believer our security or glory must never be found in external things, even the things that God has done. When the apostle Paul summarized his guiding passion for life and ministry in Philippians 3 he said simply that it was to know Christ. Everything else in comparison was only rubbish, to be discarded in preference to exploring the depths of friendship with Jesus.

Then he gives us advice that every branch needs to learn thoroughly: We must always forget the things that lie behind us and press on toward the real prize to which God calls us. It's not just failures and sins that Paul was forgetting, but successes and joys as well.

Never is that danger greater for a believer than at the onset of spiritual winter. As we've seen, the harvest is a time of euphoria. Almost daily, opportunities to touch people with God's power fill our lives, and we watch God do amazing things through us. In such times righteousness seems to flow from us like a raging river; so wrapped up are we in God's working that temptations stay far distant. Even our most difficult moments are swallowed up by this overreaching joy.

But like all seasons, harvest too runs its course. Suddenly the opportunities aren't as laden with power as they had been previously, and they get fewer and further between. We don't seem as effective as we used to be, and we have to redouble our efforts just to get by. Temptations return with a vengeance, and every little thing that goes wrong irritates us.

What's happened? Why is my joy slipping away? Why am I not as effective as I had been? It's easy to panic if we don't recognize a shift of season. Our first conclusion is that something is wrong with us. We know the frailties of our flesh, and they provide a ready source for personal blame. But in doing so we forget that God's work through us comes only by his grace. We didn't earn it the first time and we certainly won't now. We try repentance, but it doesn't seem to be the answer. While it might refresh our walk with the Lord, we still watch helplessly as the harvest withers. Suddenly other people are being more effective than I am. What am I going to do?

Most of us prefer to hide the fading. If we don't let anybody see it, they won't know that the harvest is over. So we cover it up, most commonly with busyness. We push through by our own effort what had seemed so graced before. But one thing is so very odd about our approach to the fading of harvest: I've never seen it duplicated in the vineyard. No farmer I know ever tries to hold onto the harvest, hiding its end lest someone think him a failure. Every farmer celebrates not only the harvest, but also its end.

The onset of winter is not something to be lamented—far from it. These are the days where the vineyard is restored for a new year. The activity is not as fast, and the farmer has time in the winter to give attention to other needs in the vineyard. The pace slows, and I've never met a farmer who wasn't relieved to have the crop in and winter approach. This is not embarrassment; it is nature's way, which is to say quite accurately that it is also God's way.

Any act of ministry in the kingdom of God is not open-ended, going on until the second advent. God harvests in specific seasons through specific people. If we recognize this fact we can allow specific harvest times to come to completion—to celebrate and let go. Yet who does that today? Most ministries keep going on far after God's harvest, institutionalized into lifeless programs. The early church didn't do that. Paul and Barnabas went out on their first outreach through Asia and then came back, because "they had been committed to the grace of God for the work they had now completed." They didn't start a denomination or build an outreach center.

Their task was done. They could celebrate it and get on to what else Jesus wanted them to do. They didn't do everything they could have done in Asia. Their time there had not been without trouble and failure. Not everyone was touched. But that particular harvest was over. It was time to let it go.

God does a work, mines it for its maximum usefulness, and then lets it go to raise up other ministries. How many people are trapped administering programs that have long since been lifeless? Can't we find the courage to say that something can be finished without being a failure?

We can't live in harvest all of the time, not without destroying the life of the branch. Those who define normal Christianity in the days of harvest will be frustrated most of their lives. Such times will come to an end, not by your failures, but by God's design. When opportunity around you slows, when you don't seem to be as effective as you have been, when God seems a little harder to get to, don't panic. It's time to get on to a new season, where your life can be refreshed and renewed and a future harvest assured.

A new season is at hand, and that is not failure unless your priorities are skewed. If you look for fruit in the middle of winter, you will by that definition be a failure. But if you are continuing to pursue your friendship with Jesus, you'll find it just another season to enjoy him. Unlike Moses, whose glory really faded, Paul says that we serve a covenant whose glory only increases. But don't judge that by externals. The true glory is the depth of friendship which Christ builds within our lives and the shaping that makes us more like him. That process passes through a variety of seasons, some more glorious than others in external matters, but all of them inviting us to greater touches of his grace.

Winter is a glorious time when God reshapes us from the effects of ministry past to release us to more fruitful days ahead. In doing so it tests the affections of our heart. Have we done what we've done because of our love and obedience to Christ, or has it been for our own sense of fulfillment and success? The onset of winter will let you know for sure.

If you have a hard time letting go because you need your busyness to feel important, then perhaps the reshaping is more needed than you know. I've done it. In times past I've come to the end of harvest's euphoria to a slackened pace that makes me feel worthless. Instead of seeing my increasing ineffectiveness in areas in which I had previously been competent as an invitation of God to restoration and refreshing, I took it as a threat to my calling and ministry.

Instead of letting God deal with those insecurities, I've looked for other ways to busy myself: Join another committee, plan another outreach, start another Bible study. I didn't like the quiet. I wanted to be fruitful for God, and in doing so I resisted his work. Burying myself in busyness, I tried to run from the pruning he wanted to do in me.

But faithful God that he is, he was patient with my misdirected zeal. He even blessed some of those outreaches and Bible studies in ways that still amaze me. But I have since learned that when things slow down, God is addressing something inside. He's moving me to a new place of dependence. Don't worry about work that seems undone, God has it for others to do.

Don't be surprised if after your greatest victories comes what you might perceive to be your greatest failure, but if it's just fall moving on to winter, don't be alarmed. The attention now will shift away from developing fruit and spreading leaves. The priority that takes center stage now is that vital link between vine and branch. If you have the courage in these days to set aside the ministries that God has brought to completion in your life, you'll have more time and energy to devote to deepening your friendship with Jesus.

These are the best days for personal retreats and extended time in his presence. As things grow quiet, you'll see more clearly God's direction in your life, and even some of your own less-than-pure motives that have sneaked in or been exposed by the growing season. Don't fear it or resist it. Finding that you've done things for God with less than absolute purity does not negate your obedience or destroy its effectiveness. It only provides the opportunity for the Father to do an even deeper work in you in the winter ahead.

38

THE COLDER THE BETTER

Be still, and know that I am God.
PSALM 46:10

What is more serene than the earth under a blanket of freshly fallen snow? Though we may appreciate that such a scene best when looking out on it from the comfy confines of a winter cabin with a roaring fire in its hearth, the morning after a snowstorm is an awesome sight. The vivid blue sky almost pours down through the trees and the sun reflects in splendor off the white blanket below.

But to really experience its beauty you must go out in it, not because you have to get to work, but just to admire it. That's when you notice the stillness. Nature has come to a standstill. The only sound to be heard is snow crunching underfoot. Have you ever noticed how most people who behold such a scene speak in muted tones, not wanting to defile it with harsh voices?

Take that same image into the vineyard. In our valley it is not snow-covered. It has snowed only once on our vineyard, and only four inches at that. Mostly our winters are filled with a low, gray overcast that swaddles the vineyard into the same serenity of the most ideal winter landscape.

Quiet and stillness is winter's glory, but it is brought about once again by a seemingly hostile climate. This is the second season born of hostility. The heat of summer sought to destroy

273

the vine's fruitfulness, but persevering in it only helped bring the fruit to completion. Winter is also a hostile climate, except that this time we don't prevail by perseverance but by patience and rest.

I realize this is a difficult season to sell. Few of us look on winter with great longing to be refreshed and rested. Instead we dread the harsh climate and endure it by looking forward to the warmer days of summer. But it is just the opposite for a vine. Summer was the season of warfare as it battled the hostile forces bent on destroying our fruit. Fall, too, was a time of multiplied activity and intensive effort. The cold of winter lulls the vine to a much-needed rest.

So does God with us, but not because he turns cold and unresponsive. Quite the contrary, it is during this season of rest and restaging that God draws even closer to us, putting a greater priority on our relationship with him and his Son.

There are two ways that God brings us to winter. One is circumstantial, as we saw in the last chapter; the external trappings of our spiritual life become less effective. The second is by calling, where God directs us to lay some things aside and for a time give greater attention to our relationship with him. Both signal an end of a season of fruitfulness in order to prepare for another.

There are many instances of such seasons in Scripture, though given their nature we don't always get a great deal of detail with them. Moses on the back side of the desert was in a time of transition, from a prince in Pharaoh's court to an ambassador and deliverer on God's behalf. The children of Israel passing through the wilderness also comprised a winter season as God sought to forge a people who could go into the Promised Land and be fruitful.

Jesus' experience in the wilderness after his baptism also provided God an opportunity to prepare him for his public days of ministry. We don't know what happened in the wilderness, since Scripture only details for us the temptations of the very last day. But Luke tells us that Jesus went out full of the Spirit and returned in the power of the Spirit. Jesus recaptured similar moments when he withdrew from the crowds to lonely places for prayer.

Because of these examples the winter season is often referred to as a wilderness experience, and though I won't begrudge the term I will take exception to some of what has been taught as a wilderness experience. If by wilderness we mean a time where God calls us to a season of undistracted attention away from the busyness that ensnares us, I will wholeheartedly agree.

But I've heard many people define the wilderness as a time when God withdraws his conscious presence from us in order to deepen our faith. Nowhere does Scripture suggest such an idea. God wants to increase our dependence upon him, not teach us how to live without him. I will grant you that God will allow certain methods we've used to touch him to dry up, but only so that we'll come looking for him in fresh ways that he wants to reveal himself. In fact, many of our winters may begin just that way: The old patterns have grown lifeless, and God beckons us to a fresh discovery.

The rest of winter is not the result of burnout. The vine is not wasted from its fruitfulness, and in fact has more strength reserves at the end of fall than at any other time of the year. If autumn was particularly dry, my father would give his field one last irrigation. The farmer ensures that dormancy comes as part of the normal growth cycle, not as the result of carelessness or starvation. A healthy vine rests while a starved vine withers, and the distinction between these two, though not always evident in winter, will be obvious next spring.

There is the prevailing view in the body of Christ today that burnout is an essential cost of doing business in the kingdom of God. I disagree. Burnout is the expression of a life that has not trusted in God's strength but its own. It has run on its own motives or has propped up some activity far longer than God graced it. I know, for I myself have fallen prey to it, as most believers have. We need to recognize that those on the verge of burnout are not healthy people before they go out in a smoldering blaze. Admittedly, that recognition is not easy, for burned-out people always look their best the day before they crash. They are so willing and helpful that they usually serve as a model for others, the epitome of a zealous believer. But if you listen closely you'll see weariness, complaints that others aren't doing their part, or a family crying out for attention.

Rather than being applauded, these people should be lovingly confronted. Their response to God's work has not been borne out of intimacy with him, but out of insecurity in themselves. Burnout is resolved not by "getting away from it all" but by repenting and letting God change our motivations and our responses to him. God still loves us and will still take a burned-out believer into winter to prune away the dependence on self-effort, but only if we can recognize it as a problem. Those in professional ministry are especially at risk of finding their identity in their achievements rather than in their relationship to Christ. Yet what more can you be than a son or daughter of God?

When you recognize the onset of winter in your spiritual life, give in to God's call to stillness. Find extra time to seek his face, and be patient when it may not come with ease. This doesn't mean that we abandon all our responsibilities and go sit in a desert, but it does mean that we rest from our labors and stop striving so hard for success that we miss God drawing us. It's not that God can't speak to us in our hyperactivity but rather that we are incapable of hearing him and responding.

Among the leadership teams in our church God has established the freedom for people to take a leave of absence when they sense that God wants to reorder their life. Though they are still an active part of the fellowship, they back away from the demands of a leadership role. They do it without judgment or suspicion, because we recognize that to stay fresh with God we've got to periodically let him reorganize us. It's a good test for anyone to see whether or not he can lay aside what God has done in him. It's good for people around them, too, because it shows whether people have become dependent upon God or on the vessels he uses.

Winter is God drawing us to the quiet, where he does his deepest work. I've never heard it scientifically explained, but every farmer knows that the colder the winter is, the better the crop will be in the season to come. Mild winters lead to average yields. It seems the further the sap is driven into the vine, the more explosive its return.

The more we let God slow us down, and the more we let him put us on the sidelines, the better we will come out of it empowered for the days ahead. We need to welcome the stillness, for only then can we hear the depths of God's heart and find his true leadings.

39

THE PAUSE THAT REFRESHES

He makes me lie down in green pastures, he leads me beside quiet waters.
PSALM 23:2

I've seen worn-out grape branches. Either by overuse or because insects have eaten out the inside, they are weakened. These are not easy to see under the profuse canopy of leaves that hides the branches much of the year, but once the leaves have fallen off they are easy to spot. Most of the branch is no longer connected to the vine; it holds on only by the lightest touch.

Once a branch has overspent itself, it is worthless. The canes that spring from it are weak and lifeless, and most of them could never reach the wire to be used again for another year. Many of these I've cut off with a saw to allow a new branch to grow from that side of the vine.

Fortunately, God doesn't deal so severely with worn-out believers, or we would be in real trouble. Yet, I have no doubt that he laments them just as much as the farmer does a broken branch. "Harassed and helpless, like sheep without a shepherd" is how Jesus described one crowd of people. You can always tell a shepherdless sheep just like you can tell a gardenerless vineyard: They are weary and worn-out—surviving, coping, and all the while slowly dying.

The slowed days of winter fly in the face of our frenetic pace of life. This is the gardener leading his vineyards to rest in the same way the shepherd takes his sheep to green pastures and quiet water. There they lie down to rest. The waters that nurse them there are quiet, not raging.

If we learned this well enough, perhaps the expression "to be busy for God" would be an oxymoron. It is the world that invites us to busyness. Take it from one who used to find most of his identity in a crammed schedule, proving by activity his worth to God. It is a fool's trap that has made busyness a coveted merit badge in the kingdom of God.

God doesn't want our busyness; he wants our *obedience*. But how can we be obedient if we're not still enough to hear his voice? That's not to say there won't be periods in our obedience when activities will press from every side, but we just shouldn't pitch our tent there. God will lead us through it and then back out again to lie down in green pastures. I fear sometimes that we are reacting to the lazy Christian epidemic by becoming something gruesome on the other extreme.

So complicated do we let our lives become that we are always exhausted. Running on increasing doses of adrenaline, we miss the voice that comes only in the stillness.

Winter depicts the vineyard at rest. During these months two important things will happen. The first one we're considering here—the vines will be refreshed by the rest. It's time for a break. The second thing we'll examine in the next chapter—the vines are pruned to make them more fruitful. The two go together. Only out of rest and quiet can we let the Lord shape our lives according to his will. For there is our strength.

> *In repentance and rest is your salvation, in quietness and trust is your strength, but you would have none of it.*
> ISAIAH 30:15

Why then do we resist this so in our attempts to compress fruitful activity into virtually every moment of the day? Even most of my recreational pursuits have an alternative agenda, either to keep my weight in check or to develop relationships with others. None of this is bad in itself, but it does keep my life so cluttered with objectives, that it's rarely quiet enough to hear the voice of God that wants to shape my life.

We are a society that resists the quiet. At every point our senses take in a wide array of sights and sounds. That may be why our worship and prayer often take so long to connect: We have to get past all the clutter that fills our mind.

Part of the reason God instituted the Sabbath was to demonstrate the connection between rest and our relationship to God. He didn't suspend activity that day as a religious exercise, but that by quieting our hearts we could commune with him better. He even gave instructions about Sabbath years: Take a whole year off; cancel debts; trust God to provide. But there's no record that Israel ever did it. They probably couldn't agree on which year was the seventh.

The writer of Hebrews tells us that God was making available to his people a rest in which we cease from our own labors. We've already seen throughout our study of the year's seasons how we must rely on God's power to bring fruitfulness and fulfillment in our lives. We cannot do it by our own strength. The lesson we learn now in winter applies throughout the year: God must do the work.

This doesn't mean we become spiritual couch potatoes, sitting back and assuming that God will accomplish what he needs to. No, he wants to work *through* you. Ceasing our own labors means that we give up our wearying agendas, and instead embrace his. Certainly there is work for us to do. Paul found no conflict between the rest of God and "to this end I labor, struggling with all his energy, which so powerfully works in me" (Colossians 1:29).

But Paul was pursuing *God's* objectives and not his own, and I doubt he did it around the clock. Effort can be intensive without being all-encompassing. Remember, we were created to romp in a garden, not toil from sunrise to sunset, and that which God calls us to do embraces the former and not the latter. Jesus said that his yoke was easy and his burden was light. Instead of being drained by it all, we should, like Jesus with the woman at the well, be nourished by our obedience.

That makes a good indication of whose strength we're living on. Are we being exhausted or renewed? If exhausted, we had better find out what God *really* wants us to be doing, and cease from our own labors.

> *The fruit of righteousness will be peace; the effect of righteousness will be quietness and confidence forever. My people will live in peaceful dwelling places, in secure homes, in undisturbed places of rest.*
>
> ISAIAH 32:17,18

God doesn't need a bunch of weary, worn-out vines as a showcase for the glory of his kingdom. That is not an attraction to unbelievers. One of my neighbors had a bad experience somewhere with seeing someone's life swallowed up by the demands of her Christian activities. There's no end to her boasting of all the free time she has because *she* doesn't go to church. Scary, isn't it?

Obviously there are aspects to this rest and refreshing that we need to find every day in our lives, but in the winter of our spiritual growth there is a heightened need for us to draw away and let the Lord refresh us by lying down in his green pasture and drinking of quiet waters.

We need to learn to cultivate quietness in our life. We need to put away the clutter that ravages our spiritual sensitivity and come to the fountain where God refreshes his beloved. One of the tools that can help with stilling our hearts is fasting. Depriving our flesh its appetites may heighten its complaints, but it also heightens our sensitivity to God.

In India, in the region where the vineyards grow, it never gets cold enough to send the vines into dormancy. So after the harvest the farmers induce dormancy artificially. By stripping off the leaves, pruning the roots, and depriving the vine of water, they can stimulate dormancy without the cold weather. This still produces the same effect: The vine rests. Fasting does that spiritually. Deprivation of our physical appetites can open the doors to a deeper touch with God, if it is based on our willingness to surrender to him, and not as a mere exercise in spirituality.

God has promised us seasons of refreshing in this life so that our lives don't look as harassed and helpless as the world's. Here is where God does his deepest work in us, renewing our relationship with him and pruning our activities to restage our priorities for another season of fruitfulness.

40

SUBMITTING TO THE MASTER'S PRUNING

He cuts off every branch in me that bears no fruit, while every branch that does bear fruit he prunes so that it will be even more fruitful.
JOHN 15:2

The sap slows to nearly a standstill. It is now the middle of winter. The dried leaves have all fallen, and only the canes remain. Now the winter labor of the farmer can begin. There's one major activity which the farmer attends to in the winter, and it is the only one out of the entire year that is specifically highlighted in John 15. That's not surprising, since there is no action the farmer will take in a year that will have more impact on the health and fruitfulness of the vine than *pruning*.

Most of the time the farmer cares for the vine by protecting it from the enemies that want to destroy it. But pruning gives him the opportunity to shape the vine to make it as fruitful as possible. That's why my father hated to hire any outsiders. Hasty and careless pruning by those who only wanted to get the job done could ruin the vine for seasons to come.

So on cold winter mornings during our Christmas school break and on weekends thereafter my father would take his four sons into the vineyard to prune. Bundled up against the cold, we could barely move, but with pruning shears in hand we would follow.

A vine in winter is a confusing array of light tan canes that sprawl from a vine like broken watch springs. All emerged last spring as flexible green tubes, but they have now become woody sticks that shoot from every corner of the vine. Small dark-brown buds are spaced several inches apart down the entire length of every cane, some of which stretch to 12 feet or more in length. The buds are about half the size of a pencil eraser and quite hard. In each bud the bunches of fruit for the coming year are already formed. During the summer, while the current crop was ripening, next year's was also developing. That's why grapes are considered a two-year crop.

That next crop is all right here even in the middle of winter. Each bud contains one primary bunch, fully formed, albeit at microscopic size. In each bud there are also one or two secondary bunches that will sprout if something happens to damage the first. The only problem is that there are too many bunches for the vine to carry to harvest. Each cane holds 20 to 25 buds, and there are anywhere from 40 to 60 canes on each vine. There are far more buds on the vine than it will be able to sustain.

Unpruned grapevines will grow into the next season. In fact, in one way they'll look healthier than a pruned vine. Foliage will burst forth everywhere, and so will the small grape bunches. But most will fall off, and those that don't will stay small and not ripen fully. The vine will be overwhelmed, and the next season there will not be any grapes at all, for no new bunches will be formed in the buds that summer because the vine is far overextended. That's why pruning is so essential to vine growth.

Snip. Snip. Snip. The shears tear into the vine, reducing the proliferous number of canes to only five! That's all the vine will be able to support in the coming year. The rest are cut off and dragged to the middle of the row, where they will be chewed up as compost. What remains is a vine radically transformed from confusion and chaos into a simple, stately form with five canes arching gracefully into the winter sky.

Leon Morris in the *New International Commentary* points out why God prunes us:

> *Left to itself a vine will produce a good deal of un-productive growth. For maximum fruitfulness extensive pruning is essential. This is a suggestive fig-ure for the Christian life. The fruit of Christian service is never the result of allowing the natural ener-gies and inclinations to run riot.*

So God prunes us, and that process is not without its discomfort. Where all the canes are cut off, open wounds remain. They will heal soon enough, but we now see why pruning can only be safely done in the dormancy of winter. Only after the sap has slowed and the vine is at rest will pruning do the least amount of damage. Damage? Yes, prun-ing is organized destruction.

Even the Greek word used of pruning in John 15 conveys that meaning. Everywhere else in the New Testament it is translated "destroy" or "demolish." John 15 is its only posi-tive use, but it does show the objective of the pruning. The number of canes which the vine needed last year to provide foliage for last year's crop to ripen is now a threat to the vine in the year ahead if they are all allowed to bear fruit.

It is surgery of the highest order, and unless the branch is at rest when the process begins, this cutting would destroy the branch itself. But now during winter the sap is not flowing (or else it would drain the vine's strength), and diseases and pests that would infect the wounds are also dormant.

Pruned correctly, the vine's growth will be spread out evenly over the vine; it will carry the right amount of fruit that it can take to term, and its shape will facilitate the other aspects of care which the farmer will give the vine over the coming growing season.

What a marvelous picture of the surgery that God has to do periodically in our lives! He prunes us so that we bear even more fruit. This means he cuts away things that clutter our lives. Yes, it wounds us, but these are the wounds of a friend, who cuts softly and tenderly, realizing that separation is painful and will cause hurt.

He prunes us while we are at rest. In an environment where we are being refreshed by his presence, the wounds are not so painful nor so likely to be used by the enemy to engender bitterness or rebellion in our lives. In the climate of quiet and peace he can prune us with minimal damage.

And so he cuts. First, to rid us of those canes that are broken or unhealthy. Part of pruning is for God to cut away where worldly passions and distractions are siphoning off our spiritual life. Attitudes surface that we either had not recognized before or had disguised by our rationalizations. During pruning we will have a keener sense of our sinfulness, because God is calling us to repentance and to cutting ties where the enemy keeps a foothold.

God is serious about our sin, not holding it against us, but neither wanting us to hold onto it in the mistaken notion that grace will cover it. Sin, if we refuse to let God cut it away, will eventually catch up with us and destroy us. To show how serious God was about it, Jesus said:

> *If your right hand causes you to sin, cut it off and throw it away. It is better for you to lose one part of your body than for your whole body to go into hell.*
>
> MATTHEW 5:30

Second, he cuts to restage our lives under his agenda. Growth and harvest have a way of multiplying opportunities in our lives, but those opportunities have the capacity not only to spread our lives so thin that we are fruitless, but also to distract us from our friendship with Jesus. If you want to stay busy even as God leads you to winter, you will have plenty of opportunity, but take them at your own peril.

Since there are two or three branches on each vine, each branch will only be allowed to keep two or three canes for the coming year. Pruning allows God to set our focus, so that we can concentrate on what he wants us to do rather than trying to do everything we can. Better to do few things fruitfully rather than a lot of things that only turn out to be empty foliage.

I know people like that. In fact, I've been like that myself. Externally I looked productive, busily rushing from one meeting to another or jumping from one project to the next. Leaves everywhere! How intoxicating busyness can be. But I couldn't find the fruit. My spiritual life was so diluted by my myriad of activities that none of them were bearing anything more than paltry, unripened fruit.

Busyness is not the goal of a conscientious believer, fruitfulness is. Not every request that comes my way is God's will for me to accept. Good opportunities are not necessarily godly ones. Pressure from others is not the direction of the Holy Spirit. Almost monthly I'm asked to serve on someone's board or help out with some activity. I can't do it all, and I periodically need to draw near to God to let him cut away those things that he doesn't want me involved in.

"The grace of God . . . teaches us to say 'no,'" Paul wrote to Titus; no to the worldly passions that destroy us and no to the opportunities that overwhelm us. Notice that it's not *fear* that teaches us to say no, but *grace*. Because we can trust God and know that he will lead us into the fullness of joy, we are free to say no even to the things that we desire, whether good or bad.

Jesus said no to the enemy's temptations, knowing that God's way was better. He didn't rush to Lazarus' side when he first heard he was sick. He stayed two days longer to finish what he was doing before he joined the friends he deeply loved. Given Paul's explanations in his epistles, he didn't rush either to churches that desired him to come, following God's agenda instead.

The first pastor I worked with in Fresno was a master at this, and I wish I had learned it better from him. He could refuse the pressures and expectations of others and stay in the corridor of his own obedience better than anyone I've ever known. We need to have the same freedom in the body of Christ; to say no by God's grace to someone's request without having our love or our appreciation for his or her ministry questioned. It hurts me deeply when I have to refuse a request to help out another ministry and hear later that it was supposedly due to my lack of support or value of that ministry.

There's just too much going on for all of us to participate. We've got to free ourselves and each other to be focused toward those few things that God has really called us to. That's the only way to be fruitful: Draw near to God and let him show you what his plans are for you. His grace will teach you to say no.

But say no you must, for unlike the grapevines I approached with my pruning shears, which had absolutely no say in the matter, it seems we do. God's pruning requires our submission. We have to willingly let go of that which he wants to prune from us, and even after he prunes it he won't prevent us from grabbing it back. He will only continue to gently call us to lay it down.

The life that listens to God is not a whirlwind of activity, but a focused life. It results in simplicity, power, and joy. Don't resist God's pruning. It is your fulfillment and fruitfulness he is working to enhance.

41

TIED TO
THE WIRE

*Everyone who competes in the games goes into
strict training. They do it to get a crown that
will not last; but we do it to get a crown
that will last forever.*

1 CORINTHIANS 9:25

In my father's vineyard a long, shiny wire runs the length of each vineyard row. Held in place by stakes driven into the ground next to each vine, it is a simple but lifesaving tool: It supports the canes above the vine so they won't break under the foliage and fruit of the new season.

All of that fruit weighs a significant amount, and since the canes arc gracefully up from the vine, the load will pull them to the point where the cane will either split or break from the branch altogether. Either way, the fruit is lost, a victim of the cane's success.

So the last thing the farmer does in winter is to wrap the canes around the wire. Two canes from each vine run down the wire in one direction and three go in the opposite direction. When a row is tied on the wire it looks as if an unending cane stretches the length of the field. Everything is in a straight line, and any canes left untied look so out of place that they are noticeable from a great distance.

This tying is not a difficult task for the farmer, but it is for the canes. They are almost a year old now and not at all as pliable as they used to be. Their woody grain makes them quite rigid, and the farmer's attempts to curve them back to the wire and wrap them around it is often met with resistance. The canes try to slip from the farmer's grasp and protest with popping and snapping as he reins them in.

Here's where the worker must be careful. If he pulls on a cane too abruptly or at the wrong angle the cane will break off, and one-fifth of the crop of that vine will be lost, since there are no other canes to replace the broken one. (Remember, the excess canes were pruned away earlier.) The farmer must take the cane in hand and curve it gently back to the wire in an arc that will not break it. Gentleness is the key to training.

The cane would rather remain free, able to reach out to the heavens unrestricted by the wire and the other canes it is tied with. It doesn't know how much it needs the wire, for it doesn't need it right now. Only when the fruit begins to ripen will it need that support. By then, however, it will be too late to wrap the cane on the wire without breaking off most of the new growth. God does the same with us. I see two applications of this in believers today. First, there is the believer who has strong calling and vision, but who never sees it fulfilled. He usually has had a number of starts, but never found his way to fruitful completion. Years later he has the same vision but is no closer to actually fulfilling it.

All too often we sense God's calling in our heart, and then set out to accomplish it in our own way. Though we may find some measure of external success in our own efforts, the biblical fruitfulness we anticipate never comes. Unless our calling is reined in with godly supports, that will always be the case.

The second application is even more tragic. The history of the body of Christ is littered with people who were not strong enough to withstand their own success. We all know those who started with wonderful ministries only to be swallowed up by success. Either pride or sin ran rampant beneath the surface. All too many times people have told me such a story and ended it with, "I just don't understand. How can God use someone like that so powerfully and have it end this way?"

Behind every story like that is a testimony of someone who stepped out unsupported in his or her growth and fruitfulness. Most were Lone Rangers. People who separate themselves from others should always remain suspect, since God gave us specific structures that support his working in us.

I realize I risk alienating some people by the word "structures." For those people who have tasted too deeply of institutionalized structures which have preserved a form of godliness long past the time God's power inhabited it, such a term can be disconcerting. But it doesn't need to be. God has given us structures that can support the work he is doing in our lives.

The apostle Paul wrestled with that issue in his letter to the Corinthians. He used an analogy of a boxer that can without discipline go through all the right motions but still not achieve the prize. Therefore he trained diligently in spiritual matters to ensure that his vision followed through to fruitfulness. And so must we.

The support of God's work in us is first secured by our continued friendship with Jesus. Structures of personal worship, Bible study, body life, and service must continue to hold primary importance in our growth. Too many people replace ministry for relationship, and soon everything dries up.

Specifically, however, there are three things that support God's work in us.

First, pray! Just because you know what God wants to do, don't assume you know how he wants to do it. Wherever God is calling you to focus, make sure that this goal stays at the top of your prayer list. Salt it with prayer all the time. In doing so, listen to God. When he wants to accomplish something in your life he will give you simple steps to follow to bring that plan about.

Don't be surprised if those steps don't look like they are direct ones to what he has promised. But follow them anyway. Who would have thought that Paul's missionary trips would be launched from little-known Antioch instead of Jerusalem? But he was in Antioch in response to God's working, and Antioch became the great mission church of first-generation Christianity.

If you want to participate with one of our worship teams on Sunday mornings, we'll first look to see if you're there early to pray with our existing teams and to help them set up the sound system and transparencies in our rented quarters. We want to see you worshiping aggressively already without having to lead. Those who sit and wait for it to happen are usually disappointed. God will give you a place to start if you're willing to follow him.

Second, be obedient. Write down the things God speaks to you and follow through with them. I don't know how many times I've sensed God's voice about something but plodded along by my own wisdom having forgotten what it was he told me to do.

Third, invite some other believers to come alongside you in prayer and honest dialogue as God fulfills his work. They can help confirm the validity of what you're hearing, thereby ensuring that it is not a result of a wild imagination. They can also hold you accountable to the steps of obedience that God gives you.

You don't need many such fellow believers—only two or three with whom you can be blatantly honest and who will respond in kind with you. Most people who falter lack this depth of insight and honesty. They may have many people watching from the outside or commenting as "yes people," but they have no one close enough to perceive the dangers and encourage them when they begin to fall. Without supportive relationships of loving believers few of us will follow through enough to really find fruitfulness.

The emphasis here is on *supportive* relationships. Too many of us have had experiences with believers judging us, criticizing us with jealousy, or wanting to use us for their ends. Supportive relationships are built on encouragement. Though they embrace genuineness and honesty, they come out of a sincere concern for your welfare and growth in Christ.

With your canes firmly wrapped around these supports you can rest confidently, knowing that God will be able to complete his work in you. Take hope; winter is now almost over. Rested and restaged, the vine is ready for another season of growth.

We have now come to the waning days of winter. It is only mid-February, but in the short winters of California's San Joaquin Valley, spring is just around the corner. It has already been in the 70's earlier this afternoon, urging the winter to succumb to the ever-lengthening days.

It's just after 5:30 in the afternoon and the long, yellow rays of the setting sun have surrendered to violet-tinted shades of pink. The evening chill comes quickly, and I zip up my coat against the light breeze, pulling the collar up around my neck, then thrusting my hands into its pockets.

This is where we began many pages ago. We've come around to it again, for spring with its burst of joy and fresh vision is just around the corner. A new year in the vineyard is about to begin!

Finale

GO AND BEAR FRUIT

The seasons of the vineyard demonstrate different ways that God works with us, but of course he is far more creative than the illustration allows. We have looked at some of the ways God works in our lives, not only so we won't be surprised when they happen, but also so we'll know better how we might respond to him.

But don't be surprised if they don't fit in so neat a box. Rarely do I find my life definable in exclusively one season or another. God's work in me at any one time may be a blending of different facets of these seasons. In my own life I find God calling me to endurance in some areas where fruit is maturing; but in other areas where my own efforts have taken over for God I see him with pruning shears in hand. In still others fresh growth is breaking out.

I still encounter circumstances I can't fully define. I sometimes endure periods where I'm not sure at all what God is doing, but by hanging in there I'll see how it all works out. But this is all part of the dynamic of following after God's heart in this age. In the very same chapter of Ecclesiastes that began our study of the seasons, where Solomon outlined how God does different things at different times, he concludes with an interesting statement: "He has made everything beautiful in its time. He has also set eternity in the hearts of men; yet they cannot fathom what God has done from beginning to end."

Even though we may not understand it now, God moves with a plan, and what burns in our hearts is far larger than our mind will comprehend. It is sufficient for us to know that he will make all things, including our hopes and visions, beautiful in his time.

In the meantime, pursue your friendship with Jesus at all costs. Continue to carve out meaningful time with him regardless of the distractions of this age. Settle for nothing less than fullness of joy welling up within and seasons of fruitfulness when you can see his glory produced through you and made available to a dying generation.

Jesus' simple summary of John 15 will suffice for this work as well: "Go and bear fruit." When it's all said and done, what matters is the fruit we have borne for the kingdom of God, purchased by our friendship with him and expressed in our transformed lives. He is fully capable of leading us to that.

My prayer is that this passage, John 15:1-17, will fill your heart with a desire never to settle for anything less than a fullness of joy in your relationship to him, and the fruit that results from such fulfillment. Every time you read this passage, I hope it stimulates hunger in your heart and a broadened perspective of what it means to be a branch on the vine of the Father's vineyard.

> *I am the true vine,*
> *   and my Father is the gardener.*
> *He cuts off every branch in me that bears no fruit,*
> *   while every branch that does bear fruit he prunes*
> *   so that it will be even more fruitful.*
>
> *You are already clean*
> *   because of the word I have spoken to you.*
> *Remain in me, and I will remain in you.*
> *   No branch can bear fruit by itself; it must remain*
> *   in the vine.*
> *Neither can you bear fruit*
> *   unless you remain in me.*
>
> *I am the vine;*
> *   you are the branches.*

If a man remains in me and I in him,
  he will bear much fruit;
  apart from me you can do nothing.
If anyone does not remain in me,
  he is like a branch that is thrown away and withers;
Such branches are picked up,
  thrown into the fire and burned.

If you remain in me and my words remain in you,
  ask whatever you wish, and it will be given you.
This is to my Father's glory, that you bear much fruit,
  showing yourselves to be my disciples.

As the Father has loved me,
  so have I loved you.
Now remain in my love.
If you obey my commands,
  you will remain in my love,
Just as I have obeyed my Father's commands
  and remain in his love.

I have told you this so that my joy may be in you
  and that your joy may be complete.
My command is this: Love each other
  as I have loved you.
Greater love has no one than this,
  that he lay down his life for his friends.
You are my friends if you do what I command.

I no longer call you servants,
  because a servant does not know his
  master's business.
Instead, I have called you friends,
  for everything that I learned from my Father
  I have made known to you.
You did not choose me, but I chose you
  and appointed you to go and bear fruit—
  fruit that will last.
Then the Father will give you
  whatever you ask in my name.
This is my command: Love each other.

Acknowledgments

No one person writes a book. There are so many who contribute to its formation and content. Allow me to thank a few.

- My father, Gene Jacobsen, who (after the Scriptures themselves) was my primary resource for the nature and growth of grapevines. He has spent all his life teaching me God's ways as revealed in the vineyard.

- Elaine Roberts, personal friend and personal editor, who reads just about every word I write before anybody else, not only improving them significantly but also making me think a bit more deeply.

- Bill Jensen of Harvest House for entrusting me with his idea for a book on God's vineyard.

- Eileen Mason, editor at Harvest House, who, along with her staff, shaped much of the final outcome of this work. She not only lends me her wisdom and counsel but offers me more encouragement and patience than anyone deserves.

- To Savior's, one of the most incredible churches in the world, which allows me to be a friend among friends, helping to equip my life and release my call wherever God desires.

And most of all, to my wonderful wife, Sara, and my two children, Julie and Andy, who with grace and support pay a greater price than anyone else in allowing me to bring to completion what God speaks to my heart.

Other Good Harvest House Reading

A PASSION FOR GOD'S PRESENCE
by *Wayne Jacobsen*

Clothed in expensive architecture, elaborate programs, and impressive statistics, the modern church has all too often traded the presence of God for the nakedness of religious form. Jacobsen gives a clear and inspiring view of what true intimacy with God entails and offers a blueprint that every person can use to build that intimacy.

SILENT STRENGTH FOR MY LIFE
by *Lloyd John Ogilvie*

Gladness . . . refreshment . . . encouragement . . . renewal . . . these are the rich rewards of quiet time spent with God. Daily time spent with God, alone in His presence, satisfied by His Word, makes our hearts stronger and our vision clearer. *Silent Strength* is designed to help you maximize your time with our Lord. As we glimpse His power, we find ourselves ready to meet the challenges of the day with a strength that is beyond our own, a silent strength that comes from God alone.

THE DAILY BIBLE
New International Version
Compiled by *F. LaGard Smith*

Unlike any other Bible you have ever read, *The Daily Bible* allows you to read the Scriptures chronologically as a powerful, uninterrupted account of God's interaction with human history.

You will see events from Creation through Revelation unfold before you like an epic novel, conveniently organized into 365 sections for daily reading. Gain a better overall perspective of Scripture by reading the Bible in the order the events occurred from the widely acclaimed New International Version.

GOD'S BEST FOR MY LIFE
by *Lloyd John Ogilvie*

Not since Oswald Chambers' *My Utmost for His Highest*
has there been such an inspirational yet easy-to-read de-
votional. Dr. Ogilvie provides guidelines for maximizing
your prayer and meditation time.

THE FATHER HEART OF GOD
by *Floyd McClung, Jr.*

The Father Heart of God is a book about the healing power
of God's love. In its pages you'll discover how the loving,
compassionate Father Heart of God enables us to overcome
insecurity and the devastating effects of some of life's most
painful experiences.

Dear Reader:

We would appreciate hearing from you regarding this Harvest House nonfiction book. It will enable us to continue to give you the best in Christian publishing.

1. What most influenced you to purchase *The Vineyard*?
   - ☐ Author
   - ☐ Subject matter
   - ☐ Backcover copy
   - ☐ Recommendations
   - ☐ Cover/Title
   - ☐ _____

2. Where did you purchase this book?
   - ☐ Christian bookstore
   - ☐ General bookstore
   - ☐ Department store
   - ☐ Grocery store
   - ☐ Other

3. Your overall rating of this book:
   - ☐ Excellent ☐ Very good ☐ Good ☐ Fair ☐ Poor

4. How likely would you be to purchase other books by this author?
   - ☐ Very likely
   - ☐ Somewhat likely
   - ☐ Not very likely
   - ☐ Not at all

5. What types of books most interest you?
   (check all that apply)
   - ☐ Women's Books
   - ☐ Marriage Books
   - ☐ Current Issues
   - ☐ Self Help/Psychology
   - ☐ Bible Studies
   - ☐ Fiction
   - ☐ Biographies
   - ☐ Children's Books
   - ☐ Youth Books
   - ☐ Other _____

6. Please check the box next to your age group.
   - ☐ Under 18
   - ☐ 18-24
   - ☐ 25-34
   - ☐ 35-44
   - ☐ 45-54
   - ☐ 55 and over

Mail to: Editorial Director
Harvest House Publishers
1075 Arrowsmith
Eugene, OR 97402

Name _____

Address _____

City _____ State _____ Zip _____

**Thank you for helping us to help you
in future publications!**